PRESSURE

PRESSURE

LESSONS FROM THE PSYCHOLOGY
OF THE PENALTY SHOOTOUT

GEIR JORDET

Published in 2024 by New River Books
www.newriverbooks.co.uk

10 9 8 7 6 5 4 3 2 1

A CIP catalogue record for this book is available from the British Library.

ISBN: 978-1-915780-21-8
ISBN: 978-1-915780-24-9

Printed and bound by CPI Group (UK) Ltd, Croydon CR0 4YY

This FSC label means that materials used for the product have been responsibly sourced.

To Yanique

Contents

Foreword
by Arsène Wenger

A penalty shootout is the highest moment of pressure in a footballer's life. It's a mental test. Not a technical test.

Penalties show how the mental aspect can interfere with technique. When I saw Harry Kane miss a penalty for England against France in the 2022 World Cup, I would have understood if the goalkeeper had stopped it. But Kane missed the target altogether. That shows how much pressure was on him.

With penalties, players have to try to make themselves immune to the external world. The circus around them should not influence what they have decided to do. External factors contribute to internal pressure. And blocking those factors out is the key to lessening your internal pressure. You have to control yourself to focus on what you want to do.

But, you never know. Penalties is always a poker game.

I don't like it when goalkeepers move out and stand in front of the ball. Now we have created a new rule where the keepers cannot behave like clowns. However, what the goalkeeper is doing on the line is fine. I like that he is trying to have an influence. That is part of the emotional intensity that people want to see as well.

My teams would practise penalties. We took penalties in

training. Not too much, but a little. I would try to make the level of concentration in training match as closely as possible the level in the game. Rewards helped: prizes increased people's concentration.

In the break before a penalty shootout, the clarity of organisation is important. I tried to have the names of the penalty takers ready early. And then to agree with the players about the order. Because some players will be, like: "I'll take the last one." And I would say: "No, you're taking number two!" The manager has to decide.

At that moment, I would also be trying to strengthen the players' determination and their belief. I would tell them: this is now our opportunity to show them that we are mentally stronger. Focus on what we have in front of us now. Forget the past and focus on the moment.

At Arsenal, I was involved in 15 shootouts. I won the first two, then lost four in a row, but won eight of the last nine. I had not thought about this, but Geir Jordet reminded me.

Today, the use of data and analysis has completely changed. When I was a player, we never saw opponents taking penalties. You maybe knew the team's main penalty taker, but you ignored the others. We didn't have specialist goalkeeping coaches. We now have much more information. Sometimes we don't see the evidence that is right in front of us. We can easily get into a routine way of thinking where the penalty shootout is not as important. We are tempted to focus much more on other aspects of the game. Yet players need to be conscious that penalties decide big successes and big failures. Much more than we expect.

Penalty shootouts are important now and will be more so in the future. At FIFA, we have increased the number of teams in the World Cup from 32 to 48. That means one more knockout stage, and another chance for teams to have penalties. Also, from 2025, we will have a Club World Cup with 32 teams, where there will also be penalties. We need to give this part of the game serious consideration, as Geir Jordet does in this book.

Roberto Baggio says that he still thinks about the penalty he missed in the 1994 World Cup. That tells you one thing: it's worth being prepared.

Arsène Wenger, Chief of Global Football Development, FIFA,
and former manager of Arsenal FC (1996-2018)
March 2024

Introduction

"Only big players can miss penalties because small players don't take them."

Ante Milicic, coach of the Australia women's team, 2019

Imagine this. You are 23 years old. You have one chance to deliver. One shot, with the whole world watching. If you are successful, it's only what everyone was expecting. You might get a respectful nod, at most. If, on the other hand, you fail, it will shatter the dreams of millions, including your teammates, family and friends.

You failed last time you were in this situation. The fallout was devastating. But eventually people forgave you. If you fail this time, no one will forget. It will define you forever. Your name will forever be synonymous with this moment of failure.

In addition, you're exhausted. You've just completed two hours of hard, physically strenuous work, at the end of a whole month in which you have been on constant duty with your team.

When you are about to deliver your shot, there is an opponent in front of you, smiling. Next come cruel words and disturbing gestures, with one aim only – to get inside your head, trigger your worst fears and knock you off balance.

And one final thing: this is a situation you and your team

have not prepared for. You're thrown into this situation without rehearsal. Why? Because your boss does not believe such moments can be practised.

Dread. Anxiety. Fear.

Welcome to the penalty shootout.

When Kylian Mbappé walked from the centre circle to the penalty spot on December 18, 2022, this was his situation. This was the World Cup final, between his France and Argentina.

To say that everyone he knew was watching him at that moment would be no overstatement. There were 1.5 billion people tuned in on television.[1]

A nationally record-breaking 29 million viewers were watching in France alone.[2]

Mbappé was up against Argentina's goalkeeper, Emi Martínez, one of the most notorious trash-talkers and penalty-taker disruptors in the world. And the French team was woefully unprepared – their manager had stated numerous times his belief that it is impossible to practise penalties.

The last time Mbappé had been in a penalty shootout for France was in a round of 16 match in the 2020 European Championships, held in 2021. All the opponents from Switzerland scored, all Mbappé's teammates scored, but Mbappé missed. The aftermath was ugly. He was blamed for the loss. Fans questioned his character: he was an egotist, in it for himself, not a team player. It was said that he didn't care enough. He was racially abused. Eventually, he met with the president of the French Football Federation to discuss whether he would retire from the French team. He played on, but the consequences of taking part in a penalty shootout were painfully clear.

One year on, he was back at the penalty spot. But with even higher stakes. The World Cup trophy on the line. Mbappé was France's biggest star, the one everyone expected would deliver.

He had everything to lose.

I have always been fascinated by penalty kicks. More precisely, I have been fascinated by missed penalty kicks. The idea of having to do something which everyone reasonably expects you to manage, then failing to manage it, and your failure affecting everyone around you… this scenario has always seemed uniquely terrifying to me. My obsession with it began when I played football myself. Although I was a decent youth player, scored quite a few goals and often captained the teams I played for, I feared penalties. I never volunteered to take them. There were two occasions, however, when I could not avoid them.

The first was when I was 15 and played a tryout game for the Oslo regional team. Being picked to play for this team had been my dream for years. I had already failed at the trial stage once, and leading up to this tryout game I was more nervous than ever.

It didn't seem to show, though – or not at first. I played the game of my life. Dribbles, passes, everything clicked. I even scored a nice goal.

Then my team got a penalty.

I walked away, as I normally would. Others could take care of it. The coach saw it differently. "Geir Jordet will take it!"

On the one hand, I didn't even know that the coach knew my name, so that was something. On the other hand… take a penalty? In *this* game? Dread washed over me. But I had no choice. So I grabbed the ball.

My hands were shaking so badly I could hardly keep hold of it to place it on the spot. I walked back, having no real idea what I would do. But I was able to take aim. That memory is clear and vivid – I aimed for just inside the right post. I ran up to the ball as quickly as I could and shot. The ball slowly rolled into the net.

Relief. I had scored. My teammates were happy, the coach seemed impressed. But there was something about this penalty that only I knew. The ball had entered the goal just inside the *left* post – the opposite side from where I was aiming. I had missed my intended target by about seven metres. Complete fluke.

I made the team. I kept quiet about the penalty, though. Until now, in fact.

My second penalty was in a shootout. I was 17 and playing in what at the time was the biggest international youth tournament in the world, the Norway Cup. I was in a good U19 team, with several Norway youth international players. We felt that we had a shot at winning the whole thing. We breezed through to the round of 16 and confidence was high. But that game went to extra time, and then to penalties. I missed and we went out.

The small consolation was that someone else on our team missed his penalty too. Moreover, the other guy was a more senior player, and he probably felt a bit more responsibility for his miss. Yet for me this was still the summer that I crushed the dreams of my teammates and friends. Because that is what it feels like to miss a shot in a penalty shootout. I never took another penalty kick.

My curiosity about penalties did not leave me, though. On the contrary, I grew more and more fascinated by the penalty shootout and the uniquely distilled nature of its drama. In the summer of 2004, having completed my PhD in psychology and football, and while I was waiting to start in my first academic job, the European Championships for men took place in Portugal. Most people remember this tournament for the classic victory of the under-dogs – Greece, who beat the hosts 1-0 in the final. For me, it was the tournament that marked the start of my professional quest to understand the psychology of the penalty shootout.

There were two dramatic shootouts in the 2004 Euros quarter-finals. First, Portugal beat England 6-5. Then, two days later, the Netherlands beat Sweden 5-4. Everybody was talking about David Beckham, who was probably at the time the player with the highest profile in the game. Beckham was chosen to take the first penalty in England's shootout against Portugal. The Portuguese goalkeeper, Ricardo, came to greet him at the penalty spot prior to the shot, taunting Beckham, gesturing and trash-talking to him. A few seconds later, Beckham fired a shot that went between one and two metres over the crossbar – a huge miss. I watched it live on TV and could hardly believe it. But we had seen it before. Being a superstar is a liability in a penalty shootout. The pressure is higher on them than on others. And extraordinary players suddenly become very ordinary.

Norway is a small country and there were not many specialists in football psychology at the time, so the day after the game I was called up by a national radio station and asked if I would talk about the shootout we had just witnessed. Right before we went on air, the host told me another guest would be joining the discussion, linking in from a remote studio. It was Henning Berg. Oh, OK. Berg was a huge figure in Norway. He had just retired as a player after a distinguished career: 100 caps for his country, playing in two World Cups. He also played 66 games for Manchester United in the Premier League.

I was the first one up on the radio show. "How could someone like Beckham miss?" was the question. I delivered a couple of my pre-rehearsed psychological observations and speculations: "The pressure on Beckham is enormous. He is the biggest superstar in the game. Everyone expects him to score, he probably started to overthink his kick, and…"

A loud and scathing voice interrupted me.

"That's nonsense. Completely wrong!"

It was Henning Berg.

"I played with David Beckham for three years," Berg continued. "I know him very well. He's extremely mentally strong. His miss had nothing to do with pressure."

I was so stunned, I didn't even hear the rest of what he said. There was no way I could question Berg's authority – nor his self-certainty. I had nothing to counter with, and barely said a word after that. I left the radio studio feeling pretty crushed.

But I also felt determined. Despite Berg's two-footed challenge, I did believe that penalty taking was, to an important degree, about pressure and the management of pressure, and that penalty shootouts had a psychological dimension that might deserve attention. I certainly knew I wanted to delve deeper into this topic. And so began a period of intense exploration. I sought out the existing studies – and found that these typically featured student footballers being recruited to a penalty simulation task in a laboratory. I didn't get it. How could they come even close to simulating the real pressure of a major penalty shootout? I knew that I needed to focus more on what actually happened in real-world shootouts. My interest rapidly became a mission. I watched videos, read memoirs, interviews, explored the drama and emotions involved in penalty kick experiences and tried to identify the behaviours that might mean something. I asked myself: what were players who scored doing differently from the ones who missed?

It certainly seemed that it would be useful to know. In the World Cup for men, there have been 35 penalty shootouts since this method of deciding a tied game was introduced to the tournament in 1974, which means that 20% or one in five of all World Cup knockout games go to penalties. The number of penalty shootouts in the European Championships is higher (26%) and for the Copa América higher again (30%). For women, the equivalent percentages are 11% in the World Cup, 15% in the European Championships and 30% in the Copa América Femenina. This means that any team going into one of those tournaments with an ambition to go all the way is being very naive if it doesn't expect and plan to feature in at least one penalty shootout.

Meanwhile, with respect to penalty kicks awarded within regular game time, at least one penalty is given in 27% of the matches in the top European leagues for men.[3] Given that more than half of all football games are either tied or decided by only one goal, it stands to reason that any penalty kick awarded is likely to play a major part in the outcome of most games.[4] Again, understanding penalty taking in all its dimensions would seem like a good idea.

My first breakthrough came after I started my job in the autumn of 2004 at the University of Groningen in the Netherlands. The Netherlands and England have very similar penalty shootout histories: traumatic and painful. Leading up to the 2004 Euros, the Netherlands had participated in four big penalty shootouts – in the Euros in 1992, 1996 and 2000, and in the World Cup in 1998. They lost all of them. The most excruciating loss was probably in Euro 2000, when they were the host nation. They faced Italy in the semi-final at the Amsterdam Arena. During regulation time, the Dutch missed two penalty kicks, the score remained 0-0 and the match went to a penalty shootout. In that, three of four Dutch penalty takers missed. Italy won comfortably. Consequently, when the Dutch team won their penalty shootout against Sweden in the quarter-final of Euro 2004, it was a cathartic moment for a country obsessed with football.

Even before starting my new job at the university, I had begun thinking about doing some type of study of penalties, together with my new Dutch colleagues. Upon arriving, I found out that one of those colleagues, Chris Visscher, had connections that could gain us some access to the Dutch team. Coincidentally, I also personally knew some of the Swedish players who took part in that Euro shootout. My thought was that maybe I could get them to speak to me about what they went through. It was a long process and took all our powers of persuasion, but eventually we secured interviews with players from both sides, and I had the material for a unique study, exploring in depth the players from two top-level teams' experiences of facing each other in a penalty shootout.

What was excitingly clear to me was that the penalty shootout in football is a natural laboratory for the study of pressure and human performance. Moreover, it's a laboratory with some enormous advantages. Firstly, it can do something that regular laboratories cannot – produce high levels of raw, real-world pressure that would be impossible, and surely unethical, to induce in participants in regular studies. Here, in other words, is pressure in the wild, naturally occurring and ready to be examined.

A second benefit is that we can use the penalty shootout to study the effects of pressure on elite, high-performing individuals. This is an exclusive group who would be hard to draft for university lab studies.

And third, even though the binary outcome of a penalty kick or a penalty shootout is simple – score or miss, win or lose – the cognitive, emotional, social, technical and tactical variables surrounding penalty taking are incredibly rich, offering us a uniquely rounded and illuminating picture of the pressure experience.

Those years in the Netherlands were the beginning of an enduring passion which led me to publish numerous academic research studies on penalty shootouts. In the process, I interviewed more than 30 top-level players in depth about their thoughts, emotions and experiences during penalties, and conducted detailed video observation of more than 2000 penalty kicks. And I got to test my predictions in practice while consulting with over 20 elite teams, including Germany men (for the 2022 World Cup), Great Britain/England women (for the 2020 Olympics), the Netherlands men (for the 2006 World Cup), Norway men and women (regularly over the past decade), as well as several leading European clubs from the Premier League and other top leagues.

In this book, I will present the highlights of my research. I will dig deeply into the constituents of pressure, how it manifests in penalty shootouts, and describe and explain how the world's best (and some of the worst) penalty takers cope and maintain performance under some of the most extreme pressure conditions that exist in sport. Most of my research is on men, which is related to the historical lack of availability of video and data from the women's game. Hopefully there will be more research on women and penalties in the near future.

However, the focus is not only on footballers and their penalty kicks – it is as much on the experience and management of stress itself. As we shall see, the way that successful penalty takers perform under pressure is not only about a physical act, a kick at a ball. To be perfectly honest, I am personally not even that interested in the penalty kick itself. What happens to the ball after the foot has struck it is not my primary focus. It is all about the pressure that is on *before* the kick, what players think and feel, what they do, how they relate to and communicate with others. This is where the magic happens. And this is where the broader lessons are. Not many of us will be asked to take a penalty for our country in a World Cup shootout. But all of us will face pressure of some kind in our lives, and maybe it would be useful to know what we can do to prepare ourselves, overcome our fear of failure and survive, and even thrive, in those big-pressure moments.

This has become a lifelong mission for me, yet it might never have been so if it had not been for that on-air tackle by Henning Berg. In a full-circle moment, exactly 10 years after that crushing radio experience, on June 1, 2014, Legia Warsaw had just beaten Lech Posnan 2-0. This was the last match of the season, and they were now handed the trophy as the 2013-2014 winner of Ekstraklasa, the Polish league. I was at the stadium and found myself in the dressing room after the match, celebrating with the players and my good friends, the coaches of Legia Warsaw – Pål

Arne Johansen, Kaz Sokolowski and their boss, the head coach… Henning Berg. The following year, Legia Warsaw became Polish cup champions. The most dramatic match was the quarter-final, where Henning Berg's men won after a very well-executed penalty shootout.

In that 2022 World Cup final, Kylian Mbappé did not just take France's number one shot in the penalty shootout, he also took *two* penalty kicks in the game – one 10 minutes before the end of regular time and one two minutes before the end of extra time. Each kick was a make-or-break shot, where missing would almost certainly have meant that France would lose the game. This is the penalty kick. One small act, massive repercussions. And, accordingly, immense amounts of pressure.

Even though France ended up losing, Mbappé scored on all three of those occasions, producing one of the most extraordinary performances under pressure ever seen in football.

What did he do differently from the year before with those kicks?

That, ultimately, is the subject of this book.

Chapter 1

Feeling the pressure

"Penalties look so simple, that's why they're difficult."

Johan Cruyff

The penalty shootout was adopted by FIFA in 1970 as the official way to decide tied football matches in knockout competitions. The first shootouts were, perhaps inevitably, raw, unpolished events, rough at the edges. Penalty takers had not learned about how one should or shouldn't behave in this extraordinary new scenario. Referees were inexperienced and very loose in their control of the situation and the actors involved. Watching film of those shootouts now, they look unvarnished, unmediated – and actually rather magical, especially if you happen to be a researcher with an interest in pressure and its effects. Here is performance under pressure in a very pure form.

Watch, for instance, the shootout at the end of the 1980 Cup Winners' Cup final between Arsenal and Valencia.[5] The game had finished 0-0 after extra time so for the first time a major European club final would go to penalties.

Valencia naturally sent down their most trusted penalty taker for their first kick. That was Mario Kempes, one of football's brightest superstars, a World Cup winner with Argentina in 1978, the top scorer in that tournament, with six goals including two in the final against the Netherlands, the winner of the South American Footballer of the Year award. He missed. It was the first time the world had seen one of the game's living legends get stripped of their dignity by the ruthless spectacle of a penalty shootout. And it would certainly not be the last.

A little later, with the score still level after the designated five kicks for each team, confusion seemed briefly to reign about what should happen next. Should each team's first five kickers cycle through again? Or did the remaining players now have to take a turn? While the goalkeepers stood together discussing the matter, coaching staff ran down to the referee for clarification. Carry on through the team, was the instruction.

Valencia took their sixth penalty and scored. Graham Rix, 22 years old at the time, had played well in the match and now stepped up for Arsenal. Rix needed to score to keep Arsenal in the contest. If he missed, the cup was Valencia's.

Rix arrived in the penalty area with the air of someone for whom this couldn't be over soon enough. As he stepped up to place the ball, he looked at Carlos Pereira in the Valencia goal and attempted some cheekiness by miming a side-foot shot before the ball was down. Looking at it now on the video, the joke is sort of funny and sort of not; mostly it oozes nervous energy. Naturally. They were all nervous, and they were showing it in different ways.

Rix then took only a few steps back from the ball and, on the referee's signal, immediately sprinted in. Not a bad penalty kick, but the goalkeeper went correctly and made a relatively simple save. Arsenal were beaten – the first team to know the unique pain of surrendering a European final on penalties. As the jubilant Valencia players rushed past him to mob their goalkeeper, Rix, with his socks around his ankles, could only stand still, bent over in an altogether new form of mortification.

Or wind forward a little from there to 1984 and watch the shootout to decide the final of the UEFA Cup (the Europa League, as we now know it) between Tottenham and Anderlecht. By today's standards, it's incredible how impatient and rushed these players seem. Nine of the 10 penalty takers react to the referee's whistle as if it were the crack of a starting pistol. Because the referee in this shootout blows as the players are walking back from the ball, they don't even pause or gather themselves in any way, not even for a second, before they begin their run-up. Moreover, four of the five Tottenham players turn their backs on the goalkeeper when walking away, so the referee's signal produces from them one fast, fluid and surely quite hard-to-coordinate movement: walk, turn around, run, kick. The only Spurs player who does not turn his back on the goalkeeper, Gary Stevens, starts his run-up before the whistle has gone, making the referee appear to react to *him* rather than the other way around. Stevens then becomes the only player in major penalty shootout history to kick the ball at the same time as the referee blows. He scores and the Belgian goalkeeper, Jacques Munaron, understandably protests bitterly afterwards, but to no avail.

The Belgian players are also fast, although not quite as fast as the English. And the only player in the shootout who notably takes a little bit more time is Enzo Scifo. He is only 18 years of age, yet incredibly composed prior to his run-up. His one-second pause after the whistle feels like an eternity compared with the rest. Scifo will go on to have an impressive career and earn 84 caps for Belgium. However, Tottenham win the penalty shoot-out, 4-3, and the trophy.

Or wind back again and watch what happens when Uli Stielike takes his kick for West Germany in the shootout to decide the

1982 World Cup semi-final against France, in Seville, Spain. This is the first time penalties have been used to decide a World Cup game, and as such, the first time this supremely edgy drama has been played out on the global stage.

The teams are exhausted after 120 minutes of intensely competing for a place in the final. (At one point, France led 3-1 in extra time, only for West Germany to pull back to 3-3.) In the centre circle, instead of the shoulder-to-shoulder team formation we are now used to seeing during penalty shootouts, the players are spread around, laid out on the ground. No attempt to preserve their muscle tone, no attempt to appear ready or competitive. They have simply given in to their tiredness and sat down.

Uli Stielike is the third penalty taker for West Germany, and the sixth in the contest. Nobody has yet missed. When Stielike walks up to the ball, he does not look confident at all. He too reacts quickly to the referee's whistle, but walks relatively slowly towards the ball while looking at the goalkeeper. With his last steps, he looks down, then delivers a shot at medium height, but only a metre or two to the left of the goalkeeper.

Penalty saved. Yes – a German has missed a penalty. Savour this moment because it won't happen again at a major tournament for another 34 years.

But watch Stielike. Even before the goalkeeper has fully landed from his dive, he has slumped to his knees with his hands covering his face. Then he surrenders to a combination of shame and gravity, falls flat on the grass and rolls himself into a tight ball of pain. For a full 10 seconds, he is curled up next to the penalty spot, until his own goalkeeper, Harald Schumacher, comes and literally lifts him off the ground before half carrying, half dragging him out of the way. Pierre Littbarski, who is next up to kick for West Germany, then takes the still demolished Stielike in his arms, holds him and consoles him.

Meanwhile, Didier Six of France is stepping up to take his penalty – and he misses, too. But the TV audience doesn't get to see that because the cameras are still focusing on Littbarski's nursing of Stielike. The first the viewers know of Six's miss is Littbarski's exhilarated reaction to it. What the audience *does* see, before the replay of Six's miss, is Six, too, falling to the ground, hiding his face in his hands and curling into a ball inside the six-yard box. Six also stays down for 10-15 seconds, before he is urged to get up by his goalkeeper, and eventually makes it to his feet. He doesn't make it out of the penalty area, though. Six is actually still standing inside the area, watching, hunched over and defeated, as Littbarski hammers his penalty into the top right corner. Meanwhile, further up the pitch, Stielike remains curled up on the ground for the rest of the shootout, peeking out now and then to see what is happening, but mostly hiding his face in his hands. In the end, France miss again and West Germany win, but the memories of Stielike's and Six's pain and the intensity of their reactions will endure. And for Six, who did not just miss but also lost, the trauma was not left behind in Seville: "I had difficulty finding a job, because they said, 'That one is unstable.' And all of that has come from this missed penalty kick."[6]

If there was one thing the world very quickly learned from this painful footage, it was that a penalty shootout is a merciless beast. Here was a format which, in a split second, could turn men into mice, superstars into scapegoats and international-level performers into balled-up figures on the ground.

Stielike and Six were among the first to show intense, negative post-miss trauma and shame in penalty shootouts, but they are not alone. For simple descriptive analyses in this book, I have gathered videos of every single shot (718 in total) from every single penalty shootout in the World Cup, European Championships and Champions League for men since the beginning in 1970 until

2023. This shows that 53% of the players who have missed their penalty behave in a similar way by making themselves look smaller, falling to the ground, hiding their faces in their hands or looking down and not facing teammates as they walk back.

Penalty shootouts are unforgiving and ruthless. What was clear from these displays of post-shot emotion was that how you emerged from your encounter with the beast of the penalty shootout was going to vary significantly depending on how you handled the pressure – whether you coped with it or whether you choked on it.

Football and choking

There are plenty of examples of choking in elite competition but the most vivid tend to be in individual sports: the golfer Jean van de Velde squandering a three-shot lead at the 18th and final hole of the 1999 British Open; Jana Novotná losing a commanding lead over Steffi Graf in the final set of the 1993 Wimbledon women's singles final; the Australian swimmer Cate Campbell going into the 100 metre freestyle final at the 2016 Olympics as the heavily backed world record holder and finishing fifth, "possibly the greatest choke in Olympic history," Campbell herself reckoned afterwards.

Identifying examples of choking in team sports such as football is more complicated. Teams that dramatically collapse at the biggest stage in the most important moments look like strong contenders: AC Milan, who lost a 3-0 half-time lead in the 2005 Champions League final in Istanbul, and the penalty shootout that followed; Bayern Munich, who had a 1-0 lead in the 1999 Champions League final at 90 minutes, but three minutes later had lost 2-1; Brazil, who, as host nation, were humiliatingly trounced 1-7 in the 2014 World Cup with a place in the final at stake. However, all these examples might not be choking but the consequence of outstanding performances from their opponents – Liverpool, Manchester United and Germany, respectively.

Penalties, though, both in regulation play and in game-deciding shootouts, are the moment when football suddenly approaches the condition of an individual sport – a direct face-off, with most of the pressure on the kicker. Typically in football matches, about 80% of in-game penalties are scored – though we'll see in due course that there is large individual variation and those percentages drop for penalty shootouts in major competitions. Nevertheless, when the kicker arrives at the spot, there is an expectation that they will score. The odds seem to be stacked in their favour. I have had the privilege of attending penalty training sessions at the elite level, and can tell you that the same thing happens every time. Everyone scores, more or less. To be precise, in a squad with about 20 players, if each player only has one kick, often 19 or 20 will score. The penalty skill performed without the pressure, and without an audience, is relatively easy. However, add a crowd, a TV audience, consequences, pressure... well, as at no other moment in football, the game suddenly dramatically changes and the odds for choking skyrocket.

Just to be clear, a missed penalty is not always a choked penalty. It might be a great save, or bad luck or an inexplicable absence of skill on the kicker's part, with anxiety playing little or no role at all. (That, essentially, was Henning Berg's view of that Beckham penalty miss in the 2004 Euros, though I disagreed and still do.) Certainly, a penalty can be a surprisingly complex event, with layers that need to be carefully identified and analysed before any conclusions are drawn about cause and effect. Nevertheless, it's evident that penalty kicks and penalty shootouts present a unique setting in which to observe what happens to performance in the presence of acute stress and anxiety. And it's not always pretty.

Acute stress

On a normal summer day in the Munich area of Germany, around 20 people are admitted to hospital needing medical attention for cardiovascular issues such as heart attacks or strokes. On June 30, 2006, however, that number more than tripled, surging to 64. So what made that particular Thursday different? Well, there was at least one thing: it was the day Germany's World Cup quarter-final against Argentina went to penalties.

Heart-related hospital admissions spiked on every one of the seven days that Germany competed in the World Cup that summer – 43 admissions for the tournament opener against Costa Rica, 49 for the group stage game against neighbouring Poland. But the match with the penalty shootout in it (which Germany won, almost needless to say) spiked highest.[7]

This is by no means just a German thing. In the Netherlands, when their men's team lost on penalties to France in the quarter-finals of the 1996 European Championships, 14 more people than normal actually *died* due to heart attacks or strokes.[8] And more than 20 other studies document the same morbid effects from all over the world – simply watching an exciting game can have devastating consequences.[9] When you read studies like that, you start to wonder whether watching penalty shootouts should itself be categorised as an extreme sport.

And if that's the effect of merely watching these events, what sort of stress is being experienced by the people who are participating in them? Players who have taken penalties in a shootout sometimes provide very telling descriptions of what it felt like. Stuart Pearce, who took, and missed a shot for England in the 1990 World Cup semi-final shootout against West Germany, expressed it like this: "All you need to do is walk fifty yards, take a penalty and score. That's the worst part of it, that bloody walk from the halfway line. Why do they make you stand there, so far away? God only knows which masochist decided that. It is clearly someone who has never been in this nerve-jangling position because it heightens the tension to an unbelievable degree."[10]

Similarly, one of the players I interviewed about his experience of being part of a penalty shootout in a European Championships game told me he was almost overwhelmed with anxiety: "When we were in the centre circle I became incredibly nervous. I thought it showed on TV that my legs were shaking, that is how nervous I was."[11]

Occasionally, images emerge from the scene in the centre circle during shootouts that beautifully illustrate some of the acute stress these players experience in that phase of the event. One of my personal favourites is of Brazil's Marcelo. He is a highly accomplished, vastly experienced footballer – 386 official games for Real Madrid, 58 caps for his country. Yet his body language when he stands in the centre circle during penalty shootouts is akin to that of a petrified child. Facing Chile in the shootout to decide their 2014 World Cup round of 16 match, every Brazilian player in the group is clearly affected by the pressure, but Marcelo still stands out. A photograph reveals him, at this high-pressure moment, to have taken a firm hold of two of his teammates' shorts, one with his left hand and the other with his right hand.

You can see him do something similar at club level with Real Madrid in a penalty shootout in the 2011-2012 Champions League. This time the item that Marcelo has a reassuring hold on, while he is sitting on his heels, is the thigh of his teammate Pepe.

Most people will probably relate. Touch is comforting and it does make you feel safe to hold onto something when you are under stress. For me, for example, when I give presentations or speak to large audiences – one of my regular pressure moments – it is always calming to have a slide-clicker control in my hand. Slide-clicker, Pepe's leg – same thing, maybe.

When we are put under serious pressure – and this is not just penalty takers, it's all of us – our heart rates increase, our breathing becomes faster, our muscles tense and butterflies start flinging themselves around in our stomachs. Pressure, like threat, sets off a cascade of psychophysiological processes: our adrenal glands release cortisol into our bloodstreams;[12] our pupils dilate to admit more light while our peripheral vision blurs and our perception narrows, perhaps causing us to experience "tunnel vision";[13] our hearing alters, it feels almost as if our ears are covered, and we can have trouble locating the source of specific sounds;[14] and our attention gets funnelled onto whatever we perceive to be causing the stress, impairing our working memory and our cognitive flexibility and making us rigidly focused.[15]

Some of these processes are helpful for performance. For example, the narrowing and focusing of one's attention and energy might be useful because there are clearly occasions where being less distractable is advantageous. However, these psychophysiological processes also have the capacity to backfire on us because of other, less welcome consequences: insufficient situational awareness, flawed situational judgment, more cognitive errors, increased risk taking and decrements in fine motor control.[16]

These stress reactions are universal human responses, likely true for all high-stress situations, whether it's stepping up to take a penalty with a World Cup final place at stake, striding out onto a theatre stage on opening night, or standing up at the table to deliver a speech at your best friend's wedding. Unfortunately, we have yet not been able to strap psychophysical measurement devices to players who are getting ready to take a big penalty kick, but we have systematically tapped into their thoughts and emotions. What specifically do we know about penalty takers' experience of pressure at the penalty spot?

In our interviews with the 10 players who were involved in the Euro 2004 quarter-final shootout between Sweden and the Netherlands, we provided them with a list of 24 emotions, 14 of which were positively toned and 10 of which were negatively toned. The participants were asked to think back to the penalty shootout and identify from the list the emotions that applied.[17] Although the players also experienced positive emotions (determination was most popular – identified by eight players), the emotion that featured most prominently of all was anxiety. Indeed, it was the only emotion on our list that all 10 of the players said they had experienced. Not surprising.

However, on closer inspection, the anxiety was not something stable that endured throughout the shootout.[18] Rather, it was constantly evolving, coming and going, depending on the way events unfolded. One player told us that his experience of anxiety was most intense early on: "I was the most nervous here, between the first and the second shot. Yes. Most nervous. Absolutely. Absolutely. No doubt." But the anxiety disappeared as soon as one of his teammates missed: "First, I felt bitter and angry, but then the nervousness went away. I became much calmer."

Interestingly, for several of the players, the anxiety seemed to be more pronounced and present when they were standing in the centre circle than when they approached their shot. Waiting and watching other players taking shots, with its associated powerlessness, was perceived as very difficult: "When one of them or one of us shoots, then the tension is a lot higher than for that person who is going to take the penalty. Because it is not in your hands [to control]." This is an important part of the threat involved in a penalty shootout for these players – potentially very negative outcomes if it goes badly, and very little control to influence it.

In our interviews with penalty takers, three players explicitly said that their anxiety gradually decreased between the centre circle, the walk and the penalty spot: "When [the shootout] started I was indeed stressed. I had some of those small shivers then. When I walked to the ball, it was over." If anxiety was less present during the walk, it is probably because the players at this point could actively take some measure of control. Their performance had started, and they could focus on what was familiar: taking the ball and attempting to put it in the net. That said, players were nervous during the walk as well, but, unlike Stuart Pearce, they did not single out the walk as the most stressful phase. The players' experience of anxiety during the walk varied much more than one might have assumed.

That their performance starts the moment they step out of the centre circle is consistent with some of the leading theories about anxiety in sport, which predict anxiety to be highest immediately prior to the onset of competition and then to dissipate once the competition has begun.[19] Thus, when the players arrived at the penalty spot, they experienced less worry, being preoccupied instead with adopting a constructive focus. Two players said that they needed to have the right feeling before they could take their shot: "I would only take it when I was ready to. You have to take the time to do that. It was very important for me to have that feeling." Four players even talked about being calm at the penalty spot ("I was calm, very calm, just shoot it in, very relaxed"), while two others clearly experienced anxiety: "When you are walking towards the ball things are going fine, but at that moment when you put the ball down, you get a special feeling in your body." Two others indicated that their anxiety progressively decreased on their final approach to the penalty spot: "At a certain moment, I put the ball down and everything was just gone. Before that moment, I was really very nervous and tense."

Anxiety is a normal reaction in pressure situations. The

question with respect to how it will impact performance is: how do you interpret it and what do you do with it? Later, I will show how elite athletes, and particularly penalty kickers, are able to gain control when faced with anxiety, and hence perform better. But first we need to look at what can happen when penalty takers allow anxiety to take over.

Overthinking

In the penalty shootout to decide the final of the 2020 European Championships at Wembley, Marcus Rashford of England faced the Italian goalkeeper Gianluigi Donnarumma. Rashford can't have known it but he was about to set a record. After the referee had blown his whistle, the England player stood still for 11 seconds before he started moving towards the ball. In all the 718 penalty kicks taken in the World Cup, Euros and Champions League for men between 1976 and today, no other player has paused as long as this before making their move.

So what kept him? The day after the final, Rashford put it like this: "Something didn't feel quite right. During the long run-up I was saving myself a bit of time and unfortunately the result was not what I wanted."[20] In his book published the year after, Rashford said a little bit more: "Normally I don't get nervous when playing football. But that day, when I picked up the ball to take my penalty, I felt different, as if something was off."[21]

Further, as he was addressing the ball, he seems to have set himself a tough challenge: "For some reason, my brain wasn't telling me 'Just try your best,' like it normally did. Instead, it was saying: 'You have to be perfect.'" He then did something new: "I tried a different penalty style from the ones I normally do. I did a stuttering run-up, where I paused a little bit on my way to kick the ball, trying to get Donnarumma to move early and make the penalty easier."

Towards the end of the run-up, he seemed to hesitate a little before reaching the ball. His shot struck the foot of the post. Miss. England never recovered in the shootout. Both Jadon Sancho and Bukayo Saka missed as well, and Italy became European champions.

Eleven seconds is by far the longest Rashford has paused before a penalty shot in his whole career. He usually takes quite long pauses – but not that long. On his last 10 penalty kicks prior to the penalty shootout against Italy, he paused for about 5.7 seconds on average (see diagram below). He scored on every single one of those 10 kicks but missed the kick against Italy.

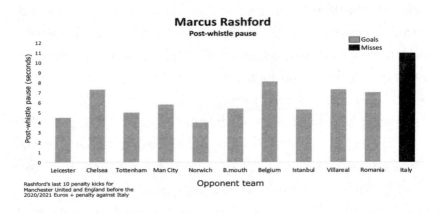

Marcus Rashford
Post-whistle pause

Rashford's last 10 penalty kicks for Manchester United and England before the 2020/2021 Euros + penalty against Italy

So did that extra-long pause contribute to impair his performance at that crucial moment? Before trying to answer that, here is another example of something similar, from the 2023 Women's World Cup. In that tournament, there were several dramatic and spectacular penalty shootouts. The first was between Sweden and one of the big favourites in the tournament, the USA. The Americans were the reigning champions, having defeated the

Netherlands in the 2019 final. On that occasion, Megan Rapinoe scored the first goal with a brilliant penalty shot. The 2023 World Cup was her last appearance for her country prior to her international retirement, which she had announced before the tournament. When she stepped up to take shot number four in the shootout against Sweden, many things were in play: this moment in her personal story, her huge profile in the game and the expectation of pretty much everyone that she would score. A lot to carry. Massive pressure.

Prior to her kick, everything looked normal. Rapinoe was obviously nervous, but that was to be expected. The referee blew the whistle and Rapinoe paused. She always does this, so nothing to worry about. Or was it? She paused for 5.7 seconds after the whistle. This was longer than she had waited in any of her last 20 penalty kicks (see diagram below).[22] And she missed. Blew the ball high over the crossbar. The first time in 16 kicks she had missed, and the first time in 21 kicks that she had missed the goal altogether.

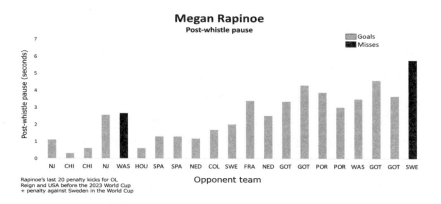

Megan Rapinoe
Post-whistle pause

Rapinoe's last 20 penalty kicks for OL Reign and USA before the 2023 World Cup + penalty against Sweden in the World Cup

Why did this happen to both Rashford and Rapinoe? Here were two experienced penalty takers, faced with probably the most important single kicks of their careers. And they both took the longest time that they had ever taken prior to their shots, and they both missed.

It is time to speculate a bit. When players pause for an unusually long time before they start their run-ups, it sometimes (but certainly not always) indicates that they have walked into the trap we call overthinking. And overthinking is consistent with some of the classic theories about why people choke under pressure.[23]

The overthinking theories of choking essentially propose that performance anxiety causes a performer to disrupt what otherwise is an automatically run skill. Instead of exclusively attending to the external information relevant to performing the task well (the lie of the ball, the position of the goalkeeper, the area of the goal one is aiming for, and so on), attention is turned inwards to the production of one's own movements. Suddenly, with pressure and anxiety, performers find themselves consciously controlling and/or monitoring decisions and movements which they would normally perform without thinking. What usually is smooth, natural and effortless becomes measured, restrained, complicated. And performance suffers.

This type of choking was first studied in 1984 by one of the world's leading social psychologists, Roy Baumeister. Over six experiments, he found support for the links between pressure, self-consciousness and low performance (choking).[24] Later studies have elaborated on these findings. For example, in an experiment with dribbling the ball, it was shown that an expert's performance is harmed when they turn their attention to monitoring the step-by-step performance involved in that skill, while less experienced performers, on the contrary, benefit from such skill-focus.[25]

Support for the operation of this theory during penalty kicks was found by a group of Dutch brain researchers. They used a sophisticated optical brain-monitoring technique called fNIRS to estimate the concentration of haemoglobin in the blood across different areas of the brain, and to monitor how this varies with different conditions, emotions and penalty kick performances. Among their significant findings was that experienced football players with anxiety showed a relatively higher left temporal cortex activation. Since that's an area of the brain linked to self-instruction and reflection, the implication was that these players had stopped executing their skills automatically and had started thinking about them.[26]

For Rashford and Rapinoe, it is possible that these theories can explain their missed shots. The extraordinarily long pauses could indicate that they took time explicitly planning, controlling and monitoring the details of their movements going into their penalty kicks. Rashford's statements seem to support this. He clearly felt the pressure: "something didn't feel right" and "something was off". He then focused on the ingredients of the skill: "have to be perfect" and "tried a different penalty style from the ones I normally do". This seems consistent with the "turning inward", overthinking, theories of choking.

To be fair, the margins in these shots are incredibly small and to interpret the specific cognitive mechanisms involved is inevitably speculative. Those two big misses might still just be coincidences, the mess-ups that happen every now and then for no real or determinable reason. Having said that, both Rashford's and Rapinoe's penalties were anomalies. Their pauses were much longer than the ones they normally took before taking penalties, and missing the goal entirely is equally rare for the pair of them. Besides, Rashford's statements clearly express that, for him, this shot was different. That miss, along with Rapinoe's, does bear many of the traits of a classic overthinking choke.

Meanwhile, there are theories about why performers choke which imply an almost *opposite* view of the mechanisms involved. Let's have a look at some of those.

Ironic processes

Elite-level penalty takers don't just wish not to miss their shots; they *intensely* wish not to miss them. Our interviews with players who have taken part in major shootouts are resoundingly conclusive about this. One player said: "You don't want to ruin it all. You don't want to not go through to the next round because YOU missed. So, you just hope that you will not miss your penalty. And you think: Don't miss, don't miss, don't miss, DON'T MISS! That's all I'm thinking."[27]

Ironically, though, this adamant desire not to miss could be something that makes missing more likely. Ample research (and perhaps your own experience) shows how instructing yourself *not* to do something will, under physical or cognitive load (e.g. performance pressure), increase the probability of doing the very thing you were trying to avoid.[28] A series of studies by a research group from the Free University of Amsterdam has shown that football penalty takers are at least as vulnerable as anyone else to such ironic processes.[29] Experienced football players were given different instructions for their kicks performed in a laboratory. Ironically, players who were instructed not to shoot within the reach of the goalkeeper ended up both looking more at the goalkeeper and shooting more towards the goalkeeper than players who were instructed to shoot as accurately as possible or towards the open areas of the goal.

Quiet eye and disordered eye behaviour

In the 2023 Women's World Cup penalty shootout between the USA and Sweden, the first three US penalty takers, Andi Sullivan, Lindsey Horan and Kristie Mewis, gave a dazzling demonstration of composure and narrow focus. Their facial expressions clearly betrayed that all three of them were nervous, but they displayed an almost identical pre-shot routine that most likely kept those nerves under some type of control: a three-second pause after the referee gave the whistle, a deep breath prior to the run-up and eyes firmly locked on the ball throughout. Result: three goals. Three impressions of a team and penalty takers who have prepared and rehearsed for the unique demands of high-pressure penalty kicks.

Sweden scored twice and missed twice with their first four shots, while Megan Rapinoe missed for the US team, the incident we encountered above. This meant that if Sophia Smith scored with her penalty, the USA would be through to the quarter-finals. A massively important shot, but with a positive incentive – if you score, you win.

Like her teammates, Smith paused after the whistle for three seconds. She also took a deep breath. However, in contrast with the others, who all had their gaze steadily focused on the ball throughout those pre-shot seconds, Smith's eyes suggested enormous uneasiness. She constantly shifted her gaze – from the ball to the goalkeeper, back to the ball, back to the goalkeeper, continuously readjusting. Then she ran in. The Swedish goalkeeper went early to the penalty taker's left, but Smith went right. However, the ball was poorly struck and went way clear of the post. Miss.

Does this type of eye behaviour play a role in penalty kick performance? Before I say anything more, I need to stress that there are no absolutes with respect to what works and does not work in the lead-up to a penalty kick. Rapinoe had the opposite type of gaze from Smith's, steadfast and locked on the ball, and she missed as well. Nevertheless, some behaviours may make success more or less likely. What does the research say?

Much work has been done on athletes' performance under pressure and something called "quiet eye". Quiet eye is defined as the duration of the final visual fixation on a relevant target prior to the initiation of the final movement.[30] More than 30 studies have been conducted and together they document a significant positive effect of a longer quiet eye period for performance across many different sport tasks.[31] This means, the longer performers can maintain a focused and still gaze, aimed at their target, the more likely they are to deliver a good performance.

Several studies also show that when athletes are put under pressure, they reduce their quiet eye duration. For example, in a study of basketball free-throw shooters, conversion rates decreased from 68% under low pressure to 57% under high pressure.[32] The quiet eye duration also dropped significantly across those conditions, suggesting that pressure causes the free-throw shooters to maintain their last visual fixation for a shorter time, and that this may contribute to a disrupted free-throw performance.

However, not everyone under pressure suffers quiet eye reductions. Studies show that when athletes are put in the same pressure situations, some will interpret the stressful situation as threatening (and negative), while others will interpret it as challenging (and positive). The ones who feel threatened are more likely to show short quiet eye periods, while those who feel challenged have longer quiet eye periods.[33] Thus, with the proper mindset, the negative effects from pressure can be countered.

Why do quiet eye reductions impact performance? Researchers link this to distraction theories of choking, which posit that anxiety or fatigue increases a performer's distractibility. This means that in situations of pressure, anxiety disrupts one's ability to maintain visual attention (eye fixation) on the key information for your performance.[34] Penalty takers under pressure are more likely to be distracted and not optimally attend to the most relevant aspects of their situation – the ball, the goalkeeper, the area of the goal they want to shoot for. Result: more missed penalties.

Avoidance gaze behaviour

"I can't bear to look." We've all felt it, possibly said it, maybe even hid our eyes accordingly. And that includes football managers and coaches during penalty kicks.

When the final of the men's Euro 2020 between Italy and England went to penalties, the late Gianluca Vialli, assistant coach to Italy's manager Roberto Mancini, firmly took up a position with his back towards the field, and did not turn around until Italy had won. Zlatko Dalić, the manager/coach for Croatia, who faced Russia in a penalty shootout at the quarter-final stage of the 2018 World Cup, sat on the bench throughout the torment with his face hidden behind his hands. Croatia also ended up winning. Liverpool FC's Jürgen Klopp routinely assumes the back-to-the-pitch position when his team gets decisive in-game penalties. He did this when James Milner took a late penalty against Swansea in November 2015; and when Bukayo Saka made it 3-2 to Arsenal with a 75th-minute penalty at the Emirates Stadium in October 2022. Finally, Chelsea women's manager, Emma Hayes, could be spotted looking down or looking away from the penalties in the Champions League quarter-final against Lyon in 2023. All coaches who turn away pick up quickly on what's happening, of course, from the reactions of people around them and the crowd. But they prefer not to see it with their own eyes.

Players do the same. When Bayern Munich received a late and potentially decisive penalty kick in the 2012 Champions League final against Chelsea, Bastian Schweinsteiger could be seen sitting on the grass at the opposite end of the pitch in the Bayern penalty area, with his back towards the action. The penalty didn't go in, and Schweinsteiger later found himself taking, and missing, a penalty in the shootout and ending up on the losing side.

In the 2014 World Cup, Kun Agüero stood with his Argentina

teammates in the centre circle during the penalty shootout in their semi-final against the Netherlands. However, while the others were nervously watching the kicks, Agüero had turned his back and was looking the opposite way. Chelsea's Portuguese defender Ricardo Carvalho adopted the same position in the 2008 Champions League final against Manchester United, and England's Paul Ince was heavily criticised in the English media for sitting down in the centre circle with his back to the penalties during the epic shootout against Germany in the semi-final of Euro 96. Even back in 1980, in the early days of this kind of drama, at the Cup Winners' Cup final, the TV cameras picked up Paul Barron, the reserve goalkeeper for Arsenal, standing on the sideline with his back towards the ongoing shootout.

The cocktail of unpleasant emotions these players get served when participating in a penalty shootout can be explosive, and some clearly decide that the best thing to do is not watch at all. This "perceptual avoidance", or "experiential avoidance",[35] is something everyone can probably empathise with. We have all done more or less the same at some time or another, whether we are about to drive past a squashed animal on the highway, or about to witness a particularly gruesome scene in a horror movie, or (yes) when our team is about to take an important penalty kick in a football match. We look away to spare ourselves the trauma.

And fair enough. Watching a penalty shootout is a stressful business: it makes sense to protect yourself. And that goes as much for those watching on the sideline as for those of us in our living rooms. However, there is obviously a difference if you are there as a member of the performing team. Maybe we should draw the line at perceptual avoidance in that case. If you're a player who is active in the shootout, your actions and behaviours are always likely to speak to and affect the other performers. You cannot not communicate.[36] And maybe you need to be wary of conveying emotions that will negatively impact your teammates.

We will return to this in Chapter 4, when we consider ways in which penalties are actually a team game. In the meantime, what are the penalty takers themselves doing with respect to their gaze and their natural instinct for avoidance? Obviously you can't take a penalty with your back towards the ball…

Or can you?

Two years after Paul Ince sat down in the centre circle, looking the wrong way, he found himself involved in another penalty shootout for England. This time it was in the magnificent (for the neutral, certainly) clash with Argentina in the 1998 World Cup quarter-final. And this time, Ince did not remain watching for the duration of the shootout, because he had to take a shot. When he walked towards the ball, he gave a little smile. Confidence? Or an attempt to mask a lack of confidence? Difficult to tell. However, what happened then, although in some ways mundane and undramatic, could provide a clue.

After players have placed the ball on the penalty spot, they essentially have two ways to walk back to the spot from which they later initiate their run-up. They can walk backwards, while keeping their face in the direction of the goalkeeper (I call this approach looking). Or they can turn around and walk away with their back towards the goalkeeper (avoidance looking). This latter strategy gives the penalty taker a relief from watching and engaging with the goalkeeper, and it's fully consistent with the "perceptual avoidance" theory described above. This is the strategy Ince used. He put the ball down and immediately turned his back on the goalkeeper when he walked away to prepare his run-up. With this he gave himself a pause from looking. He extended the period of perceptual avoidance. Then he turned around to face the ball, and the goalkeeper. Finally, he quickly ran towards the ball. And missed.

What exactly do we know about this visual strategy in a penalty shootout? In 1982, when France's Alain Giresse was first up in that first ever World Cup penalty shootout, he initially stood with his back towards Harald Schumacher, the German goalkeeper. Giresse said about this: "I don't want to look at Schumacher. I don't want to. I look away. You never know, he might have thrown me off, with gestures, so, I didn't look at him."[37] In our interviews, several players talk about how stressful it is to watch the goalkeeper as one prepares one's shot. For example, one player looked away after observing the goalkeeper's actions. The goalkeeper had taken his time getting into the goal, had ostentatiously thrown his drinking bottle away and had then verbally queried the shooter's placement of the ball. "Usually I don't turn when walking back from the ball," the player said. "But it felt good to have a second where I did not have to look at him".

We know that under the conditions of greatest intensity in a penalty shootout, players engage more in avoidance looking than in other situations. We published a paper in 2008, showing that up until that time, when players in the major tournaments took one of those extraordinarily high-pressure shots where a miss would instantly mean their team lost, the players turned their backs on the goalkeeper on 44% of their shots.[38] This was significantly more than when players had shots where a goal would instantly produce a win (14%), and also higher than where their shots would make no immediate decision (30%). It really does seem that when the pressure is at its highest, football players seek relief by looking away.

There are also some distinct national differences when it comes to avoidance looking. In 2009, I published a paper entitled "Why do English players fail in soccer penalty shootouts?"[39] I looked at differences between countries with respect to several variables and behaviours. Players from what are traditionally considered strong football nations with the most competitive domestic leagues, among whom England definitely figured, showed more avoidance behaviours than players from other countries. For example, 57% of English penalty takers turned away from the goalkeeper when they walked back from the ball. This was by far the highest proportion among the eight European countries examined in the study, and considerably more than the country with the second-most avoidance looking (see diagram below).

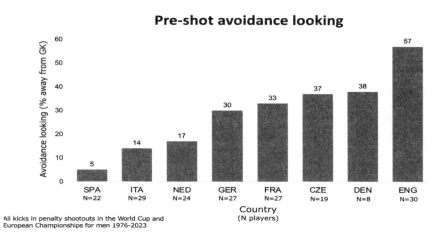

Pre-shot avoidance looking

All kicks in penalty shootouts in the World Cup and European Championships for men 1976-2023

I concluded in that paper that English players probably experienced more pressure than players from other European countries, pressure which had its roots in very high (perhaps unreasonably high) national expectations, the long gap since their last big tournament win (the 1966 World Cup) and the unique ruthlessness of the English media. These factors had likely produced a stronger stress experience for English players at high-pressure moments, with increased anxiety and other disruptively unpleasant emotions. And perhaps that was why they had tended to turn around.

But does avoidance looking impact performance? It depends. My analysis of all the penalty shootouts in major tournaments for men between 1976 and 2023 shows that players doing avoidance looking score on 72% of their shots, while players who don't avoid, those who walk backwards while facing the goalkeeper, score on 74%. That's a small and statistically meaningless difference. However, a series of laboratory studies from English, German and French researchers has found that goalkeepers who are up against penalty takers who look down or away feel significantly more confident than against those who keep looking at them.[40] Other studies show that goalkeepers will actually perform better against penalty takers who look away.[41]

Ricardo, Portugal's goalkeeper in the 2006 World Cup penalty shootout against England, may have felt superior when he looked at players such as Frank Lampard, Steven Gerrard and Jamie Carragher and they did not look back: "They didn't want to look me in the eye," Ricardo later said, sounding quite pleased about it.[42]

However, apart from what gaze behaviour communicates to the opponent, a key question, I think, to ask is *why* players turn their back to the goalkeeper prior to their shots. Is the turn a deliberate and planned part of a rehearsed strategy for coping with the pressure? Or is it a more spontaneous reaction to reduce discomfort? I would argue that the former can be adaptive and smart. When players strategically and deliberately look away, they take control, feel more in control and possibly even *gain* more control. A curious part of our video analyses of approach and avoidance looking in major penalty shootouts is that when the forwards in our sample avoid looking at the goalkeeper when walking back from the ball, they score significantly more goals (87%) than when they maintain their gaze towards the goalkeeper (70%).[43] Forwards are typically more experienced goal-scorers and penalty takers. Consider the Polish super-striker and specialist penalty taker, Robert Lewandowski. He always turns away from the goalkeeper prior to his penalty kicks. This is an integrated part of his routine, which provides a moment of rest for his attention before he goes into top gear and executes his shot. Other masterful specialist penalty takers who often turn around are Brentford's Ivan Toney (occasionally, against goalkeepers who are loud and take up a lot of space) and the brilliant Néstor Ortigoza, of San Lorenzo and Paraguay, who always turns away from goalkeepers prior to his shot. For these players, avoidance looking is probably the wrong word. A more appropriate term might be strategic disengagement (see more on this in Chapter 3).

What about those whose visual avoidance is unplanned, a spontaneous reaction? These players are maybe less experienced penalty takers, and may feel somewhat overwhelmed by anxiety, and thus compelled to seek a moment of relief. Looking away is not necessarily bad for these players either; it might just not be enough, and while trying to feel better they are also distracted from their task. When they turn to face the goalkeeper again, the situation is still there, they are not done with it, and now they need to confront the fear that they have been reactively avoiding – the Paul Ince scenario. Temporary relief does not necessarily yield results.

With this said, since we first published our findings on pressure and gaze behaviour in 2008, there has been a clear change in players' actions. With some notable exceptions like the ones mentioned above, hardly any players turn their backs and use the avoidance gaze strategy any more (see diagram overleaf). Pretty much every penalty taker now continues to face the goal while stepping back from the ball.

Why? One reason may simply be that some high-profile, respected and successful players have started to behave in a certain way and others have copied. For example, in the mid 2000s, Cristiano Ronaldo broke through and set new standards in many aspects of the game, including his extremely determined and deliberate pre-shot penalty routine, which involved a very dominant, confident-looking, backwards walk, with his gaze assertively directed forward towards the goalkeeper. Maybe it's all on Ronaldo.

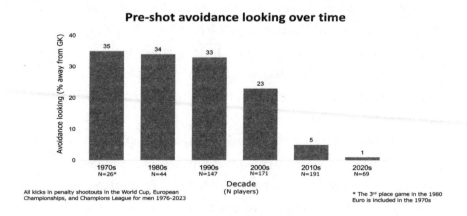

Pre-shot avoidance looking over time

All kicks in penalty shootouts in the World Cup, European Championships, and Champions League for men 1976-2023

* The 3rd place game in the 1980 Euro is included in the 1970s

Secondarily, it is not entirely unlikely that the published research by us and others from around 2008 onwards has brought awareness to these two ways of walking back from the ball, and prompted players to stop avoidance gaze because they want to appear more dominant, confident and in control.

Whatever reason, it is interesting how a single way of doing things can suddenly emerge, spread and ultimately come to dominate in the world's biggest sport. Penalty takers are particularly vulnerable to the emergence of such sudden orthodoxies, because penalties are at once so vitally important for the outcome of many games, yet at the same time so under studied among coaches and analysts. In that context, a certain behavioural imperative can quickly become firmly established, even though few, if any, know exactly why.

Still, this much needs to be acknowledged: our binary measure (either turn one's back to the goalkeeper or not) lacks some nuance and is unable to distinguish more subtle forms of avoidance looking. Recently, researchers rightfully critiqued our research and suggested a more fine-grained head direction coding protocol.[44] In their subsequent study of all penalty kicks in the German Bundesliga between 2011 and 2016 (400 kicks), they found that players who oriented their faces away from the goalkeeper or directed their gaze downward for a considerable duration of time prior to a kick missed significantly more shots than others. This suggests that penalty takers' looking behaviour may indeed give away something about how successful they will be. However, again, there are no absolutes, and correlation does not imply causation – I would never dream of telling Lewandowski to stop looking away from the goalkeeper because researchers say he should.

Speeding up

In the 2006 World Cup quarter-final penalty shootout between England and Portugal, Jamie Carragher took shot number four for England. He put the ball on the penalty spot, turned his back to the goalkeeper before he walked away, then instantly spun to sprint towards the ball. Carragher's shot was hard and down to his right. Ricardo, the Portuguese goalkeeper, was left standing. Goal.

Except not. The referee blew his whistle and pointed to the penalty spot, indicating that the penalty needed to be retaken. Carragher had committed a rare thing in a penalty shootout: a false start. So impatient to go, to get the shot over and done with, he had gone too early, before the referee had signalled. Now he had to line the ball up again. He repeated his strategy. He turned his back on the goalkeeper. As he was walking, the whistle came and he instantly turned again, rushed towards the ball and shot, this time to the other side. Ricardo saved it.

Are English players more in a hurry than players from other countries? In the aforementioned 2009 study on the English, I also measured the players' reaction time to the referee's whistle. The answer was clear. In the period 1976 to 2008, English players took on average 0.28 seconds to react to the whistle, which indeed was significantly quicker than players from most of the other countries (see diagram below).

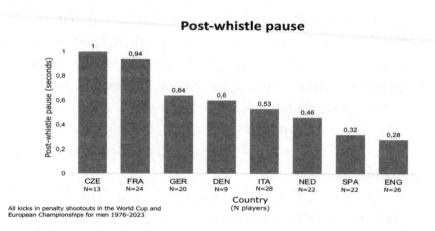

Post-whistle pause

All kicks in penalty shootouts in the World Cup and European Championships for men 1976-2023

Is 0.28 seconds quick? When Usain Bolt ran the 100 metres in 9.58 seconds in Berlin in 2009, for the current world record, his reaction time to the starting gun was 0.15 seconds. Thus, in comparison to the fastest man in the world, the English players are relatively slow. But compared with other penalty takers they are extraordinarily quick. They do not wait at all after the referee's whistle.

With that said, in our studies of penalty takers prior to 2007, most players took less than one second to react to the referee's whistle (0.7 seconds on average).[45] This is absurdly quicker than athletes from other sports, in similar situations. For example, a study of NBA basketball players showed that the mean time from when the players received the ball from the referee – at which point they were free to shoot – until the ball was released was about six seconds.[46] A study of rugby players in the 1999 World Cup shows that they took between 10 and 11 seconds after they had walked back to stand still and concentrate before they started moving towards the ball.[47] And many elite rugby players take longer than that – up to 15 seconds.[48] Meanwhile, golf players sometimes stand over shots for as long as 20-30 seconds.

This begs the question: when athletes in all these other sports are taking up to half a minute to focus themselves before their comparable performances, why do football players take less than a second? Why, in football, is the referee's whistle so often interpreted as an instruction to kick rather than what it is – the signal that grants permission to kick? Why are footballers in such a rush? I think a part of the answer is that football penalty takers have been less aware and deliberate about their pre-performance routines than players from other sports. They have no plan or strategy – apart from where and how to shoot, and the whistle then becomes the starting gun. However, also, penalty takers in penalty shoot-outs are under extreme levels of pressure, and this might show in their timing. An indication of this can be found in how some of the English players who have missed penalties over the years have described their experiences. Chris Waddle, who missed in the 1990 World Cup, said afterwards: "I just wanted it to be over."[49] Gareth Southgate, the England manager since 2016, famously missed his penalty in the 1996 Euro semi-final against Germany, and said this: "All I wanted was the ball: put it on the spot, get it over and done with."[50] And, Steven Gerrard, who missed in the 2006 World Cup quarter-final against Portugal, gave perhaps the most colourful description of them all: "Jesus, I wish I was first up. Get it out the way. The wait's killing me. I could hardly watch as Simão scored… I was ready. Elizondo wasn't. Blow the whistle. F****** get a move on, ref! Why the wait? Jesus Christ. I was screaming inside."[51] What all these players have in common is an intense dread, urgency and a desire to end the wait and stop the pain.

That people speed up under pressure is not unique to football, or to penalty kicks. There are several studies documenting and illustrating how athletes rush and speed up when they are not able to control themselves under high pressure.[52] In general, research shows that when people are given the choice to wait for something painful or get it over with quickly, many choose to get it over with quickly.[53] In one study, in 70% of the cases people dreaded mild but painful electric shocks so much that they wanted to receive more pain right away rather than to wait for less pain in the near future. It's possible to dread the anticipation of the pain more than the pain itself.[54]

The question is whether speeding up to cope with pressure is helpful or harmful to performance. In 2009, thinking about this issue, we published our study of every kick in all the major men's penalty shootouts that had taken place up to that point (37 penalty shootouts and 366 kicks).[55] The results showed that those players who instantly ran towards the ball after the whistle scored significantly fewer goals (less than 60%) than those who paused for just a moment before moving towards the ball (more than 80%).

Things then started changing. The media picked up our study and put out stories with titles such as "Why pausing on penalties could help England win" (*Daily Telegraph*) and "In penalty kicks, tortoises fare better than hares" (*Wall Street Journal*). Around the same time and over those next few years, several of the most profiled players, Cristiano Ronaldo, Nani and Neymar, started taking three- to five-second pauses prior to their kicks. For example, when Neymar scored the winning goal in the penalty shootout in the 2016 Olympics final against Germany, he paused for almost five seconds before his run-up. Since then, players seem to have started taking considerably and progressively longer time after the referee's whistle. Whether because of these pioneers, the publication of our research, or for some entirely different reason or combination of reasons, the penalty takers over the next decade (into the 2020s) more than doubled their average post-whistle pause time to more than two seconds (see diagram below).

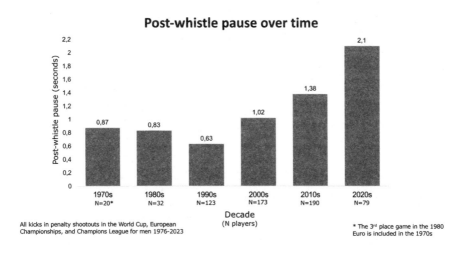

Post-whistle pause over time

All kicks in penalty shootouts in the World Cup, European Championships, and Champions League for men 1976-2023

Decade (N players)

* The 3rd place game in the 1980 Euro is included in the 1970s

When players tended to take a very short time, there clearly were performance decrements for the shortest post-whistle pauses. But as we have seen previously, there might also be a performance decrement for the longest post-whistle pauses. This would be especially true where a long pause introduces the possibility of our old foe, overthinking – as we already saw, perhaps, in the instance of Marcus Rashford's 11-second pause at the 2020 Euros. Thus, observations of the time players take may identify two different ways to choke: 1) too little attention to the process (a short pause is linked to under-performance), and 2) too much attention to the process (a long pause is linked to under-performance). Generally, our more recent data shows that when players take longer time, they perform better. However, taking a long time does not come with any guarantees. There are enough instances where players take a long time and miss to serve as a warning – one could also take too much time.

Nevertheless, in an analysis of all major international penalty shootouts during the past three years, for both women and men, players who took longer time to respond to the whistle tended to perform better, and players who took the longest time scored 78% of their penalties.[56] Those who took the shortest time scored 51% of theirs. These effects can also be observed on a team level. For example, in the 2020 Olympics, there were five penalty shootouts (two for men and three for women). All shootouts were won by the team that on average took the longest time after the referee's whistle.

Note that it does not follow from this that all short pauses are a bad idea. Some of the players taking virtually no time at all, such as France's Kylian Mbappé and Antoine Griezmann, are experienced penalty takers who *always* take short pauses. This is part of their routine, and what works for them. The critical component is what players *do* with the time they take, which we'll come on to in Chapter 2.

Shot importance

Some penalties are more important than others. At the 1994 World Cup, which took place in the USA, Brazil played Italy in the final in Pasadena. The match took place on a smoking-hot July day in front of 94,000 people and a global television audience later estimated at two billion.[57] To cater for the European broadcasters, kick-off was at 12.30pm local time, when a temperature of 27 degrees Celsius in the shade turned to more than 40 degrees under the Californian sun. When extra time still couldn't produce a goal to separate the sides, the game went to penalties – the first time a shootout had been used to decide the destiny of the world championship.

The shootout got off to a shaky start. Franco Baresi missed the first kick for Italy, then Márcio Santos did the same with Brazil's first shot. Viewers wondered whether they would ever see the ball hit the net in this match. Finally, both teams got on the scoresheet. But when Daniele Massaro missed Italy's fourth kick and Dunga scored for Brazil, it was all on Roberto Baggio to keep Italy's hopes alive.

Ponytailed Baggio, the Juventus striker, was the shiniest star of the tournament – reigning FIFA World Player of the Year and holder of the Ballon d'Or. He had scored five times in this tournament already. Score again now, and his team were still in it; miss, and Brazil were world champions. There had arguably never been a kick with so much riding on it. A kick to save the World Cup.

Yet as he stepped up, Baggio appeared serene and focused. Composed movements, not much facial expression. His run-up was long and he started moving towards the ball immediately after the Hungarian referee gave the signal. Calm first step, then another seven quick steps. And then he struck the ball hard.

Baggio seemed to know as soon as it left his feet. The ball flew over the crossbar. Way, way over the crossbar. Not just a miss, a spectacularly dramatic miss. While the Brazilians swarmed around him in a crazy mix of relief and euphoria, Baggio quietly bowed his head.

Five years later, Baggio published his autobiography. In a book with the telling title *Una Porta Nel Cielo* ('A Hole in the Sky'), he revealed how much that one shot had affected him.[58] "I failed that time. Period. And it affected me for years. It was the worst moment of my career. I still dream about it."

The relative importance of a shot has an impact on the outcome of that shot. Penalties are scored significantly more from in-game penalty kicks than in penalty shootouts. Multiple studies demonstrate this. For example, a study of the French domestic Cup competitions showed an overall penalty conversion rate of 73.1% in penalty shootouts (252 shootouts/2504 kicks), against a regular penalty kick conversion rate of 76% in Ligue 1 at the time.[59] We also know that penalty takers who take regular in-game penalty kicks and who feature in penalty shootouts score about 4% more goals with their in-game shots.[60] The penalty shootout adds pressure and performance suffers.

Back to Roberto Baggio. He is not alone in missing the type of penalty he missed. Shots where a miss instantly produces a loss, and a goal merely continues the shootout, are defined by the potential negative consequence. I call this a negative shot. Our analyses of all major penalty shootouts show that players only score 63% of negative shots.[61] This is significantly less than the opposite type of shot – when a miss merely leads to more shots, and a goal instantly produces a win for your team. Those are converted 89% of the time. Shots with more neutral direct consequences, where both a goal and a miss will merely continue the shootout, are scored 72% of the time.[62]

The results from these analyses have been replicated in a study of French cup competitions, which found that in situations with the maximum at stake, players scored on just 56% of the kicks.[63] However, it was not replicated in a study with a large sample from 115 European competitions over a period of the last 11 years.[64] Of course, in my studies, we're looking solely at a highly elite sample of players in the top three tournaments in the world, where the consequences of failure could be fundamentally different from domestic penalty shootouts at lower levels.

So what these numbers seem to be telling us is that, for players in penalty shootouts at the highest level of performance, when the prospect of winning is there to exert its allure, performance rises (or is maintained at a high level). But when the prospect of losing looms over a player, performance suffers and the possibility of choking increases.

Or, to put it another way: the penalty shootout is a mental game. What strategies can be put in place to prepare for that challenge? And is there anything we can learn from those strategies about coping with pressure in general?

Chapter 2

Controlling the pressure

"Something that has made me so successful in penalty kicks for so long is the realisation and the acceptance that I will miss them."

Megan Rapinoe

Some people like to describe the penalty shootout as a lottery. Frequently they say this when their team has just lost on penalties. Fabio Capello: "Penalties are a lottery."[65] Louis van Gaal: "It is a matter of being lucky, a lottery."[66] Guus Hiddink: "You can't blame anyone if they miss a penalty. A penalty is always a lottery."[67] And Danny Murphy: "When it comes to penalties, it's a lottery... anyone can miss."[68]

Christian Karembeu, the former France international, took it up a notch in his description of a penalty shootout: "It is loading a bullet into the chamber of a gun and asking everyone to pull the trigger. Someone will get the bullet, you know that. And it will reduce them to nothing."[69]

Lottery, Russian roulette... well, choose your metaphor. But the sense is the same: the resignation of control. Surrendering your agency to other powers that you are helpless in the face of. We know that having control, or a sense of control, is a fundamental part of coping with penalty kicks under pressure[70] – of coping in any kind of pressured situation, in fact. And feeling in control comes from believing that an outcome can be influenced by your own effort – i.e. believing that it *isn't* a lottery (or a game of Russian roulette), or certainly not entirely so. In our psychological examinations of penalty takers in shootouts at the highest level, players who believed a shootout was all about luck were more likely to experience harmful anxiety than those who said it was all about skill.[71] Similarly, those who didn't especially rate their own skills as a penalty kicker experienced more anxiety. So the lottery analogy is clearly not the penalty taker's friend here. What can we do about that?

In this chapter, I will examine ways that football players can regain a sense of control over the penalty-taking situation, and themselves, and cope better with its demands. And maybe we will find that these techniques can have broader applications for pressure situations in our own lives.

But first let's try and find out the extent to which skill does play a part in the penalty shootout. To what extent *is* it a lottery, in fact?

The Messi problem

We generally agree that the world's best football player over the past 10-15 years is Lionel Messi. But how good is he at penalties? There are benchmarks we can measure this against. The most basic one is the percentage of penalty kicks that have been scored in the top 30 European leagues in the past 3-4 years: 78.6%.[72] In the 2022-2023 season, Messi's last season in Europe before he moved to Inter Miami, he played in Ligue 1 in France. There, the average penalty success rate that season was slightly higher: 79.7%.[73] And the average success rate across their careers for all the players in Ligue 1 that year was even higher than that: 81.9%.[74]

And Messi? Well, he has taken 140 penalty kicks in his career, of which 109 resulted in goals, giving him a success rate of 77.9%.[75] So Lionel Messi, the best player in the world this past decade, and a prolific goal scorer, is a below-average penalty taker.

Actually, there is a large constituency of excellent players, and habitual goal scorers, who all have surprisingly average penalty records. This includes some of the leading goal scorers in Europe over the last years, such as Ciro Immobile (82.8%, from 93 penalty kicks), Edinson Cavani (81.6%, from 76 kicks), Kylian Mbappé (80.4%, from 51 kicks), Marco Reus (79.2%, from 24 kicks), Radamel Falcao (79.1%, from 67 kicks), Thomas Müller (78.9%, from 38 kicks), André Silva (78.4%, from 37 kicks) and Pierre-Emerick Aubameyang (78%, from 50 kicks). Other top-level strikers are clearly below average, such as Sadio Mané (73.9%, from 23 kicks), Joselu (69%, from 29 kicks), Victor Osimhen (68.4%, from 19 kicks), Lautaro Martínez (65.2%, from 23 kicks) and Alexis Sánchez (47.6%, from 21 kicks).

Even the players from the past decade many would consider the best-performing penalty takers in the big European leagues only come in at or just a hair above average: Cristiano Ronaldo (84.9%, from 192 kicks), Zlatan Ibrahimović (83.2%, from 102 kicks), Neymar (81.3%, from 91 kicks), Mo Salah (80.4%, from 51 kicks) and Karim Benzema (79.2%, from 53 kicks).

What does the research say about the impact of skill on penalty kicks and penalty shootouts? Skill, of course, is difficult to quantify and measure. In our earliest studies, we used position as a proxy for skill. It would make sense that more offensively oriented players (midfielders and forwards), who are much more experienced shooters than defenders, have better penalty-taking skills. Our results showed that forwards (80% goals) scored more than defenders (67.7% goals).[76] However, in studies with in-game penalty kicks (thus not penalty shootouts), position differences only seemed to play a marginal or insignificant role. In an examination of 833 penalty kicks over eight seasons of the Primeira Liga in Portugal, forwards scored on 79.6% of their kicks, midfielders on 78.7% and defenders on 75.4%.[77] And in a report from InStat, the sport analytics company, on more than 100,000 penalty kicks, the difference is even smaller, yet in the same direction: forwards 76%, midfielders 75-76%, defenders 73-74% and goalkeepers 72%.

Another recent study gathered 1711 penalty kicks (both in-game and shootout) taken in the World Cup, European Championship, Champions League, and Europa League from 2005-2006 to 2019-2020.[78] Again, there was little or no difference in penalty kick outcomes from various measures of skill. Player market value, for example, does not seem to matter at all. Players who are worth €35m or more score on 74.9% of their attempts, those worth €10-35m score on 74.8%, and those worth less than €10m on 73.2%. None of these differences were statistically significant.

However, players on stronger teams scored somewhat more of their penalties (76.4%) than players on weaker teams (71.2%). When only looking at cup tournament shootouts, where sometimes teams from very different levels compete against each other, there are more pronounced team quality differences. A study of 1067 penalty shootouts held between 2004-2005 and 2017-2018 in 14 different cup competitions showed that the presumed better teams, the favourites, won 559 penalty shootouts (52.5%) and the outsiders 506 shootouts (47.5%).[79] These latter results appear to indicate that players on better teams do better with penalty kicks. But this does not automatically mean that this difference is all down to skill. Those big-team players may also be better under pressure and therefore better at handling the unique challenges of penalty shootouts.

So, in general it appears that your overall skill as a footballer, comparatively speaking, plays a role in your ability to convert penalties, but a relatively small one. Whether it's Lionel Messi stepping up, or a player of less abundant gifts, penalties seem to be a leveller of the playing field.

But just because everyone seems to have almost the same chance of scoring at the outset of the shootout, does that make it a lottery? Or are there things players can do to take control of their own destiny? Let's look, for a start, at different approaches to the penalty kick itself – and at the players who seem to have penalties sorted.

Specialists

The most impressive penalty takers, in my opinion, are those who have consistently taken penalties at the highest level over many years, and who still have a clearly above-average success percentage – the specialists. Harry Kane is one such, with a total conversion rate of 86.6% (82 attempts) and an exceptional 89.2% rate on his 37 attempts in the Premier League. And Robert Lewandowski is another – an impressive 89.7% from 87 attempts, predominantly in the German Bundesliga.

Yet although Kane and Lewandowski are clearly quite similar in that they cope with the pressure of the penalty moment, they have very different penalty kick techniques. Kane typically adopts what we label the "goalkeeper-independent technique". This is where the penalty taker decides beforehand where and how they intend to shoot. Most players go about it this way. Choose your spot, step up, aim and kick for it. Deciding in advance where to shoot simplifies the task to some extent. This style of kick also has the advantage of being relatively easy to execute adequately. However, it is difficult to execute exceptionally, the way Kane does it.

Where to shoot, though? Aim high is the received wisdom. Studies of penalties in the English Premier League and Portuguese Primeira Liga suggest that kicks should be directed towards the uppermost zones of the goal, and that the risk of going high and missing is lower than the risk of aiming low and seeing the goalkeeper save it.[80]

In our data from major penalty shootouts, we find (as you might expect) that there is no significant difference between shooting left (70.7% goals) and shooting right (71.2% goals). Best success rate, however? Straight down the middle, into the hole where the goalkeeper was standing until he dived. According to our numbers, 77.9% of penalties struck down the middle go in. Antonin Panenka was clearly onto something. It was 1976 when the Czechoslovakian midfielder wowed the world with his daring penalty innovation, luring the goalkeeper to go early and then gracefully chipping the ball into the middle of the goal – the style of penalty that still bears his name. (The move, which Panenka had allegedly practised for two solid years, won Czechoslovakia the European Championships, defeating West Germany.) Goalkeepers have a bias for action, going left or right as people generally expect them to, rather than standing still, which comes at the risk of looking foolish or, worse, indifferent.[81] However, the odds do suggest that goalkeepers are wise to mix it up a bit and stay in the middle at least occasionally.

A huge challenge for players using the goalkeeper-independent technique is if the goalkeeper goes correctly. In fact, this is where proponents of the lottery metaphor will get my support. Most goalkeepers by far will commit to and move towards a side before the ball is struck, which means sometimes they will pick the correct side, other times not. In our analyses of major penalty shootouts, if goalkeepers pick the wrong side, e.g. they go left, but the ball goes right, penalty takers score on 91% of their shots. If goalkeepers pick the correct side, only 54% of those shots are scored. Think about this for a moment. This means that something you as a goalkeeper-independent penalty kicker cannot control, the side that the goalkeeper goes to, cuts your odds of scoring with your penalty almost in half. This is an important reason why penalty takers often feel such lack of control in this situation.

However, if you have a powerful foot, like Kane does, even though you cannot fully beat those odds you can greatly bend them in your favour. Across his career as a penalty kicker, when the goalkeeper goes to the wrong side, Kane scores on 95% of his shots. However, when the goalkeeper goes correctly, Kane still scores an impressive 81% of the time. This is considerably higher than most players' 54%. His penalty-shooting skill is simply that good.

Not many players are able to deliver goalkeeper-independent shots consistently of that high quality. However, another exception is Dominik Szoboszlai, the Hungary captain. Szoboszlai joined Liverpool in 2023, but two years earlier, aged just 21, he was playing for RB Leipzig in a Champions League group stage game against PSG. Trailing 2-1, Leipzig were awarded a late penalty and a chance to equalise. Szoboszlai immediately grabbed the ball and took up position by the penalty spot. At which point he found himself face to face with PSG's Neymar, who seemed interested in having a word with him from very close range.

In the post-match interview, Szoboszlai revealed what was said in the exchange: "Neymar was asking me: 'You going to score?' I said, yes. He said to me 'Are you sure?' I said, yes. I never miss. It is how it is."[82]

Szoboszlai was as good as his extremely confident word. He struck the penalty hard and low to his left, just inside the post. Although the goalkeeper, Gianluigi Donnarumma, dived the right way, the shot was too hard and too precise to be stopped.

How could Szoboszlai have been so sure of himself? A game-saving last-minute penalty in a high-stakes match carries the kind of pressure that can break even elite penalty takers, whether or not Neymar is on hand to try and get inside their heads. Plus Szoboszlai was up against the formidable Donnarumma – all 1.96m of him.

Well, despite his young age, this was not Szoboszlai's first penalty kick. Prior to this one, he had taken 10 penalties for senior teams. And, exactly as he told Neymar, he had scored with every single one of them. A 100% record. Of course, 10 kicks is a ridiculously small sample. But what is interesting is that of those 10 kicks, eight of them were shot in exactly the same place, to his left. Since then, Szoboszlai has taken another six penalties, all of them also struck to his left. This makes 14 shots to his left, with two to his right (see illustration). That makes him extremely predictable. He could just as well have told the goalkeeper beforehand where he would shoot. However, because his shots are hit with such precision and pace, they are very hard to stop. Even the one penalty out of those 16 that he missed was not reached by the goalkeeper. It struck the foot of the post. I asked a goalkeeper, Ørjan Nyland, who was Szoboszlai's teammate at Leipzig but is now playing for Sevilla in Spain, how these penalties could be stopped. Nyland said: "Even if you know where he shoots, it is incredibly difficult to stop. His right foot is just really outstanding. It also helps him that he has an enormous belief in himself, he's mentally strong and is not affected by his surroundings or the preparations that goalkeepers have done in advance."

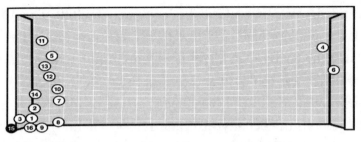

Dominik Szoboszlai's career penalty kick placement
(chronologically, with 1 being his first kick, 16 his last as of November 2023)
○ Goals
● Misses

This is goalkeeper-independent penalty taking performed at its very best. Pick the spot, then hit the spot, hard and accurately. Other elite penalty takers who have perfected this technique are Chris Wood (90.6%, from 32 kicks), the Paraguayan penalty specialist Néstor Ortigoza (91.8%, from 49 kicks) and Olivier Giroud (89.2% goals, from 37 kicks). All these players are highly effective in the firmness and accuracy of their kicking, and accordingly don't have to worry too much about what the goalkeeper gets up to.

Robert Lewandowski does it differently. In 2014, the Polish striker arrived at Bayern Munich from Borussia Dortmund. His first official game for his new club was a cup tie against the lower-tier club Preussen Münster. Bayern were comfortably 4-1 ahead in the 91st minute when they got a penalty, but Lewandowski hadn't got on the scoresheet. Here was his chance to score a debut goal. Despite the scoreline, Lewandowski was visibly nervous as he waited for the referee to blow the whistle. He then reacted quickly, took a few steps to the side and accelerated towards the ball. The shot was low and to his right, but he didn't strike it cleanly enough and the goalkeeper was able to grab it fairly easily. It was the last kick of the game. Clearly embarrassed, Bayern's big new signing put his arms to his head and then walked around, shaking his head, talking to himself, with a sheepish smile on his face. When I met Lewandowski in Munich to interview him for the Amazon documentary *Lewandowski – Unknown*, he said this about that incident: "This was the lesson that I had to change something. I started after this penalty to try to find a new technique."[83]

Now fast-forward to May 2016. Bayern are playing Ingolstadt, and a win will confirm them as league champions. After 15 minutes, they get a penalty and Lewandowski steps up. He seems extra restless leading up to the shot, breathing heavily a few times, while the referee gets himself ready. He then performs a run-up, but not with his usual acceleration. This time, he maintains an even speed at first, then actually decelerates, taking an extra-long second-to-last step and pausing before he reaches the ball. At this point, the goalkeeper, Ramazan Özcan, takes a big anticipatory step to his right, upon which Lewandowski finishes his run-up and calmly places the ball to the other side. Lewandowski has just become an official adopter of what is called the "goalkeeper-dependent technique" and will go on to become arguably its most lethal practitioner.

With this technique, the kicker keeps his eyes on the goalkeeper's movements immediately prior to and during the kick, and adapts the shot accordingly, sending it (ideally) wherever the goalkeeper isn't. This strategy gives the penalty taker a lot more control, ultimately, than the goalkeeper-independent technique, but only at the expense of some initial control. Essentially, you let the goalkeeper make the decision about where you're going to shoot. It's a very sophisticated technique, because the goalkeeper will normally be looking to commit to a side as late as possible, so the penalty taker may only have a few tenths of a second at their disposal to read this movement, make a decision and finally execute the kick. Often, the ball is struck without directly looking at it, which brings its own extra stresses; and perhaps in a situation with a title or trophy at stake and with millions of eyes bearing down on the scene, which brings even more pressure.

Over the next seven and a half years, Lewandowski took a total of 62 penalties with this technique and only missed four of them – a 94% conversion rate. Given the high competitive level at which those kicks were taken (Bundesliga, Champions League, international matches), this is an outstanding record. Moreover, he ended up putting the ball to the side which the goalkeeper dived in only 16% of these shots.

Variation helps penalty takers keep ahead of the opposition. After 80 goalkeeper-independent penalties, Harry Kane suddenly switched and waited for the goalkeeper before his penalty in the quarter-final against Arsenal in the 2023-2024 Champions League. And, across his career, Lewandowski has taken 21 kicks where he picked his spot early and blasted it, scoring 17 of them (81% goals).[84] But this means that when Lewandowski decides beforehand where to shoot, he is no more than an average penalty taker. When he lets the goalkeeper make the first move, he is an incredibly good penalty taker.

Lewandowski is also incredibly good at not disclosing the thinking behind his methods. When I interviewed him for that documentary, I asked him five times to describe the details of his focus as he begins the run-up to his penalty kicks. He dodged the question five times. Fair enough. The more secrecy and uncertainty players can build around the way they take their penalties, the higher the probability of them continuing to score them.

Another player who used the goalkeeper-dependent approach was Diego Maradona. He took a total of 109 official penalty kicks in his career (82.6% goals), but for Napoli, at the height of his career, he did better (93.1% goals, from 58 attempts).[85] This is how Maradona spoke about his goalkeeper-dependent technique: "It's very, very difficult. I've missed a lot of penalties, and they've saved a lot of them, but I've also scored plenty… Generally, I manage to win at these things, because I do this, I stand on my leg and I watch the keeper."

Here is a list of other excellent penalty takers who, like Lewandowski and Maradona, all regularly or occasionally employ, or employed, the goalkeeper-dependent technique:

Michel Platini 95.7% (46 kicks)
Raúl Jiménez 94.4% (36 kicks)
Ivan Toney 93.8% (32 kicks)
Sébastien Haller 93.3% (30 kicks)
Bruno Fernandes 89.8% (59 kicks)
Erling Haaland 89.4% (47 kicks)
Mikel Oyarzabal 88.9% (36 kicks)
Gabriel Barbosa 86% (50 kicks)

The broader lesson is that being prepared to accept some initial vulnerability and sacrificing short-term control and comfort might be an excellent way ultimately to gain *more* control and achieve better outcomes. However, this is contingent on having a highly specialised skill, and being able to place yourself in a productive mental state at the moment of the performance.

How can such a mental state be achieved? Where else within the act of taking a penalty can a sense of control be gained?

Pre-shot routine

January 2015. Tottenham v. West Bromwich Albion. Penalty to Tottenham. The 22-year-old Harry Kane appears focused. This is his first penalty kick in the Premier League. What does he do? He puts the ball on the penalty spot and calmly walks back. He adopts a standing pose, almost like a sculpture, staring at the ball, with his left foot ahead of his right, slightly leaning forward, both arms straight down. He starts his run-up by pulling back the left foot that initially was leading. Then, in a few short and rapid steps, he accelerates quickly towards the ball and hits it with pace. Goalkeeper-independent shot. Goal.

Fast forward almost nine years, and 70 further penalties, to August 2023. Bayern Munich v. Augsburg. Penalty to Bayern. The 30-year-old Harry Kane appears focused. This is his first penalty kick in the Bundesliga. What does he do?

He puts the ball on the penalty spot and calmly walks back. He adopts a standing pose, almost like a sculpture, staring at the ball, with his left foot ahead of his right, slightly leaning forward, both arms straight down. He starts his run-up by pulling back the left foot that initially was leading. Then, in a few short and rapid steps, he accelerates quickly towards the ball and hits it with pace. Goalkeeper-independent shot. Goal.

Spot the difference? There isn't one. For Kane, stability is key. He always sets up his penalties in the same way. The foundations of his behaviours leading up to the shot have been the same for nearly a decade. In his words: "Everyone has a different way of taking a penalty. My personal way is routine, same sort of run-up, same sort of angle, obviously pick a spot, and go with it."[86]

This does not mean there is no room for adjustment, if something can be beneficial. In his first year in the Premier League, Kane would hear the referee whistle and then almost immediately start running towards the ball. The next year, he introduced a deep breath and would wait a moment, before starting the run-up. Then, in the 2016-2017 season, he took it one step further: the starting position and the run-up were the same, but when the whistle went,

Kane would take a deep breath with a powerful exhale, look up to the goalkeeper, take another deep breath, look down at the ball again, and only then start his run-up. Those breaths, executed in the same way and order, have been his practice for the past eight years.

The stability of Kane's pre-shot behaviour is reflected in the time he takes before starting to move towards the ball after the referee has whistled (see diagram below). Although there has been a slight increase in time over the years, the duration of his post-whistle pauses reflects permanence and solidity, at a moment when the pressure is truly on, and the chaos and spectacle around him would distract and fluster most people.

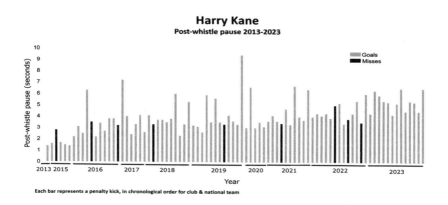

Harry Kane
Post-whistle pause 2013-2023

Each bar represents a penalty kick, in chronological order for club & national team

With that said, the spectacle could also get to Kane. There are outliers, some unusually long pauses, seen as occasional spikes in the diagram. The biggest of those spikes – a wait for more than nine seconds – was at Norwich in 2020, in the 83rd minute with Tottenham 2-1 down. Extra pressure? Well, maybe, but a close inspection of the video suggests to me that, amid all the noise, Kane simply didn't hear the whistle. Then, after a long period of standing and waiting, he glanced over at the referee and realised that the whistle had already gone. Only at that point did he start his breathing routine, which he executed as normal. Hard shot to his right. Goal.

A stable and steady pre-performance routine is a way to achieve more control in a high-pressure situation. There are countless ways to compose such a routine. Arsenal's Martin Ødegaard was not initially a regular penalty taker, but started taking some kicks in 2023, both in penalty shootouts and in games. He shared with me how deliberate his behaviours are, prior to his penalties.

"I know how to place the ball on the penalty spot. I know what to do when I walk back. I take sufficient time. And I know what to do when I run up to the ball, and what I think and focus on then. So that is all I focus on really, and not much else. You don't know if the ball will go in or not, but until I strike the ball, I have a good grip on what to do."

This clearly helps him to adopt a proper and productive mindset in these high-pressure situations: "There is this sharp and focused feeling. I am concentrated. I only focus on what I am supposed to do."

Control is a critical part of this: "I decide about the ball. I want to be the one who controls the situation, and not let the situation take over. The thought behind all these things I do is that I want to control it. That I command the situation."

He also explains that this is not something that just comes naturally; he works on it: "I think you just have to find your zone and be comfortable with that. This is something that I have trained so that I feel in the right zone."

Routines help performers concentrate more effectively on their tasks and channel their attention in those critical moments immediately prior to a performance. Studies also show that having a distinct pre-performance routine minimises distractions, increases one's feeling of control and reduces anxiety.[87] A meta-analysis of 61 studies with athletes from different sports concluded that pre-performance routines have a significant and robust effect on performance.[88] The exact components of each player's routine are different – how they walk back, take up position, start the run-up, the number of steps they take, whether they look at the ball or the goalkeeper. There is not necessarily *one* correct way to do it. What matters is that players feel comfortable with their individual routine, spend time in training rehearsing it, polishing it and making it robust.

Kane is the shining role model for this approach.

Ball placement

Our study on preparation times and performance showed that players who take more time physically placing the ball on the penalty spot scored more goals than those who took shorter time.[89] This could indicate that it pays to deliberately, carefully and meticulously make sure that the ball is properly placed.

Manchester City's Erling Haaland has taken this up a few levels. Haaland is an excellent penalty taker. Despite his young age (23 at the time of writing), he has taken 43 penalty kicks at senior level and scored 38 of them – a respectable 88% conversion rate. At the beginning of his career, Haaland employed a goalkeeper-dependent technique and was effective but unpolished and raw. For example, his very first senior penalty was in April 2018, for Molde against Lillestrøm in the Norwegian Eliteserien. He looked up before reaching the ball, saw the goalkeeper move early to his left, then smashed the ball into the top right corner. Was it strictly necessary to place it there when the goalkeeper was already lured away? Perhaps not. Nonetheless, the then 17-year-old Haaland said this about the penalty after the game: "The goalkeeper went left, so I put it to the right."[90]

A few months after that, he took a decisive penalty in an U19 Euro qualification game for Norway against Italy. Now he had added a pre-shot jump to his technique. Upon landing that jump, though, Haaland accidentally and subtly touched the ball with his right foot, before striking it with his left. Technically that was an illegal double-touch, but the referee missed it and the goal was allowed to stand. After that, Haaland stayed with a pre-shot pause where he simply dragged his foot prior to reaching the ball. He scored his next seven penalties, executing the goalkeeper-dependent technique to perfection – the goalkeepers going to the wrong side six out of seven times. He was asked after a game: "What's your secret?" The response: "I look at the goalkeeper."[91]

After his transfer to Borussia Dortmund in Germany, Haaland initially continued his flawless penalty record, but then ran into some difficulties. First, he missed a penalty against Augsburg in January 2021. The goalkeeper stood longer than Haaland may have preferred, and he powered the penalty against the crossbar. A couple of months later, he was up against Sevilla and their goalkeeper, Bono. There is one potentially powerful countermeasure against goalkeeper-dependent tech-niques and that is a well-timed pre-shot deception movement on the line. Bono performed an exquisitely timed left-right-left feint that may have bewildered Haaland, who shot right. Bono easily caught it. However, Bono had come off his line too early and the referee ordered a retake. The second time, Halaand scored, although Bono went the right way that time too and got a hand to the ball. In an interview with Norwegian TV after the game, Haaland appeared both cheeky and confident when he said: "I missed when he cheated… I scored when he didn't cheat."

However, maybe that incident got to him more than he admitted. A month or so later, Haaland changed his penalty technique completely. Against Werder Bremen in April 2021, he simply hit the ball cleanly and drilled it relatively high to his left. When the following season started, he had developed a smooth run-up, with no pause, but looking at the goalkeeper nearly all the way, before finally lowering his gaze to get a clean hit on the ball. These behaviours are very uncharacteristic of someone using the goalkeeper-dependent technique – there is no jump, stop or pause. You would assume, in fact, that Haaland had already committed to his shot and transitioned into the ranks of goalkeeper-independent penalty takers. However, the goalkeeper went in the wrong direction for nine of his next 11 penalties. Either Haaland is blessed with an inordinate amount of luck, or he can stealthily perceive the goalkeeper's movements, possibly using his peripheral vision while seemingly looking down at the ball, without losing the pace in his shot. Honestly, I do not know exactly how he does this. And he for sure will not tell me.

What is easier to ascertain is that in 2021, Haaland made a big change to his pre-shot routine that has stayed with him since. Prior to this, he put the ball on the spot, walked back (with his face towards the goalkeeper) and waited for the referee to blow his whistle. Then, suddenly in a game against Mainz, he remained standing with the ball in his hands at the penalty spot, looking at the referee. Only when he saw that the referee was about to blow did he put the ball down and walk back. He continued doing this. Sometimes, he would put the ball down on the spot and pick it up again, then repeat this a few times.

Other times, he would seemingly be preoccupied with something: wiping his nose, spitting a few times, or pulling his socks up. Why did he spend so much time by the penalty spot? Presumably this was intended to give him more initiative and control in a situation where the penalty taker never knows how long the goalkeeper will stall and the referee will wait. With such a routine, Haaland could adjust the ball positioning up until the last second and take control of the decision about when to start his run-up. After he changed his routine, he not only took substantially more time after the whistle (see diagram below), he also scored his next 15 consecutive penalty kicks. [92]

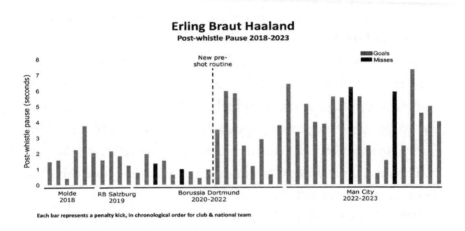

Each bar represents a penalty kick, in chronological order for club & national team

Thus, with Haaland, we see how even the simple matter of placing the ball on the spot can become another facet of the pre-shot routine and another opportunity for the penalty taker to seize control of the extremely pressured situation in which they find themselves.

Post-whistle pause

Yasuhito Endō is a Japanese football legend. With 150 appearances for Japan, he is their most capped player of all time. He played more than 1100 professional football games and retired in 2024 at the age of 43.

But when he featured in the 2010 World Cup in South Africa, Endō created a piece of penalty kick history. Japan and Paraguay met in the round of 16. After an uneventful and goalless 120 minutes, the match went to penalties – the first shootout of the tournament. Endō was first up for Japan. When he arrived at the penalty spot, he took a few moments to tread down the grass around the spot. Deliberate, but calm. He then put the ball down, took a glance at the goalkeeper and walked back (facing the goalkeeper). Upon reaching his run-up starting point, he locked his gaze on the ball. And then he just stared at it while standing completely still.

The referee gave the signal. Endō continued to stand still, apparently completely absorbed by the sight of the ball. And continued to stand. The television cameras zoomed in on his face. Not a single movement there. He appeared to be meditating. He stood like that for an achingly long 6.4 seconds. While the whole world was watching. Then he abruptly snapped out of it. One glance at the goalkeeper. A very short run-up. Two steps. Shot to the right corner. Goal.

To most people this penalty may have looked like an ordinary well-struck penalty. But for me, with my specialist interest, it was a simply massive moment. At this point in the history of major football tournament penalty shootouts, nobody had stood still for so long after the referee's whistle.

I toyed with running out into the street and finding someone to tell. But, of course, I still had the rest of the shootout to watch.

I met up with Endō to find out why he paused for so long. First, he said, he wanted to be unpredictable for the goalkeeper: "If I go right after a referee blows the whistle, the goalkeeper can more easily time his movements, so I try to take my time before kicking... I've waited maybe longer than six seconds for a penalty kick in the past. I rarely kick within one or two seconds after the whistle, so I think my appropriate timing is probably between six and ten seconds. It's always like that."

But what does he think about while he is waiting? "I think meditation is staying still without thinking about anything – it's really, well, close to that. So, I was focused, and of course I was standing there with confidence that I could make the kick. So those are the two most important things; to kick with confidence and being committed to successfully make the kick. I think about these two things prior to a penalty kick and I don't really think about anything else. I stay calm and still."

And that is it. He reduces his attention to the essence. Calm, confident and concentrated on successfully making the kick.

The post-whistle pause is self-paced, so in every case it is entirely up to the player how long it lasts. Historically, as shown in the previous chapter, penalty takers normally, and instinctively, take less than a second after the whistle before they start moving towards the ball. Those in a hurry, who immediately start running towards the ball, seem to miss more shots than others. On the other hand, those who get caught overthinking, might take extra time before the run-up to the ball, which could suggest that waiting too long is also not good.

The five players with the longest pauses in the history of major penalty shootouts are: 1) Marcus Rashford (England), 2) Tameka Yallop (Australia), 3) Paul Pogba (France), 4) Yasuhito Endō (Japan), and 5) Megan Rapinoe (USA).

The top-10 lists broken down by gender also clearly show that most of the long-time takers took their shots quite recently.

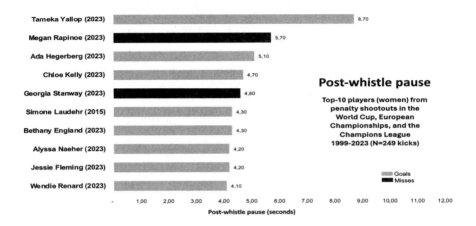

Post-whistle pause

Top-10 players (women) from
penalty shootouts in the
World Cup, European
Championships, and the
Champions League
1999-2023 (N=249 kicks)

Goals
Misses

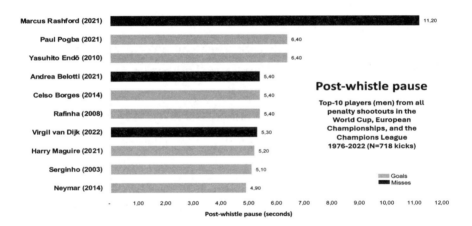

Post-whistle pause

Top-10 players (men) from all
penalty shootouts in the
World Cup, European
Championships, and the
Champions League
1976-2022 (N=718 kicks)

Goals
Misses

Given players' natural inclination to go at the moment of the referee's whistle, when they occasionally take longer time it almost always means that they are doing it deliberately. There is an intention there, not just a reaction. The function of taking a moment after the whistle is to ground yourself prior to the run-up, to achieve more control over yourself and the situation (including the goalkeeper) and to make sure that the shot is properly lined up and prepared. Here are a few examples of how elite players do this.

Celso Borges is the player taking the fifth-longest time in the history of big penalty shootouts for men. He had a very difficult beginning to his penalty kick career. At the age of 20, he missed the decisive shot in a penalty shootout for the Costa Rica U23 team in a 2008 Olympics qualification game, which to make things even worse, was against a Panama team that was coached by his father, Alexandre Guimarães. Borges told me: "It's one of the deciding moments of my career. It was traumatising. Tragic. I didn't take penalties for six months, and then, my dad told me, 'Sooner or later, you're going to have to take a penalty. It doesn't define who you are as a player; it's just a moment of the game.' All right. OK. Everybody misses. After six months, I took a penalty in a friendly shootout in Uruguay with my team. I changed side, and it worked. After that I took a lot more."

Celso Borges proceeded to become the most capped player in Costa Rican history, with more than 160 games for his country. In the 2014 World Cup, Costa Rica surprised everyone by coming out on top of a group that contained Uruguay, Italy and England, with the two latter teams being eliminated. Against Greece, in the round of 16, the match ended 1-1. Penalty shootout.

Borges remembered this vividly: "Oh boy. It was the first ever penalty shootout in the history of my country in a World Cup. I took the first penalty ever. So I was very nervous. I was very nervous. I cannot describe it any other way."

Borges did not let the nerves take over, though: "I was so set on what I was going to do. I didn't care about what was happening outside. I took my time and I'm all along just remembering what I have to do, where I'm going to shoot."

Borges scored. Costa Rica won the shootout and came up against the Netherlands in the quarter-final. Another penalty shootout. This one would not end happily for Costa Rica, but Borges was again first up and straight into the eye of the storm against the savage Dutch goalkeeper, Tim Krul: "I did everything the same. Took my time, waited a bit. A breath. And then I just took it." Another goal.

Now, interestingly, on both of his penalty kicks, after the referee's whistle, Borges took an astonishing amount of time before running towards the ball (more than five seconds against the Netherlands). I asked him why, and he said: "Yes, I took my time, which was my father's advice. He told me once the referee blows, it's not a signal for you to start running. It's a signal for you to start your ritual. It's not like in tennis, where you have, how much, 25 seconds before you have to serve the ball? You can take all the time that you want."

This, in turn, became for Borges an opportunity to influence the duel with the goalkeeper: "My father always told me, let the anxiety go to the keeper as well. What you want to do is to get the keeper to say: 'Hey, what the f…, is he never going to go?' Once they get to that thought, then I start my penalty. Once you see him break a little bit, I breathe and then I go. So that's why I take my time. It's not to rush it."

Many of the leading penalty takers in the world – Lewandowski, Kane, Giroud, Toney – now take a 3-5 second pause after the whistle before they run towards the ball. And we increasingly see young penalty takers taking a moment, and sometimes more than that. In January 2024, Jude Bellingham took his first penalty for Real Madrid. He was a young, inexperienced penalty taker (this was only his third senior career penalty), but he adopted the same ball placement routine as Haaland and Toney, where he delayed walking back from the ball, and then he took time. Lots of time. After his walk back and the whistle, he remained standing for more than 10 seconds before starting his run-up. And he scored.

It is imperative that players understand *why* they pause – that the aim is to acquire some control and composure, and that the pause mainly exists to help achieve this. Arsenal's Martin Ødegaard always takes a 2-3 second moment before he runs up to the ball. I asked him why, and at first he laughed and said, "I have listened to people like you, saying it makes sense." But then, more seriously, he told me that it was about being in control: "The referee blows the whistle, but I decide when I start the run-up. I don't just react to the referee, but it is under my direction. I am in control of that." When I asked Robert Lewandowski why he stands so long, he was very aware of the benefits for him: "I stand long after the whistle to have more time to get calm. To get more focused. And I know that for the goalkeeper this is difficult." He then emphasised that he has actively worked to get this part of his routine as optimal as possible: "I want time to work with me, not against me. It's a mentality thing. Long wait before you run. I control the situation if I have more time. I worked on this, and I found a good solution."

However, players should also be given the real option of *not* taking a pause, if they think they can transport themselves to a composed and focused state without one. If players take a pause just because the coach says so, this could add stress rather than relieve it. A study of elite archers showed that when they had to delay shooting another five seconds beyond their usual time, it drastically and negatively affected their performance.[93] Personal choice, informed by coaches' guidance, will in itself increase the perception of control and most likely increase performance.

A player's pre-performance routine will ideally be robust enough to serve in all sorts of pressure conditions, including very protracted ones. The experience of Chelsea's Maren Mjelde in the second leg of the 2023 Women's Champions League quarter-final against Lyon serves us with a good example here. Mjelde was brought off the bench with 15 minutes of normal time remaining and asked to play in, for her, an unusual role as a full-back. As she told me, "I find myself running after a really quick Lyon winger, and after 10 minutes I sense there is something wrong with my calf." Then she was moved to midfield, and her calf started protesting even more: "What is wrong with my body?" But she kept it together somehow: "At the same time, I am able to walk. And it is not over until it's over."

Indeed not. With her calf struggles, Mjelde's mindset was not at its best at this point. "In my head, it's like I don't understand, that if we get another goal, we are actually tied. I guess this is just over." Then, in the absolute dying seconds of the match, at the end of the second half of extra time, in the second of two minutes of added time, and with Lyon 2-1 up on aggregate, suddenly a Chelsea player is fouled in the penalty area and the reality dawns. "Shit. If we score now, it's actually a penalty shootout. And it tells you how many strange things happen in your head in such a pressure situation. In one moment, you think you're out. In the next moment, 'No, it's just one more goal.'"

As the referee went to the monitor to check the VAR, something else occurred to Mjelde. "I look around and think, 'OK, it's me then. I am the one to take the penalty'. Because when I look around, none of the two pre-assigned penalty takers were on the pitch. So I understood, 'OK, I just have to get ready'. So I actually start walking towards my own goalkeeper. I just need a calm place, and to take some time. I start to walk, I don't know how many steps. And when the decision is made, I have quite a long bit to walk to the opposite side, to the penalty spot. But I needed that time to get ready."

Apparently, taking time is always essential for her in these situations, and she has had some bad previous experiences: "I try to do the same in every penalty situation. And perhaps what I have the most focus on is time. I have experienced penalties where I did not take time, and that didn't go so well. I was not able to block everything out. And I was thinking, 'I just have to get this done with!' And I missed."

There was no risk of her taking too little time against Lyon: "In this situation against Lyon, I think about taking time. This is not just penalties actually; there are situations on the pitch when you have more time than you think you have. I take time and I breathe. Get the heart rate down. Many people said, 'Your heart rate must have been so high!' I replied, 'No, I actually didn't think about that. It was probably calmer than at many other times. If I had measured it, maybe it was higher than I thought, but at least I convinced myself. I had almost total control."

As it happened, time was not in short supply on this occasion. Indeed, Mjelde potentially had too much time. With the VAR check and the extended Lyon protests, a full six minutes elapsed between the awarding of the penalty and the actual kick. Interestingly, she said that her hearing capability almost disappeared in those moments. "I had this internal self-talk, where in a way, I don't hear anyone else but my own voice. It deafened everything else. It's like I almost don't hear the referee. I don't hear the crowd. I don't hear anyone. My voice is the loudest. It's a weird and absurd situation, really."

Then, finally, she was up. Whistle. A three-second wait. Then the run-up. And what a penalty. Under vast pressure to deliver, and after all that waiting around, Mjelde smashed her shot into the top left corner to make it 2-2. It was the last kick of the match.

But now there would be a penalty shootout: "After a little victory lap, I quickly felt: 'No, we are not done, we are tied. I have to focus again.' I felt a little bit invincible, and I brought that feeling with me for the whole team, in a way. Because of what I just did, it is not going to be more pressure than that."

In the shootout, Mjelde was first up: "It was good to just take my shot again, right away. The feeling of being invincible was still there. So I felt safe. You just have to do the same again. The same process. Take time, plan where to shoot and strike the ball well.

Those three things. I am pretty confident in myself then."

Mjelde scored again. She shot to her left, as with her previous kick, but low this time. The goalkeeper was after it, but it was hard and close to the post. Chelsea won the shootout to advance to the semi-final.

Can taking a pause before starting to execute one's task be used for coping with pressure outside of penalties and football? Certainly. In September 2009, at a gathering called the Vancouver Peace Summit, there was a panel discussion with, among others, the Dalai Lama, four other Nobel Laureates and respected leaders in the fields of education, business and social transformation. One of those was the German Eckhart Tolle, a well-known spiritual teacher and best-selling author. Tolle was asked by the moderator how "creativity can arise from a mind that is not completely distorted by mental constructions".Tolle closed his eyes and took a pause (who wouldn't when faced with such a question?), and then, slightly to the surprise of the audience, started speaking about football. He confided that he had listened to a researcher on BBC World News saying that those penalty takers who take a 3-4 second break after the referee's whistle were more likely to score than those who immediately started running towards the ball. There was, he implied, a clear lesson. The audience laughed warmly – not least when Tolle added that he hadn't watched a football match in about 20 years.

More seriously, Tolle characterised this pause prior to a kick as "stillness" and a "redirection of attention to within, to a deeper layer of being, where all power resides." This is more concrete and functional than it may sound. Anyone, in or outside of sport, can benefit from this. A moment of stillness prior to starting any critical task, perhaps using conscious breathing, will make it easier to ground yourself emotionally, plan the appropriate strategy and direct attention to where it is most required. (The researchers watching penalty shootouts with a stopwatch are of course in limited supply, so the one Tolle had heard on the radio was me – if there was any doubt.)

Breath

When Cristiano Ronaldo scored his decisive goal in the penalty shootout against England in the 2006 World Cup, not only did he pause for what then was an extraordinary length of time – almost three seconds after the whistle – he could also be seen taking three separate deep breaths. With each breath, his chest visibly inflated as he took air in, and the exhale was almost as forceful as some of his actions with the ball, his shoulders clearly dropping as his lungs emptied.

Long and deep breaths can be a powerful pre-performance technique in all types of pressure situations. When tennis champion Novak Djokovic is asked about his mental strength, he immediately talks about his breath: "There are different techniques. Conscious breathing is a big part, especially in the moments when you are under tension."[94] The neurobiologist Andrew Huberman showed that a "physiological sigh" – five minutes of breathing where the exhale is twice as long as the inhale – had considerable effects on the amelioration of anxiety.[95] Performers in all kinds of different high-threat or high-pressure contexts are increasingly resorting to different types of breathing techniques, and that goes for penalty takers, too.

Robert Lewandowski is one of the best penalty takers in the world, and he can be seen before every kick, deliberately engaging in deep breathing. As he once explained in an interview: "Taking a penalty in a Champions League knockout game is a big challenge, emotionally. The pressure is on. You run around a lot, you're out of breath, and you have less than a minute to calm yourself and slow your pulse down. You do that by concentrating on your breathing and finding a spot of serenity. You remind yourself of your own ability and replace pressure with confidence."[96] In his conversation with me, he said: "I started focusing on breathing the same time that I changed my technique. I know being calm in my head and my body helps me a lot. These kinds of small things give you a higher probability to score."

Costa Rica's Celso Borges has also incorporated a breath into this routine, which is part of the reason why he takes time after the whistle: "I took a breath. Inhale, exhale, OK, I'm ready. So nothing really took me out of that concentration." He also had detailed knowledge about why breathing might help: "I later found out, when I worked with a psychologist, the effects of breathing – filling up your stomach, relaxing the brain and just allowing blood circulation to flow a little bit better."

Diaphragmatic breathing, where the stomach rather than the chest moves with each breath, activates the parasympathetic nervous system, which induces relaxation. If one engages in more shallow, upper chest breathing, one will get the opposite effect – the sympathetic nervous system will be activated, which will stimulate a "fight or flight" reaction.[97] Thus, a good habit prior to a penalty kick, or for an equivalent high-pressure situation, is to take three or four deep breaths; breaths that are felt deep down in the belly. This can and should also be rehearsed away from the performance context. If your default breathing pattern is diaphragmatic, this will be a better foundation to fall back on when you are called upon to conduct deep breaths prior to performing under pressure.

Mindset

As a penalty taker, Erling Haaland is machine-like. He is lethally effective from the penalty spot. Yet penalties expose him and show his humanity. In those moments, he keenly points out, he is just like you or me. Consider what he said after taking a penalty for Norway against Sweden in June 2022: "I'm not going to lie; I was incredibly nervous this time as well."[98] Or look at what he said in November 2022 when, for the first time in his senior career, he was obliged to take a potentially game-winning penalty deep into added time. This was when Manchester City got a penalty against Fulham in the 95th minute of their Premier League game, with the score at 1-1. "Nervous. One of the most nervous moments in my life. A penalty in the last minute. Of course, I am nervous. Like everybody else would be." (He scored on both occasions.)

When I asked Haaland about these admissions, he doubled down on them even more strongly: "I am just being myself when I have commented about penalties, and I say it how I experience it. I think it's very strange if there are players who are not nervous before taking important penalty kicks. When I am asked how I was before I took the penalty, I say it how it was; I was shit nervous. It's natural that it is like that."[99]

Performance under pressure, we are strongly reminded, is not about being fearless, and without discomfort; it is about acting *despite* fear and discomfort – acting directly in the face of those things.[100] The tale of Zinedine Zidane in 2004 is another graphic demonstration of this point.

Early in the 2004 Euros, on an incredibly hot day in Lisbon, France and England faced each other in the group stage. At 90 minutes, England were leading 1-0. Then the Zinedine Zidane show began.

First, a stunning 30-metre free kick, drilled into the left corner.

1-1. Less than two minutes after that, Thierry Henry was brought down by the English goalkeeper. Penalty. Zidane stepped up. He looked confident, determined, comfortable. He performed his usual routine. Put the ball down in the same way, stepped back in the same way, stood in the same spot, ran up in the same manner. And, he buried the ball with pace deep into the left corner of the goal. An incredible high-pressure shot. France won.

However, what very few people saw was what Zidane was doing in the last seconds before his kick, while he was waiting for the whistle. This was not shown on TV, but a Swedish camera team sitting behind the goal captured it. Just four seconds before starting his run-up, and six seconds before the ball crossed the goal line, Zidane leaned down towards the ground and threw up. Not just once, but twice. The referee then blew his whistle. Zidane looked up, wiped his mouth, started the run-up and scored.

Clearly, despite appearances, Zidane was not comfortable at all in that moment. Maybe it was nerves, maybe it was the effect of 90-plus minutes of exertion in the extreme heat, or maybe he had simply eaten a bad prawn the night before. Regardless of why Zidane was feeling sick, he remained sufficiently focused on his performance and executed his shot.

Like Zidane and Haaland, most elite athletes are fully used to experiencing anxiety and discomfort. But the first step towards performing well with anxiety is to view it as normal, natural and sometimes even a helpful part of the performance, something to open your arms to. The legendary golf psychologist, Dr Bob Rotella, put it like this, with regard to the mindset of elite golfers: "They have to learn to respond to the feelings that come from uncertainty as exciting, beneficial and welcome."[101]

Yes, feeling good while performing is great and can add something to the experience right then and there. But this is not what matters. To quote the Austrian sports psychologist Peter Haberl, who has been to nine Olympic games representing the USA, working with different teams: "I don't care about how you feel; I care about what you attend to. I am interested in the function of the feeling, not the form." What is his recommended method for achieving that attentive mindset? Being present and aware, flexible, open, and using mindfulness and meditation training to get there.

Novak Djokovic is an open advocate of mindfulness training and explains his approach as follows: "I might appear locked in, but trust me, there is a storm inside. The biggest battle is within. You have your doubts and fears. I feel it every single match. I don't like this mindset that I see a lot in sports – you know, just think positive thoughts, be optimistic, there is no room for failure, there is no room for doubts. This is impossible. You are a human being. The difference between the biggest champions and the ones who struggle to get to the highest level is the ability to not stay in those emotions for too long. For me it is relatively short. As soon as I experience it, I acknowledge it, I may burst or scream on the court, whatever happens. But then I am able to bounce back and reset."[102]

Unpleasant and unsettling emotions are natural when performing under pressure. But if you accept those emotions and the inevitability of their presence, you will spend less time trying to regulate them and more time focused on what is necessary to produce your performance. The ideal is to be as fully alert to the specific demands of the moment as possible. As the NBA basketball coach Phil Jackson put it: "Being aware is more important than being smart."[103] By bringing the fullest possible attention to the present, the performer avoids worrying about the future consequences of their performance (in the case of the penalty taker, worrying about missing) and revisiting the past (thinking about that last missed penalty) and instead lasers in cleanly on the task at hand.

And then you are free to execute to the very best of your ability, despite the noise, the attention, the stakes and all the other potentially overwhelming elements of the pressure. You have, in effect, taken back control.

The England 2018 story

In the round of 16 at the 2018 World Cup, England faced Colombia. The game ended 1-1 after extra time and went to penalties. Most England fans had a strong idea about how this was likely to end.

Going into that tournament, the record of the England men's national team in penalty shootouts had been famously messy. Since 1996, they had featured in five critical shootouts and lost them all. Moreover, my analyses had revealed that England players adopted more avoidance-oriented coping strategies in those shootout situations than any other players in Europe.[104] Penalties had become a weight around England's neck. Their nemesis.

Chris Markham watched the Colombia game with colleagues in the in-house bar at St George's Park, the Football Association's headquarters. When Eric Dier converted the penalty that sent England into the quarter-finals and ended a 22-year era of consecutive shootout nightmares, everybody was, understandably, elated. About 30 minutes later, Markham's phone pinged. It was a text message from Gareth Southgate, the England manager, thanking Markham and his team for everything they had done, without which the win would not have been possible.

Later, there would be a number of people who received and/ or took credit for this penalty shootout success. In addition to the players and the coach, some people pointed to the FA's technical director, some to the performance director, others to the psychologist. But Chris Markham's name never seemed to come up. Why then did Southgate text Markham? Who is Markham anyway, and what did he do? Allow me to tell the full story of what happened *behind* the scenes leading up to that penalty shootout win, and of how England regained control of something that had been eluding them for decades.

Chris Markham is currently sporting director at Bolton Wanderers, but from January 2017 until February 2021 he was the game insights lead analyst at the FA. This new department, the brainchild of Rhys Long, head of analysis at the time, was tasked with finding and developing the types of match analytics insights that could be important for the England national teams' performances, insights which those working directly with the teams did not have the time to pursue. However, although Markham came to the FA from a job as head of performance analysis at Huddersfield Town FC, he was not an ordinary match analyst. His education was in sport psychology, completing his Master's degree in 2009. This background was probably decisive for the success with the first big project that awaited him at the Football Association.

"The first thing from the FA that landed on my desk," Markham told me, "was: 'How do we win a penalty shootout at a major tournament?'" From January 2017 until the World Cup in Russia 18 months later, Markham led a team of four analysts, and eventually a data scientist, all working with one goal: to help England overcome the dreaded penalties.

I was introduced to Markham in January 2018, and met him for the first time in April that same year. He wanted to pick my brain about everything to do with penalties, and also show me what he and his team had done so far, and how they had used my research. What he showed me then, and what I later learned about the project, blew me away. I can safely say, no other team in the history of football has ever prepared as thoroughly and diligently for penalties as England did prior to the 2018 World Cup. And no team, I would suggest, has thought so hard about, or worked so assiduously on changing, the collective perception of control.

When I later sat down with Markham while writing this book, he shared a lot more detail about what they did leading up to that World Cup. The contrast with previous England management regimes was unmistakeable. Markham: "I think I found quotes from each of the last five England managers before Gareth (Southgate), not including Sam (Allardyce), that said either the penalty shootout was a lottery, penalties are all down to luck, or that you can't practise that kind of pressure."

Over time the "lottery" narrative had built a fundamental belief that penalties cannot be controlled or trained for, creating a pervasive feeling of helplessness. Markham was very aware of those consequences: "From a psychological perspective, speaking about a lottery takes ownership away from the players. And that was the thing for me to give them back. To take control of not just the kick itself but the whole process. Initially it was about the perceived control. How can we increase the level of perceived control for the players and the staff and everybody?"

With that objective in sight, a number of different steps were taken. Here are some of the key ones:

A presentation for Southgate
At first, the team had six months to prepare one presentation for the manager, to convince him they could have an impact.

"Luckily for us, Gareth and his staff were extremely open-minded and respectful of good-quality work. But they don't suffer fools gladly, so we knew it had to be at a really high standard."

However, Markham was very aware that they were presenting a level of detail that Southgate and his staff probably had never before seen. "Talking about run-up steps, angle, pace, you know…

everything from breathing techniques, optimal areas of aiming, goalkeepers, looking at gaze masks and goggles. And that was just on the technical bit. And then player selection, gambler's fallacy, action biases and the centre of the goal being under-utilised... All these things could have easily blown them away, so I remember I went into Gareth's office, and we basically printed out and cut into bits of paper all the different topics and Gareth then prioritised, literally on the floor and table, which ones he thought were important and which ones he thought were less of a priority."

Dosage

Southgate's leadership and communication was key. Markham and his team had discovered all this fascinating information about penalty kicks, and were inclined to give as much as possible of it to the players, but Southgate kept everything in perspective.

"Gareth understood there was a huge amount of information here and some of it was really important. However, if you make too much of a deal of this to the players it will have the reverse effect and instead of decreasing the pressure it will increase the pressure. It will be paralysis by analysis. Gareth was really good, being able to get the right level of detail, the timing of detail, how it was put across to them and just make them aware of these things."

Breaking down the shootout into distinct functional units

In the beginning, they read scientific papers to understand not just the penalty kicks, but the syntax of the entire penalty shootout. Markham told me: "We looked at, I think it was nearly a hundred papers across different areas. That bit took a long time and that was when we came to one of the most influential papers, which was yours, where you broke down the different stages of a shootout."[105]

The phases we broke the shootout into were:

Roberto Baggio missed the decisive shot in the 1994
World Cup and later admitted that the moment haunted
him for years.

Kiss of life: with 1.5 billion people watching on television, Kylian Mbappé gets ready to take a penalty in the 118th minute of the 2022 World Cup final between France and Argentina. A year earlier, Mbappé had been cruelly blamed for a French defeat after missing a penalty in a shootout. The pressure on a single player may never have been higher.

Having converted that penalty, Mbappé then scores with the first kick in the subsequent shootout - his third successful kick from the spot in the game, capping a truly extraordinary display of sustained performance under pressure.

West Germany's Uli Stielike sinks to the ground in despair after missing his kick in the first ever World Cup penalty decider, in 1982 – the first opportunity a global audience had to understand fully the brutality of the penalty shootout.

A penalty shootout is an emotionally intense event into which players are often despatched with little or no psychological support and must find their own ways to cope. Here, while three teammates pray, Brazil's Marcelo (no. 6) takes a firm grip on his neighbours' shorts during the 2014 World Cup shootout against Chile.

Penalty kicks trigger an abundance of avoidance behaviours. Here is Liverpool manager Jürgen Klopp carefully not watching a penalty in a match against Arsenal in 2022.

False start: England's Jamie Carragher goes too soon and shoots before the whistle in the 2006 World Cup shootout against Portugal. The retake was saved.

Goalkeeper-independent penalty takers, such as Harry Kane, decide beforehand where to shoot, then typically keep their eyes on the ball to get a clean and accurate strike.

Goalkeeper-dependent penalty takers, such as Robert Lewandowski, watch the goalkeeper's movements and shoot accordingly.

After 22 years of hurt, England finally win a penalty shootout, defeating Colombia in the 2018 World Cup. Jordan Henderson, who had missed his penalty, takes a relieved gulp of water.

A minute earlier, Henderson is more animated. Colombia have just missed and England will win if they score with the next kick. Happiness all round, except on the face of Eric Dier (no. 4) who is the next to shoot and now knows it's all down to him.

A word in your ear: the goalkeeper Diego Alves has a little chat with Cristiano Ronaldo as the latter lines up a penalty for Real Madrid against Valencia. Alves is one of the world's most effective penalty stoppers, using all means available.

Equally Machiavellian, yet possibly even more direct than Alves, Argentina's Emi Martínez welcomes Teun Koopmeiners of the Netherlands to the spot during a 2022 World Cup penalty shootout.

Marcus Rashford sets out on the longest walk in football – the return to the centre circle after a missed shootout kick. This one was during the final of the 2020 European Championships between England and Italy.

Rashford's teammates remained in the now almost statutory arms-locked team formation in the centre circle until he reached them, making the longest walk also potentially the loneliest.

Phase 1: The break after extra time
Phase 2: The centre circle
Phase 3: The walk
Phase 4: At the penalty spot

"And that was when it started to come to life – the different areas that we need to be really good at. It is not just the kick, it is not just the psychology, there is a process that we can actually make that will take the pressure away from the players ultimately."

Process

Gareth Southgate notoriously speaks about focusing on the process, not the outcome. The same went for penalties. Markham: "We then spoke about a process we can follow and be better at. The main reason for that was our idea that the main thing we can do here is give the players back the sense that they are in control of this, that it is a skill that they can improve. If we could give the players process and ownership, they could then believe that this was something that they could control."

Analyses of own players

Markham and his team conducted elaborate and rigorous analyses of their own players' penalty kicks.

"One thing that we added was a pressure rating. Why would we look at a penalty in pre-season when John Stones takes two steps and puts it in the top corner as the same as a penalty in the FA Cup final? You have to differentiate between them. We also looked at England's penalty shootout experience. How many players were on the field in penalty shootout situations? And who took versus didn't take. We found some interesting things on some of the bigger attacking players who had clearly been avoiding taking them in the shootouts. So that gave us insight."

Meeting the players

Markham and his team presented a lot of these ideas to the players in a penalty workshop held in March 2018, a few months before the World Cup. "That was when we introduced the idea that the penalty shootout can be broken down into different areas and aspects. And we spoke about each of those in detail."

A part of this first meeting was to show a video with a lot of details about run-ups, routines, referee behaviours, team behaviours, etc. They did this to "basically say, there's way more to this than you think".

This was also the first time the players got to express their views. "Certain players with experience didn't want to take [a penalty]; certain players without experience did [want to take a penalty] and vice versa."

In the meetings with the players, they attempted to change the mentality around penalties, demonstrating to them, among other things, that England would be better prepared than anyone else.

"I think framing was the main bit. All this work... was ultimately going into building the perception that we have control over this. It is not something like a lottery; we can be better prepared than the other team because they won't be thinking about it in this much detail."

Meetings with referees

In the preparation phase, Markham also held meetings with referees to discuss the opportunities and constraints of the penalty shootout rules and regulations.

"It was all around the logistics of what-if scenarios. We discussed what we could get away with and at what point they would give you a yellow card. Around distraction, how much is the goalie going to get away with? Is he going to get away with scuffing the spot? Is he going to get away with pushing the bar?"

These discussions included trying to understand and incorporate the psychology of the referees themselves. "Look, most referees are probably not going to want to be the centre of attention at this point. So we deduced from that: you're probably going to get away with more than you think."

Notes on the goalkeeper's bottle
This was not new, but they had elaborate discussions around the information about opponent penalty takers that would appear on the goalkeeper's water bottle, which included transferring knowledge from other sports: "We looked at quarterback sleeves for the goalie and all these sorts of things."

The reaction to the whistle
They knew our studies on reaction time and performance well, but created an elegant communicative spin around it.

"We were really surprised with how quick, overall, players were and how short a time they took. As soon as the whistle went, they started running. I remember telling the players: 'The whistle is not *your* cue; it is the referee's cue. So, you can begin the run-up whenever you like.' Your routine doesn't start on the whistle; it starts when you want it to start."

Goalkeeper handoff
One of the distinct innovations that Markham and England brought to penalty shootouts was that their goalkeeper always would seek out the ball after having been in action at the goal line, to hand it over to the next teammate penalty taker. Interestingly, the idea for this came from having considered ways that the goalkeeper could engage in distraction of the opposition's penalty takers.

"Obviously, one of the things we measured in our analysis was distraction. So, we tried to categorise distraction from the goalie from low, to medium, to high. We sub-coded all those goalie distractions: waving, jumping, shouting, pointing, messing with the bar... As part of this, the goalkeeper's job was to go get the ball if he could. So, after we took a penalty, he would have to try and get it and after they took a penalty, he would have to try and get it. We wanted to mess about with them and not allow their goalie to mess about with us."

Celebration and post-miss support

Markham and his people spoke and collaborated with coaches and analysts from other sports who were part of Team Great Britain. In particular, the Olympic gold-medal-winning field hockey team, who were also involved in penalty shootouts, were an inspiration. This led to discussions around how the team could collectively respond to goals and misses.

"In Team GB, they didn't change their post-kick support. If they scored there was no positive affirmation or running and getting excited, and if they missed it was the same. It was more like the All Blacks mentality. It just is what it is. And they will always do the same no matter what. So, we'll collect the teammate, welcome them back in and we'll do the same whether they score or miss."

With that said, they were aware of other ways to respond to players who missed, and they showed videos to the players of teams where certain individuals would break out of the team huddle to collect the teammate who had missed. They then left it to the players to make a decision on what they wanted to do both after goals and after misses.

"There was definitely a discussion around that. Around how we should be showing togetherness, but it wasn't as much of a discussion around over-the-top celebrations. We didn't try and manage them and we didn't try and encourage them to act falsely, if that makes sense. But we did show them about Team GB."

Tailored training

The players and team practised penalties, but to a carefully measured degree, which was tailored to the player in question. "Players with little to no experience, such as Kieran Trippier, were treated differently to those with vast experience such as Harry Kane.

"The dosage was really important, and again Gareth and Steve Holland were excellent at managing this. Especially you can't have too many opposed kicks because of the goalkeeper, it starts getting unrealistic. Because the goalkeeper knows where the takers are going to go. So, you just end up messing about and it becomes more play than training."

They also contemplated bringing in other goalkeepers at training, to better simulate a penalty kick with an opponent who does not know the penalty taker.

"So, we talked about this at one stage but obviously [being in] Russia made it difficult. If it had been in this country like the Euros were, we could have brought goalies in from academies who would have had a higher motivation to save a Harry Kane penalty, so they would be trying really hard. But it being in Russia it logistically wasn't really going to happen."

Finally, they did their best to simulate the full penalty shootout.

"We did a proper penalty shootout with referees, a huddle, a walk, a centre circle, messing with distractions – all of that. So, a proper dress rehearsal before they left for Russia. I'm sure they would have done another when they were in Russia."

Also in Russia, the analysis team collected and coded each penalty taken and faced in training to "monitor performance and the development of routines, which ultimately played a part in deciding the order of penalty kickers in a shootout".

Roles in the break after extra time

Another innovation they introduced was structuring the roles and communication for the team gathering after extra time and ahead of them walking into the centre circle.

"We looked at things like the break around extra time. We had roles and responsibility for people, where they could and couldn't stand. It was all very structured and very regimented. Every little last thing was thought about."

The inspiration for this idea came from another sport.

"We spoke to Team GB Hockey about the penalty shootout process as a whole, designating roles and responsibility for all staff and players, even those not involved in the shootout. Roles were communicated clearly during specific team meetings and practice during training sessions."

Part of this was to divide the area around the team into different zones.

"We wanted to create clear boundaries which staff and players could or couldn't cross. You had touchlines, you had the dugout and the technical area. They created like a drinking station, a massage station, and players couldn't go on to the field, or certain staff members were told: 'You are not needed on the field at this time, because we need you in the technical area'."

One can see this plan in action in that eventual shootout against Colombia. The atmosphere in the English camp appeared composed, focused and professional. The goalkeeper only spoke to a few select people, and was approached by only one staff member at a time. The contrast with the Colombia team was visible. At one point, David Ospina, the Colombian goalie, found himself being addressed by five members of staff or teammates at once, all seemingly offering advice and opinions – impossible for him to process.

The pre-shootout huddle location

One of the questions raised in the meeting with the referees was regarding where they could and could not locate their team huddle right after extra time.

"What would you do as a referee if we went and had our huddle in the centre circle? So we're already there and the opponents have to come in after us. The referees were like: 'Probably nothing. You can go wherever you want.' Or what would happen if we did our huddle right in the corner, in front of our supporters? There were loads of things like that, logistical things that we asked about that we didn't utilise, as ultimately the players had to be comfortable with the strategy to enable them to focus on execution when the time came."

Why did this work?

Markham pointed out that the timing for such a project was perfect.

"I think it was the optimal timing, just when people were starting to buy into this, that you could be more scientific around penalties. We were doing it at the perfect time. If I was to start and do this now, we would have been way behind. So, the timing of starting this in 2017 and doing it in the lead-up to the 2018 World Cup when obviously not a lot of this was thought about, that was some of the genius in it as well. I think we were ahead of the curve then. I think it would be much harder to stay ahead of the curve now, because ultimately there are only a certain amount of things you can do. I think we got ahead, and the timing was crucial."

Personal impressions

This project was obviously a big experience for Markham, both in the short and the long term.

"When the shootout happened, I've never been so nervous. I felt sick."

Colombia's Radamel Falcao started it all with a rocket straight down the middle. Goal. England's Harry Kane came next. Routine as usual, composed and controlled. Goal. The next three penalties also went in, including the one from our old friend Marcus Rashford, with less than a one-second pause after the whistle. Colombia's manager, José Pékerman, hid his face in his hands for most of the shootout, while Gareth Southgate looked as cool and composed as his waistcoat. Then Jordan Henderson for England. Goalkeeper-independent shot to his right. The goalkeeper went early. Save. A long walk back to the centre circle. However, the next two Colombians, Mateus Uribe and Carlos Bacca, also missed, while Kieran Trippier scored to leave it all up to Eric Dier to send England through. He did. Goal. England had won their first penalty shootout since 1996.

For Markham and his team, one would have expected the party afterwards to go on all night. But in professional football, there is always the next game.

"I stayed up to like 9am that morning because we had to prepare the information on [next opponents] Sweden. So, I still don't think I've celebrated it now."

Markham remains proud of what they did, though.

"It will still probably go down as the thing I'm most proud of in my career, no matter what I achieve as a sporting director, because of the sheer scale of it. I still don't understand it now. Because we were so locked in a bubble at St George's Park. The good thing was that the brilliant team we had, that had done all the hard work together over the previous 18 months, were all there to celebrate our achievement together. That was the special bit."

Chapter 3

Exploiting the pressure

"I'm a chatty boy. I create chaos."
Emi Martínez, goalkeeper, Aston Villa and Argentina

When the Brazilian goalkeeper Diego Alves faces a penalty, he becomes the penalty taker's dearest friend. He is jovial, cheerful, generous. There is always a big, warm smile, sometimes a fist bump or handshake, often a kind embrace or hug. He will frequently grab the ball and generously hand it over to the penalty taker. He affectionately rubs his opponent's head with his gloves. He will lean in and whisper some friendly words in his ears. The penalty taker is met with charm and care. And even though they have a job to do, and this man is clearly their opponent in this setting, they seem to reciprocate in kind, often giving a fist bump back, returning the smile.

They kind of know, but if they really understood that Alves's attentions are lethal and his whispering wickedly calculated, maybe they wouldn't smile. Once Alves knows the penalty taker is listening to him – and a smile or a word back is proof of that – he knows he has opened a channel of communication that he can exploit. "I like to feel out the player in the moment," Alves has said, "find out if he's nervous. I like to talk to him, get a sense of him, to see if he's going to do what I'm thinking he's going to do."[106]

Once the connection is forged, Alves strikes, delivering a message carefully planned to irritate, undermine or sow doubt. For instance: "I told him that if he missed again, it would be terrible for him, and that I understood the pressure that he was under."

Always nice to be understood.

Does this kind of psychological manipulation work? Well, in his career, Alves has faced 69 penalties and saved 27 of them, which gives penalty takers only a 61% chance of scoring against him. This is absurdly low. So not only is Alves the proud proponent of one of the most sophisticated mind game repertoires in football, he also happens to be one of the most effective penalty-stopping goalkeepers operating at top level today.

In this chapter, we will explore what Alves and many other specialist penalty goalkeepers do to get under the penalty taker's skin and increase the probability that they will miss – and what the penalty taker can do to fight back.

With Diego Alves, we are clearly in the realm of Machiavelli. To the best of my knowledge, the 16th-century Italian author of *The Prince*, the seminal work on statecraft and power, never mentioned having a favourite goalkeeper, but Alves would surely have been a contender. Certainly if we define Machiavellianism as the strategic and not always strictly moral manipulation of others to achieve one's own ends – sneaky shrewdness, to put it more briefly – then Alves is right up there among our time's greatest goalkeeping Machiavellians.

And somewhere alongside him would surely be Emiliano 'Emi' Martínez of Argentina, the 2022 World Champion and 2023 Yashin trophy winner.[107] Born in Mar del Plata, just outside

Buenos Aires, and raised in a poor family by parents who sometimes had to sacrifice meals to feed him, Martínez left home at 17 to move to London and take up a place with Arsenal's academy. He spent the majority of the next decade on loan to other English and European clubs: Oxford United, Rotherham United and Getafe, among others.

Then everything changed for Martínez, and penalty kicks were a big part of the shift. Over a period of four years, he took part in five penalty shootouts and was on the winning side in all of them. The first was the least prestigious of these: the season-opening Community Shield match for Arsenal against Liverpool, played out at a Covid-restricted Wembley Stadium in August 2020. When the shootout started, Martínez first appeared quiet and restrained. Then, with the arrival of each penalty taker, he became more and more talkative. He began smiling and winking at them. He started approaching the penalty taker at the penalty spot and actively chatting with him as he prepared to shoot. At one point, the Liverpool manager, Jürgen Klopp, watched Martínez and opened his mouth in disbelief, then turned to one of his coaches as if asking "What is this?", and the coach just shook his head. One of the Liverpool players lifted his shot above the crossbar, while all the Arsenal players scored. The Emi Martínez Penalty Show had launched.

There has always been trash-talk in professional sports. Some athletes are famous for their verbal abuse, delivered prior to or during competition: Larry Bird and Michael Jordan in basketball, Muhammad Ali in boxing, Conor McGregor in UFC. However, in crowded sports arenas, the details of these trashy exchanges are usually drowned out. This changed during Covid. With no fans, viewers at home could suddenly hear exactly what people like Martínez were getting up to.

In July 2021, Martínez represented Argentina in the postponed

Copa América in Brazil. In the semi-final, Argentina faced Colombia and the game went to penalties. Juan Cuadrado scored with Colombia's first kick, narrowly evading Martínez's dive. Messi then equalised for Argentina. Next up was Davinson Sánchez. As he ran up, Martínez's voice carried loudly and clearly around the Estadio Mané Garrincha.

"I'm sorry but I'm eating you up, brother."[108]

Sánchez shot poorly to Martínez's left. Save.

Next for Colombia, Everton's Yerry Mina. Martínez now took his trash-talk to the next level.

"You're laughing but you're nervous. You're nervous. Hey, the ball is ahead of the penalty spot. Yeah, turn a blind eye."

Mina heard every word and when he stood by the ball, he mumbled something back, while smiling, probably attempting to appear unaffected and in control. Then he started the run-up and again a constant stream of words came from Martínez, almost as though he were providing commentary, with greater and greater intensity as Mina approached the ball.

"I already know you. I know where you'll shoot and then save it. I'm eating you up, brother."

Another poor shot, another save. Martínez then celebrated his performance by thrusting his hip forwards while rapidly pumping his arms, a move ripe with gloating machismo and vulgarity.

Colombia's next kicker was Miguel Borja. Somehow, Martínez found another level to go to, keeping the words coming with increasing force as Borja got nearer to the ball.

"Are you scared? You were running your mouth at half-time, huh? Where are you going, brother? I know where you're going. So, you like looking, huh? Come on, look me in the face. Look at me! Look at me! Look at me!"

Borja scored, with a power shot straight down the middle, but when the ball rebounded to him off the net, he aggressively booted it up into the empty stands, an indication that Martínez had got to him at some level.

By the time of Colombia's last shot, the Venezuelan referee had become acutely aware of Martínez's antics and finally made some efforts to control him. Too little, too late. Martínez moderated his behaviour, but still saved the last shot, so that Argentina won the shootout and went into the final, where they defeated Brazil and lifted their first major trophy since 1993.

But Martínez was only just getting started. A year later, at the 2022 World Cup in Qatar, Argentina competed against the Netherlands in a penalty shootout for a place in the semi-finals. It turned into the most hot-blooded, volatile and combative shootout in World Cup history. And guess who was at the centre of things…

With the first Dutch penalty taker, Virgil van Dijk, Martínez seemed well-behaved, quiet and passive. But this is just his strategy: not to come out with all guns blazing, but to make a soft start, feeling out the referee and the opponents, and then to build up from there. Van Dijk's shot was a nearly identical copy of his penalty in the Carabao Cup final with Liverpool against Chelsea nine months earlier, when he scored spectacularly with a powerful shot in the top left corner. Martínez was prepared: "I knew van Dijk. I had seen that in three finals he had kicked there."[109] Martínez appeared to be already at full stretch when van Dijk hit the ball. Big save. And even bigger post-save celebrations by Martínez.

"Saving the first penalty is like marking your territory," Martínez said later. "Scoring won't be easy for them, particularly the second penalty."[110]

The next Dutch penalty taker was Steven Berghuis. Martínez was waiting for him by the penalty spot, holding the ball out to him in his left hand. When Berghuis arrived, however, Martínez twisted his wrist and dumped the ball on the ground, obliging

Berghuis to walk 4-5 metres to pick it up. Berghuis smiled before his run-up, possibly because Martínez kept speaking to him for the duration of that little wait. He then reacted quickly to the whistle – and missed. At a moment like that, most goalkeepers give a small, joyful or determined gesture and quietly walk away. But Martínez is not like most goalkeepers. He has a wide reper-toire of ostentatious penalty save celebrations to pick from, and this time he selected a little dance, rhythmically moving his hands and legs from side to side.

Teun Koopmeiners was next up. Martínez waited for him, too, by the penalty spot, this time without the ball, but locking his eyes on him, trying to get eye contact and extending his right glove for a handshake. Koopmeiners refused to engage and Martínez was left hanging for 5-6 seconds. The referee intervened and urged Martínez to retreat to his line. No yellow card, though, not even a warning. Following the Machiavelli playbook to the letter, Martínez gets away with most of his tricks because he appears just sufficiently merciful and human to give off the perception of being on the right side of the referee's line. Koopmeiners scored. He then directed a taunt at Martínez, which was understandable after he had been so clearly targeted by the goalkeeper. But it also showed everyone that Martínez's presence was felt.

When Wout Weghorst, the fourth Dutch penalty taker, was on his way to the spot, Martínez glanced in the direction of the referee, saw that he had turned away momentarily and took his chance to try something new. He kicked the ball hard, as if passing it to Weghorst, but unambiguously missing him and sending the ball probably 30-40 metres away. Confrontational and hostile. Weghorst needed help from his teammates to get the ball back. Martínez then physically marked his territory by kissing both posts and fondling the cross bar. When the referee approached him during all this, Martínez tapped his glove on the referee's cheek – again a friendly-seeming gesture, but also assertive and domineering. Controlling the referee is essential in these situations, and Martínez plays the referee as if he were his own personal musical instrument. Weghorst scored, though, and a small fight then erupted between Martínez and Weghorst over the ball. Martínez won and could comfortably hand it over to his next arriving teammate.

By this point, both teams were engaged in something that looked more like a small war than sport. The Dutch players returning from taking their shots all went out of their way to taunt the next Argentinian penalty taker as they passed. When Lautaro Martínez started walking from the centre circle to take Argentina's fifth, and potentially decisive, shot, there were three Dutch players surrounding him, giving him the worst send-off they could muster. Hence, ultimately, when the Argentinian scored to put his team into the semi-final, his teammates did not run straight to him, as customary, but first ran in front of the Dutch team, to give them a final taunt. Only then was Lautaro Martínez mobbed.

Interestingly, though, one solitary Argentinian player went elsewhere. Lionel Messi ran directly to his goalkeeper and the two shared a long embrace on the other side of the pitch. Messi clearly recognised who had been the chief orchestrator of this shootout win.[111]

However, Martínez's masterpiece was still to come. A week later, Argentina went up against France in the World Cup final, a match which ended 3-3 and went to penalties – the third time in men's World Cup history that a shootout had decided the winners of the tournament. Martínez set the stage and took ownership of the penalty area from the beginning. While the French goalkeeper and captain, Hugo Lloris, was still in the middle of the pitch completing the coin toss to select ends, Martínez quickly walked to one of the penalty areas. Did he know? Was he guessing? Had he misunderstood a gesture from the referee?

Whatever happened, he picked the right end in advance of the toss and was able to capitalise on his early arrival. When Lloris eventually joined him and accepted his handshake, it was as though Martínez was welcoming a visitor to his own home: "You're in my house now!" With that one swift walk, he had basically created a micro-version of home advantage.

Martínez also shook hands with France's first penalty taker, Kylian Mbappé – all very friendly. He then politely asked the referee to check Mbappé's ball placement. The referee kindly obliged, walking over to the ball for a closer look and responding with a raised thumb. Now Martínez had established a connection with the referee that might benefit him later. The loose regulatory framework around a penalty shootout provides someone like Martínez with broad opportunities for manipulation. One might think that a football penalty shootout is tightly structured, but in reality it is not. The rules are only explicit on a few key points, e.g. goalkeepers must remain on the goal line until the ball is kicked and the penalty taker must kick the ball forward. But for players' behaviours prior to penalty kicks, there are few or no explicit guidelines and it's all on the interpretation of the referee. That subjectivity can be exploited by expert manipulators.

Still, Mbappé scored with his penalty, even though Martínez got a hand to it.

The next French penalty taker was Bayern Munich's Kingsley Coman. Now Martínez pushed a little bit harder, trying to meet Coman by the penalty spot, forcing the referee politely to intervene. Again, Martínez got the referee to check the ball placement, which again elicited a compliant raised thumb from the person allegedly in charge. Martínez then saved Coman's penalty and unleashed an enormous celebration – a short sprint with three huge jumps while punching his fist through the air. There was no questioning who was the dominant figure in the drama at this point.

Argentina scored and Aurélien Tchouaméni was up for France. At this point, Martínez was done with being subtle. He later admitted he had prepared for exactly this situation: "I had practised it with my psychologist: if I manage to save one I make life impossible for the next one."[112]

First, Martínez simply grabbed the ball right in front of the referee and walked away with it, as if it was his own. While the referee and Tchouaméni waited, Martínez showed them his back and took his time with the ball in his left hand while urging the Argentinian fans to make noise with his right hand. The referee, now visibly annoyed, lost patience, blew his whistle and started walking towards the goalkeeper. However, instead of handing the ball to Tchouaméni, Martínez simply threw it away, forcing his opponent to walk the extra 20 metres to fetch it. The disrespect was clear and obvious. No sanctions were given by the referee and Martínez just turned his back towards him and stepped into the goal. He was fully in control of this situation, and he knew it. When Tchouaméni had placed the ball on the penalty spot and was ready, Martínez put his hands up in the air and gave him a smug smile. Miss.

Leandro Paredes was the next Argentinian to shoot. Having just thrown the ball away from Tchouaméni, Martínez knew Lloris could potentially reciprocate. He therefore quickly grabbed the ball and handed it over himself, just as he had done in the semifinal. Proactive and effective.

After three penalties each, Argentina held a comfortable 3-1 lead. At this point, Martínez was buzzing with confidence, and he was about to unleash all of it onto his next opponent. When Randal Kolo Muani walked from the centre circle, Martínez turned to his coaches on the touchline and began intensely pointing at the French player and miming different saving actions. There was nothing subtle here – he wanted Kolo Muani to know that he was talking about him and his penalty-shooting preferences. When Kolo Muani came a bit closer, Martínez started addressing him directly, again pointing to him, then at himself, while nodding intensely and flashing a big smile, as the referee tried to hold him back.

It did not require very high-level lip-reading abilities to see what Martínez was saying: "I've watched you! I've watched you! I've watched you!" When Martínez then tried to wrestle his way past the referee to get to Kolo Muani, a yellow card was inevitable. At the goal line, Martínez continued to gesture to the Argentinian fans to make noise, while continuing to smile and verbally address the penalty taker. Kolo Muani scored, but Martínez was about to win, and he knew it.

While picking up the ball from the goal, he turned to the referee and asked: "If we score, we win? If we score, we win?" The next penalty taker for Argentina did indeed score. Argentina had their third World Cup trophy, and in no small measure thanks to the Machiavellian antics of Martinez.

What are the key ways that goalkeepers seek to increase the pressure on the penalty kicker who is facing them? And what does the data say about the impact of goalkeepers' distractions, disruptions and mind games on penalty takers' concentration, emotional state and ultimately kick performance? What follows in this chapter will not be kind, noble or civil. Vicious and obnoxious are probably better labels. But these behaviours are the reality in professional football, and whether we like it or not, we need to consider and cope with them.

Visual distraction

In the penalty shootouts of the 1970s and early 1980s, goalkeepers were well-behaved, obedient and stationary. Prior to a penalty, the goalkeeper would walk into the goal and take up position on the goal line, with no extra fuss. The goalkeepers' typical position during the run-up was standing still on the line, with their feet closely together, slightly bent forward and down, and with their hands down in front of them.

One man seems to have changed all this: Bruce Grobbelaar of Liverpool. And the occasion on which he changed it was the 1984 European Cup final between Liverpool and Roma. Liverpool had only been in one penalty shootout prior to this – 10 years earlier, in the season-opening Charity Shield match. Ominously, in the week before the Roma final, they had organised a practice shootout against their youth team, and lost 5-0.[113] Not great preparation. However, they had Grobbelaar.

The Zimbabwean goalkeeper began the shootout conventionally enough. But his demeanour appeared to change ahead of Roma's second penalty, by Bruno Conti. Grobbelaar first spoke loudly to himself as he was making his way to the goal line. Then he leaned in towards the goal net, seemed to try to put his face through it, but ended up biting it instead, before he turned towards Conti and clearly said something to him while taking a few steps in his direction and gesturing with his fingers. Conti responded by turning his back on Grobbelaar, while the referee got ready. Conti's shot sailed over the bar.

Roma scored with their third penalty, but it was ahead of their fourth that Grobbelaar performed the move for which he would become renowned. Much later, he would say: "People said I was being disrespectful to their players, but I was just testing their concentration under pressure. I guess they failed that test."[114]

Indeed. The move started with Grobbelaar casually heading towards the goal line as if he were drunk, swaying from side to side. On the goal line, he performed a series of bends and shakes, a wobbly dance routine complete with comically trembling knees. It's safe to say that no professional goalkeeper had ever prepared to face a penalty in a major final in quite this way.

Did it have an impact? It's difficult to know for sure. Ready to run up, Francesco Graziani mostly looked down – or pretended to look down. However, Graziani's gaze was in the direction of Grobbelaar for the final knee shakes, and his immediate response was to make the sign of the cross on his chest. Graziani then blasted the ball over the crossbar. While Graziani walked slowly away – going directly to the bench rather than back to his teammates in the centre circle – Ray Kennedy scored, giving Liverpool the cup and engraving Bruce Grobbelaar's name in the history books as one of the penalty mind game pioneers. And, of course, writing his name in the annals of dancing, too.

Now wind forward to 2005 in Istanbul, where Liverpool are facing AC Milan in the Champions League final. After Liverpool's epic comeback from 3-0 down at half-time, the game has gone to penalties, and Jerzy Dudek in the Liverpool goal is facing AC Milan's first shot, to be taken by the Brazilian Serginho. After Serginho has placed the ball on the spot, he never gives Dudek a glance, but turns around and walks back facing the centre circle. When he turns to prepare his run-up, he looks up at Dudek for the first time… and what a sight greets him.

Dudek is no longer a football player; he is a Latin dancer – rhythmically swinging his arms up and down while taking a few steps to his left, then a few steps to his right. Somehow, this movement makes him appear enormous. After the referee's whistle, Serginho stands in the ready position for more than four seconds – longer than almost everyone who has taken a major penalty shootout kick up to this point. And it's hardly surprising: he needs a moment to take in this bizarre visual display.

Finally, Serginho runs in, Dudek halts the wild movements and gets back to a position in the middle of the goal, bending his legs slightly to prepare for a big jump. Then the shot. Big miss. The ball flies over the top left corner of the goal. Penalty taker 0 Dancer 1.

Next up for Milan – Andrea Pirlo. For him, too, Dudek swings his arms up and down, but then he switches it up, squatting down so he is almost sitting on the goal line, then feinting very quickly left and right, several times. Pirlo seems to be suffering an information overload and shoots poorly. Dudek saves. Perhaps this is the incident that will later inspire Pirlo to describe the penalty shootout as "an endless and terrible walk into one's own fears".[115]

Then it's Kaká's turn. This time Dudek replicates Grobbelaar's wobbly legs, but with extra intensity and flair, twisting his hips downwards until he is again almost sitting on the ground and then twisting upwards again. At the end of all that, though, he dives in the wrong direction and Kaká scores. This means Dudek must now face Andriy Shevchenko, who needs to score to keep Milan in the contest. For the Ukrainian, Dudek performs something closer to his actions with Serginho, and to similar effect. The shot is more or less straight at Dudek. Save. Three unconverted penalties out of four. The Miracle of Istanbul is complete. Liverpool have come back from the dead and won the tournament. And goal line dancing has been raised to a whole new level.

Taking this artistic genre even further, Australia's goalkeeper Andrew Redmayne became a national hero when he came on as a substitute in the 120th minute of Australia's World Cup play-off game against Peru in 2022 and went in goal for the penalty shootout, which Australia won, qualifying them for that year's World Cup. Media across the world labelled him "the dancing goalkeeper" after a goal line display that included star jumps, pirouettes, squats, waving arms and even a bit of back turning, all performed in an erratic, unstructured and completely unpredictable fashion – Grobbelaar plus Dudek and then some. It only worked two times out of six, but that was enough. Redmayne later said that he had spoken with his goalkeeping coach ahead of the game and decided that "if you can make a complete ass of yourself to gain one or two per cent to distract them then [it's worth it]."[116]

That goalkeeping coach wasn't wrong. British researchers have documented that goalkeepers who engage in distracting movements will indeed draw more attention from penalty takers, and this will disturb and impair the penalty takers' performance.[117] That study was done in a laboratory with student participants though, not with elite players in the real world. Thus, in 2017, a world leading researcher on body language in sport, Philip Furley from the German Sport University Cologne, and colleagues, published a study on the impact of all goalkeeper distraction behaviours in penalty shootouts in the World Cup for men between 1986 and 2010 and the European Championships for men between 1984 and 2012 (322 shots in total). They defined goalkeeper distraction as "any kind of behavioural attempt of goalkeepers to distract penalty takers and draw attention towards themselves and away from executing the penalty kick".[118] The results showed that when goalkeepers tried to distract the penalty taker, 10% more penalties were missed than when they did not try to do so.[119]

I also did an analysis of these behaviours in major penalty shootouts. It was clear that there has been a steady increase in goalkeeper distraction behaviours in shootouts from the 1970s until the present day (see diagram opposite). While less than 10% of goalkeepers in the 1970s and 1980s engaged in such (on-the-line) behaviours, 50-60% of goalkeepers in the 2010s and 2020s did something to disturb the penalty taker.

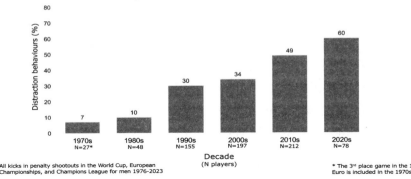

Goalkeeper on-line distraction behaviours

All kicks in penalty shootouts in the World Cup, European Championships, and Champions League for men 1976-2023

* The 3ʳᵈ place game in the 1980 Euro is included in the 1970s

Why this proliferation of goalkeeper distraction behaviours of late? It could reflect the game's increasing professionalism and competitiveness, where players are increasingly willing to do whatever is required to gain an edge. It could also reflect a widening belief that it works.

But what does our data say about it? Separating it out, we observed, across a 718-kick sample, that there was no difference in penalty-taker performance when goalkeepers quietly and instantly moved to the goal line, compared to when they moved to other locations in the penalty area prior to the penalty kick. Similarly, there was no difference in penalty-taker performance when faced with goalkeepers who stood still on the line or goalkeepers who jumped, clapped or moved from side to side. However, in those instances where a goalkeeper engaged in a *combination* of those behaviours and/or performed those behaviours in a particularly elaborate way, penalty takers scored about 10% fewer goals than when goalkeepers stood still, but this difference was not significant.

Moreover, if we examine only those shots taken after Furley and his colleagues undertook the study mentioned above (so penalty shootouts in 2013 and after), these differences are larger – a 15%

decrease in penalty-taker performance when goalkeepers combine or intensely perform behaviours compared to those who stand still. This increases to 25% difference when only including instances where the goalkeepers dive in the correct direction (which sifts out a lot of goals scored with poor shots and gives a more accurate depiction of penalty-taker performance). However, these sample sizes are necessarily smaller, and none of these findings are statistically significant, which leaves us with results in the hypothesised direction, but inconclusive.

From these analyses, visual distraction behaviours do not have an unequivocal impact on penalty-taker performance. Sometimes they will work, other times they will not, probably depending on many variables: the behaviour itself, its magnitude, its timing, the goalkeeper doing the distracting (some perform more convincingly than others in this area), and of course, the targeted penalty taker. Some players are more vulnerable to visual distraction than others. Other players may benefit from a bit of distraction – specifically those prone to overthinking. I suspect that visual distraction is most effective when performed in combination with other types of distraction, verbal, physical and functional, which we'll now come to.

Gardening around the penalty spot

In the past few years, there has been a proliferation of defending teams taking the opportunity provided by the chaos after a penalty decision, and/or VAR reviews, to do their best to, shall we say, rearrange the penalty spot with their boots. Several Argentina players tried this prior to Kylian Mbappé's critically important in-game penalty kicks in the 2022 World Cup final, and in recent times we have seen this technique performed by Premier League players at Arsenal (Aaron Ramsdale and Gabriel),[120] Chelsea (Antonio Rüdiger),[121] Liverpool (Virgil van Dijk),[122] Manchester United (David de Gea),[123] and Wolverhampton (José Sá),[124] to name just a few.

This is obviously a functional technique, because taking a shot from a scuffed-up penalty spot is more difficult than from a pristine one. But it can be a psychologically destabilising technique, too. Even if the physical damage is minimal, and the boot merely brushed over or near the spot, the penalty taker can feel indirectly violated at some level. The defender has literally stepped on the attacker's turf.

Penalty spot confrontation

Some goalkeepers take up position at the penalty spot to confront the penalty taker while he's trying to put the ball down. The Dutch goalkeeper Hans van Breukelen was one of the pioneers of this strategy. The final of the 1988 European Championships in Munich, between the Netherlands and the Soviet Union, is mostly remembered for Marco van Basten's stunning volleyed goal from the right edge of the penalty area. But let's not forget that, shortly after that, the Soviet Union were awarded a penalty, in the build-up to which van Breukelen found a moment to initiate a new approach to penalty-related psychological warfare by meeting the Soviet penalty taker, Igor Belanov, at the spot and having a quiet word with him while pointing to his own eye. Van Breukelen saved the penalty, the Dutch retained their 2-0 lead, going on to win the competition.

Ricardo of Portugal did the same in the 2004 Euros, waiting for David Beckham at the penalty spot with his hands on his hips and engaging with the England player as he put the ball down prior

– as we saw earlier – to blasting it over the bar. However, our data reveals that goalkeepers who show up at the penalty spot are not making penalty takers miss more shots than goalkeepers who stay back. For mind game specialists such as Emi Martínez and Diego Alves, the initial penalty spot confrontation is almost obligatory, but this appears to merely create a platform for other more aggressive (and effective) acts of intervention later on.

Ball possession

When a goalkeeper grabs hold of the ball just prior to an opponent's penalty, he also potentially grabs some control over the penalty taker and his concentration. He can use that control to delay, dominate or frustrate. Diego Alves likes to get hold of the ball early and then hold onto it for as long as the situation allows. He knows that this is a source of frustration and uncertainty for the penalty taker, who probably just wants to take possession of the ball and start his routine. Then, of course, the goalkeeper has the choice about how he eventually releases the ball. The theory: control the ball, control the penalty kicker. This is a subtle, but savage, powerplay.

Space domination

Few goalkeepers roam so widely around a penalty kick as Tim Krul of the Netherlands. During several penalty kicks in the Premier League, when he was the Norwich goalkeeper, the penalty taker would be more or less ready to take the shot, and Krul would be… missing. He was not even in the penalty area. He would be off somewhere taking a stroll, sometimes out to the side, occasionally even *behind* the penalty taker – anywhere on the pitch, really, as long as it wasn't predictable.

Netherlands coach Louis van Gaal famously brought on Krul in the 120th minute of the 2014 World Cup quarter final against Costa Rica, specifically to handle the penalty shootout. Nobody had ever made a specialist substitution of this kind at the highest level and van Gaal was praised widely afterwards for his imagination and boldness.[125]

Krul did not let him down. He took up more space, physically and verbally, than I had ever seen a goalkeeper occupy in a shootout. He confronted the opponent penalty takers at the penalty spot, giving them all a good talking-to, and ran all over the penalty area. At one point, Krul could be spotted doing warm-up runs back and forth in front of the penalty taker. This was his moment to shine, his 10 minutes in the limelight, and he seized it, saving two kicks and getting all the headlines after the game.

Celso Borges confirmed in a conversation with me that Krul had an effect on the Costa Rica players: "Substituting him on hit us mentally in the sense that, oh, he must be good at penalties. Then, I remember he came close to me and told me 'I know you, I know where you're going to shoot'. OK. He made us probably hesitate. He said the same thing to everyone: 'I know you'. He probably didn't even know who we were, but just the fact that he said that makes you, like, 'oh shit'. I know two guys in our team who changed the way they usually take penalties because of him. It's a mental game."

All is fair, clearly, in love, war and penalty shootouts.

Krul's legend expanded when the Netherlands ended up in another penalty shootout, against Argentina, in the semi-finals. This time, van Gaal's hands were tied, having already used up his substitutions. Krul remained on the bench and the Netherlands lost. Sometimes doing nothing at all is the best way to preserve your reputation.

Verbal disruption

What evidence is there for the impact of trash-talking and vocal distractions in general?

In one laboratory study, researchers had participants play a strategy game against an opponent named Pepper. During game play, Pepper would regularly make eye contact with the participants and offer commentary. Pepper's utterances could either be encouraging ("you're a great player... your playing has become brilliant"), or discouraging ("you're terrible... your playing has become confused"). The researchers found that those who played after having been exposed to the discouraging statements were significantly less rational and strategic in their decisions than those who were encouraged. Pepper's trash-talking had an impact on people.[126]

However, there is one detail worth noting. Pepper was a robot. A robot with head, arms, fingers, mobility and a voice, but still a robot. Even when the sender is a machine, words can have an impact on a human player in competitive situations.

What about the beliefs of the athletes themselves? A study showed that 89% of athletes thought trash-talk was an effective tool to gain competitive advantage. However, only 30% said that being exposed to someone else's trash-talk affected them personally.[127] Athletes, like anyone else, are affected by biases, and this seems to be an example of the "better-than-average bias", where people overestimate their own abilities compared to others – rather like the well-known observation that 93% of American drivers rate themselves better than the median, which, for obvious reasons, doesn't add up.[128] Building on this, the ones doing the talking might also benefit. A study found that trash-talkers *themselves* gained self-confidence from trash-talking.[129]

However, there may be a flip side. Researchers have also documented how the targets of trash-talk could be more motivated to work harder to outperform their opponents, and that they frequently did just that.[130] Targets get an extra reason to perform and put in more effort. With physical or highly automated tasks, extra effort will often be productive. Conversely, with tasks that are a bit more complex or technical, such as the penalty kick, that extra effort may be counter-productive. And it may tip over into overthinking and overanalysing which, as we have seen, can take down even the best.

Goal line deception

Jorginho is a penalty taker who had mastered the goalkeeper-dependent technique, scoring 88% of his penalties at club level and for Italy by waiting for the goalkeeper to make his move and then passing the ball into the unoccupied part of the goal.[131] However, in the 2021 World Cup qualifiers, Yann Sommer of Switzerland was ready for him. Sommer crafted a beautifully timed deception, very subtly feinting a movement to his right, strong enough to persuade Jorginho that it was genuine but not so strong that the goalkeeper couldn't then elegantly shift his centre of gravity and move to his left. Jorginho fell into the trap, directed his shot to Sommer's left and missed.

About two months after this, Italy played Switzerland again. The score was 1-1 when Italy were awarded a penalty in the 90th minute. If Jorginho scored, Italy would take the top spot in the qualifying group, with only one game to go. Confronted again by Sommer, and with memories no doubt scrolling through his mind from their previous meeting, Jorginho completely changed technique, to a goalkeeper-independent strategy – and struck the ball two metres over the crossbar. Switzerland eventually won the group and Italy did not qualify for the 2022 World Cup.

Some goalkeepers have become masters at subtle deception movements on the goal line that powerfully mislead the penalty taker. In my conversation with Fabi Otte, Sommer's goalkeeper coach at the time (for Borussia Mönchengladbach), Otte revealed that they had a special plan for goalkeeper-dependent penalty takers such as Jorginho: "There needs to be some sort of fake/feint from the goalkeeper to get him to shoot where we want him to shoot." They also talked a lot about zigzag movements and often trained penalty kicks in goalkeeper training. It helped that Sommer was "an incredible mover and very well coordinated and quick with his footwork". What's more, when Sommer stopped Jorginho in this way, other players who used a similar technique took note. In my conversation with Lewandowski, he suddenly brought up that save: "I saw the Swiss goalkeeper, Sommer, against Jorginho. That was very interesting to me. He goes very deep with his legs, shows he wants to go right, and very shortly before the kick, he goes left. Amazing. He did that really amazingly. And if you don't expect it, it can be a shock."

Timed to perfection, the goal line deception movement can be a highly effective tool against goalkeeper-dependent penalty takers. Destabilising effects can extend into future matches for the individual penalty taker and into the minds of players not even on the pitch.

Opponent analysis

In December 2006, a crumbled, sweat-soaked note with some pencil scribbles on it was sold at an auction in Germany for €1 million. The note belonged to Jens Lehman, Germany's goalkeeper, and had been used in the penalty shootout against Argentina in the World Cup quarter final that year. It had been written by the goal-keeping coach, Andreas Köpke, and contained seven Argentinian names and their predicted penalty-shooting preferences. Lehman kept it in his sock for the duration of the shootout, but took it out before every shot to check the particular penalty taker he was up against. For many, this was the first time they had seen someone using a crib-sheet in a penalty shootout. One would assume it worked beautifully, too, because Lehman went to the correct side for every single Argentina shot and ended up saving two of them. However, the pencil marks had reacted with sweat, rendering some of the words illegible. So when Roberto Ayala was up, it's believed that Lehman was unable to read the instructions. The note apparently said "right", but Lehman went left – and saved the penalty. Of course, the note might still have had an intimidating effect on the penalty takers. As Arsène Wenger told me: "Goalkeepers often get a piece of paper showing the preferences of the penalty takers. But sometimes there isn't anything on the paper; it is just to mess with the penalty takers."

There are earlier instances of goalkeepers having done their homework on opponent penalty takers. Back in 1988, Hans van Breukelen made (as noted earlier) an important penalty save for the Netherlands against the Soviet Union in the final of the 1988 European Championships, and another for PSV Eindhoven against Benfica in the penalty shootout in the European Cup final in the same year. A coach named Jan Reker helped van Breukelen with his database on penalty takers and their shot preferences.

"I created a card index in which the data was organised by country and club," Reker revealed. "I had a card for each player. I also got my information from TV. At home, I always had two videos running. At one point, I had four bins with data from 1500 to 2000 football players."[132]

Today, every professional and national team has access to enormous online video libraries with every imaginable game on file and plenty of trained analysts at their disposal. Penalty intelligence is part of this, and sophisticated data meets the gritty real world when predictions are communicated to goalkeepers on pieces of paper glued to water bottles that can be brought onto the field. However, this low-tech device can be subverted. Andrew Redmayne categorically demonstrated this.

As noted, Redmayne's dancing antics in Australia's 2022 World Cup qualifier against Peru caught the eye of all observers and may have contributed to Australia winning that penalty shootout, but let's not overlook his arguably even more outrageous action on that occasion. Pedro Gallese, his opposite number in the Peruvian goal, had two water bottles with him, one containing fluid, the other with a sheet of paper wrapped around it showing the penalty shot preferences of the Australia players. Or at least, he had two bottles before Redmayne got rid of one of them.

While Gallese was in the goal awaiting one of the Australia penalties, Redmayne simply and calculatedly grabbed the bottle with the plan on it and threw it into the stands. It took him a couple of goes, in fact. His first throw didn't clear the advertising hoarding, so he went over, picked it up and threw it again. In any event, Redmayne basically stole and threw away Peru's game plan.

It is impossible to know for sure the impact this violation had on Gallese, and on the ultimate outcome of the penalty shootout, but the fact is that the Peruvian goalkeeper went in the wrong direction for every single one of the three remaining Australia penalty takers. Redmayne later admitted to having some qualms about the strategy: "I've said to a few people it goes against every moral fibre in my body to be that kind of person and that kind of antagonist." But he justified the stunt by claiming his opponents would have done the same: "The South Americans are very football savvy, they're very street smart, they'll be the first ones to undercut you if they can."[133]

Whether judging an opponent based on the stereotype of an entire continent justifies this type of pre-emptive attack is another question.

Off-kilter positioning

There are strategies that are considerably more subtle, and less brutal, than water-bottle tossing. A fascinating line of studies shows that when goalkeepers are positioned marginally off-centre on the goal line, such that penalty takers are not consciously aware of the displacement, 60-64% of penalty shots will be directed to the fractionally more open side.[134] This is a top tip for goalkeepers, then: go off-kilter and get directly into the penalty taker's head. The data suggests that the optimal positioning for the goalkeeper in these circumstances is 6-8 centimetres in the direction of one of the posts.[135] I have not heard of any goalkeepers actually using this strategy, but I doubt they would tell anyone if they did. Got to be worth a try.

Reputation

As mentioned earlier, the reputation of an opponent can be enough to demoralise, intimidate and negatively impact a player. Simply knowing that one is up against a formidable opponent can sneak into one's head and cause one's opponent to grow before one's eyes. A line of studies indicates that knowing a goalkeeper is good at stopping penalties, or simply seeing that a goalkeeper saved the preceding penalty shot, will influence penalty takers to believe that the goalkeeper is around 6 centimetres (2.36 inches) taller than is actually the case.[136]

This phenomenon is reflected in another study of all the penalty kicks in the major tournaments (the World Cup, Euros, Champions League and Europa League) from 2005-2006 to 2019-2020 (1711 kicks in total).[137] Here, it was shown that the higher the market value of goalkeepers, the significantly more likely penalty takers were to miss the goal entirely. This was the only significant result in the study for market value and penalty outcome for both penalty takers and goalkeepers (to the surprise of the researchers). Still, it's a nice literal demonstration of the old saying about a person's reputation going before them.

Background manipulation

In 2005, the science journalist Daniel Engber produced a fascinating article about systematically distracting NBA free-throw shooters.[138] In NBA and college basketball games, home crowds have always gone to great lengths in their attempts to put opposing free-throw shooters off balance, using balloons, signs, chants and, above all, terrible noise.[139] However, free throw success percentage, home and away, does not seem to differ, suggesting the balloons and the shouting don't have much impact.

Engber then decided to go a little bit deeper to explore some of the nuances at play. He showed that arms and balloons being waved behind a target (here, the basket) do nothing more than provide a series of motion signals that effectively cancel each other out. For the shooter, all this motion becomes like a snowy TV screen, not strong enough to distract anyone. Engber's idea was to create a visual display behind the basket where the fan behaviours did not cancel each other out, but rather moved in unison to create a coherent field of background motion that was, he felt, likely to be more solidly distracting. The world behind the basket would appear to the shooter to be moving in one direction and he would likely compensate for that motion in his shooting and possibly miss. Engber pitched this idea to Mark Cuban, the Dallas Mavericks owner. Cuban went for it, and the Mavericks tried the idea out. Three coordinators organised the fans behind the basket so that everyone would wave their arms and artefacts in one direction and in unison, then in the other direction, and so forth. The Mavericks had some initial success, with the opponents making only around 60% of their free throws in the first two games, about 20% below the league average. Success!

But then they played against the Lakers, who hit 78% of their free throws, and Cuban decided to abandon the experiment, describing the initial effects as random.

Since this experiment, basketball fans have continued to promote innovations in the expanding field of distractology.[140] Among the ones who have taken it the furthest are Arizona state's college basketball team, who have come up with what they call a "curtain of distraction". This is quite literally a mobile curtain positioned behind the basket, which is then pulled away just as the opponent is about to shoot, revealing... well, all manner of craziness: roaring Santa Clauses, shouting old ladies, waving clowns, men with large bellies working out in their underwear, wrestlers, celebrities in speedos, students in animal costumes making out, celebrity impersonators... Does it work? Some statistical reports showed that in the first two years of its existence, the curtain – or what was behind it – seemed to decrease the opponent free-throw performance by 10-15%.[141] However, a report from a more recent season did not find any effect, suggesting that over time, opponents may have found ways to make the curtain of distraction... less distracting.[142]

Can such fan-based distraction stunts be performed with penalty kicks in football? In principle, of course. With that said, the fan culture in American basketball, and in particular, college basketball, is fundamentally different from that in professional football. I certainly struggle to imagine choreographed old-lady costumes and workouts in underwear at Old Trafford or Santiago Bernabéu. However, football fans show immense creativity with their taunting songs about opposing players, so maybe that creativity will one day transfer to equally coordinated penalty kick distraction displays. They could be valuable.

Run-up interference

I showed earlier how penalty takers now take substantially longer after the referee's whistle than they used to, and that this is a way for them to obtain more control over themselves and the situation. However, in all the thousands of penalty kicks I have observed, only twice have I seen a goalkeeper completely wrest that control over time away from the kicker. And both times that goalkeeper was our old friend Diego Alves.

The first time was in October 2017, against the Brazilian side Ponte Preta, and their penalty taker Lucca. Following the referee's whistle, Lucca waited, in accordance with his right. He waited a long time, in fact – just over 10 seconds. At that point, Alves decided he'd had enough. Just as Lucca was about to begin his run-up, Alves raised his hand and stepped forward, looking across at the referee and clearly protesting about the length of Lucca's delay. A small argument ensued, with Alves continuing to express his dissatisfaction, to both the referee and the assistant referee, before walking back to the goal line for a reset. Inside he must have been thrilled: another penalty taker's routine disrupted and the upper hand gained. For his second go, Lucca waited no more than 4.5 seconds, before making an uneven run-up and shooting the ball down to his left, where Alves easily saved it.

The second time was at the critical moment in a penalty shootout between Flamengo and Palmeiras for the 2021 Brazilian Supercopa. Danilo had a shot for the match and the trophy, and, after the whistle, he stood gathering himself for more than 10 seconds. Again, Alves called time on him, stepping forwards towards the ball to protest at the taker's "time-wasting", and causing everything to break down for a moment. Again, the penalty taker's routine was fundamentally disrupted. With his second attempt, Danilo paused for only 2.5 seconds and Alves once again saved the penalty. Flamengo went on to win the trophy. Diego Alves reads penalty kick situations like others read books, and he conducts them as if the players were his very own symphony orchestra.

Delay

There is a much more subtle way to disrupt penalty takers, which may be particularly beneficial for the quieter, more peaceful kind of goalkeeper who prefers not to attract fuss and attention to themselves. In May 2008, Manchester United and Chelsea met in the pouring rain in Moscow to play out the Champions League final. The game had to be decided with penalties. At the coin toss, John Terry, Chelsea's captain, was visibly annoyed. He was ready; Manchester United's Rio Ferdinand was not. Terry stood there for

a little while, together with the referees, lifted his hands in irrita-
tion, then walked away. Having to wait can be very frustrating.
And this was not the last time Terry and his Chelsea players had to
wait that night.[143]

After Carlos Tevez scored United's first penalty, Michael Ballack
of Chelsea began his walk from the centre circle. Meanwhile,
United's goalkeeper, the Dutchman Edwin van der Sar, seemed to
have placed his towel over by the corner flag. While Ballack was
walking, van der Sar was wiping his head and repositioning his
towel. This took a little while, so van der Sar and Ballack entered
the penalty area at the same time. Whereas Ballack walked efficiently towards the penalty spot, on a mission to get his kick over
with, van der Sar was seemingly out for a Sunday stroll, taking his
time getting onto the goal line. Consequently, almost 12 seconds
elapsed between Ballack placing the ball on the penalty spot
and the referee blowing his whistle. However, Ballack seemed to
work out that van der Sar was deliberately delaying matters, and
returned to the ball and respotted it before walking back again. He
then scored.

But van der Sar continued with the tactic. Where Chelsea's Petr
Cech was instantly and compliantly walking to the goal line, van
der Sar was taking his time, wiping his head with his far-away towel,
correcting his socks, asking the referee to check the ball placement,
all of which forced the penalty taker to wait. On average, van der
Sar had the Chelsea players wait for 8.5 seconds, while the United
players waited for only 0.7 seconds. Both John Terry and Nicolas
Anelka, the two Chelsea players who missed, handing United the
trophy, were forced to wait for more than eight seconds.

This was a superlative piece of indirect control taking by van
der Sar. A goalkeeper who delays takes the initiative, disrupts the
penalty taker's routine and rhythm and forces on his opponent
a few extra seconds of rumination and thinking. When all you

want to do is get something done with, being forced to wait plays unpleasantly on the nerves.

Do goalkeeper delays work? In our study on time effects in penalty shootouts, published in 2009, we found that those players who did not have to wait for the referee at all after having stepped back to prepare their run-up scored on 90% of their shots. This percentage progressively went down the longer penalty takers had to wait for the referee, dropping to 60-70% for those players who waited the longest.[144] Revisiting the data and adding shots from after we published our study, hence examining every shot taken in major penalty shootouts for men from 1976 until 2023, there is a clear and significant drop in performance for the longest waits. Penalty takers who have to wait more than eight seconds score only 44% of the time, significantly less than players in all other conditions.

Note that, importantly, this metric concerns how long penalty takers are forced to wait for the referee's whistle, not how long they choose to wait after that whistle (the self-paced post-whistle pause which we discussed earlier). The kind of wait discussed here is outside the kicker's control.

The overall trend is that the longer penalty takers have to wait for the referee – typically because of goalkeeper delays – the worse these players perform from the penalty spot. One reason might be dread, the enforced wait amplifying unpleasant and distracting feelings. The door opens here, too, for overthinking. The penalty taker might also be feeling antagonised by losing control to the goalkeeper and not sensing any means of regaining it.

In American football, there is a phenomenon that has parallels with this, called "icing the kicker". This is the practice of calling a time-out when the opposing team is about to attempt a field goal, and thereby introducing a statutory delay at a moment of potentially high tension. In the first study of this practice, researchers examined data from the 2003 and 2004 NFL seasons and found that icing the kicker reduced the chance of a successful field goal attempt by about 10%.[145] The researchers argued that having time to dwell on the kick could cause the kickers to choke. Another study of six NFL seasons (2002-2008) showed that when kickers were iced they would score 14% fewer kicks than in instances where they were not iced.[146] However, this result was not replicated in a more recent study with a larger sample, suggesting that kickers may have grown used to being "iced" and instead exploit the pause to better prepare their kicks.[147] This might happen with penalties in European football too.

In fact, a study already shows signs of this. The average waiting time between the foul being committed and the penalty getting taken has almost doubled with VAR, from 62 seconds before VAR to 114 seconds with VAR.[148] VAR reviews are a kind of automatic icing of the kicker, yet this study shows there is no reduction in penalty kick performance with longer VAR waiting times. However, these time intervals are long regardless, and it is possible that the difference between one and two minutes does not functionally matter. Nonetheless, penalty kicks taken after a VAR review were scored significantly less (71%) than after no review (81%). This might be consistent with the finding from icing NFL kickers that it is the intention and context of the delay that matters, not the actual delay. When time delays come from VAR, rather than from opponents arguing with the referee, there is real uncertainty about whether there will be a penalty kick or not, and this uncertainty may have a negative impact on the penalty taker.

Protecting against the mind games battery

Mind games are not new to football, but lately they have evolved in two directions. On the one hand, they're now more intense, volatile and brutal; on the other hand, they're more subtle, complex and manipulative. Progressive players and teams need to keep up and shield their penalty takers accordingly.

Traditionally, penalty takers rely on their mental strength and a lone referee to control opponents. Although both can be helpful, relying on this solely is naive and often insufficient. More deliberate strategies are likely to be helpful. In Chapter 4, I'll discuss how players and teams can and should take a collective approach to coping with the pressure of the penalty kick situation. But let's first look at some individual coping techniques.

Performers can compensate for the negative effects of distraction by investing more mental effort in a task.[149] This becomes easier with experience. Training will help. More experienced performers are less stimulus-driven (where attention is drawn to what the other person is doing) and more goal-directed (where attention is maintained on the task you are trying to solve). If you have been frequently exposed to distractions from other people, you are more likely not to let such distractions get to you and stay focused on your task.

For example, Kylian Mbappé's exceptional performance under pressure against Emi Martínez in the 2022 World Cup final shows a player who despite his young age has vast accumulated experience that enabled him to more effectively handle the opponents' mind games. Mbappé's second penalty kick in that final may be one of the most extreme-pressure penalties ever seen in football. To recap, the score was 3-2 to Argentina in the 118th minute (so only two minutes to go), and if Mbappé did not score, Argentina would be world champions. In addition to Argentina's goalkeeper, Martínez, there were three other Argentina players trying to get to Mbappé prior to the kick and distract him. Yet, assertively but quietly and with no extra fuss, Mbappé did what was necessary to keep the opponents at bay, seemingly without paying much attention to them. In such situations, the performer needs to produce a clear and sharp focus on the upcoming task, while staying cognitively flexible enough to fluidly handle any distraction. It is much easier to resist the distractions provided by others if you have encountered, and successfully coped with, something similar before.

Planning is important, not only for reducing practical and logistical errors, but also for the psychological benefit that arises from reducing uncertainty.[150] Mental contrasting is a technique to deal with such chaos: in other words, imagining the goal that one wants to achieve in the future and then imagining the specific path required to reach the goal, with all the obstacles and challenges to solve on the way. This strategy is shown to be substantially more effective for goal attainment than only imagining the goal itself.[151]

Further, specifically, penalty takers can protect themselves against volatile goalkeepers and other opponents by 1) delaying their arrival in the penalty area until the referee is in control, 2) delaying ball placement (Haaland's technique), 3) strategic disengagement (looking away), 4) repositioning the ball and starting the routine from scratch (which Michael Ballack and Salomon Kalou of Chelsea did, successfully, to cope with the delay tactics in the 2008 Champions League final), and 5) variation (making sure your routine has some degree of unpredictability to make you less vulnerable to goalkeepers who analyse you over time).

Is distraction fair?

Given the pervasiveness and proliferation of goalkeeper distraction, disruption and manipulation behaviours, an important question is: to what extent are these behaviours something that should be accepted in the game of football? After all, if we accept them, we also implicitly promote them, given their apparent impact on the outcomes of important games.

To what extent are these behaviours currently legal? Interestingly, following Martínez's disruptive performance in the 2022 World Cup in Qatar, the International Football Association Board, the body that determines the laws of the game, issued a clarification that "the goalkeeper must not behave in a manner that fails to show respect for the game and the opponent, i.e. by unfairly distracting the kicker".[152] Specifically, an addition was made to Law 14 ("the penalty kick"), put in effect from July 2023: "The goalkeeper must not behave in a way that unfairly distracts the kicker, e.g. delay the taking of the kick or touch the goalposts, crossbar or goal net."

The old rules were not explicit about goalkeeper mind games, so an update was understandable. However, what does it mean to "unfairly distract"? This addition allows for a lot of interpretation and subjectivity. Can goalkeepers still creatively and irritatingly take up unusual positions and move on the line before the shot? Can they speak to penalty takers? Can they move around in the penalty area before a kick? Can they take possession of the ball, and pass it to the penalty taker in ways that are just a little bit uncomfortable? Such actions are clearly intended to distract the penalty taker, but since the rule addition, most goalkeepers have still been allowed to do this. Further, I assume deceptive goalkeeper movements during a run-up would be considered fair, although some goalkeepers execute them so effectively that one is tempted to label them "unfair". Also, why are only goalkeepers' behaviours regulated? What about outfield players? As has been shown several times in this book, outfield players occasionally attempt to have an impact on opposition penalty takers: are they exempt from these rules?

Given the range of distraction on recent display on football's biggest stage, it makes sense to clarify what is allowed and not. The new ruling, needing lots of interpretation, potentially creates as many problems as it solves. So far, I am not sure if the change will make much difference, unless a) the rules are more specific about exact behaviours that one wishes to discourage, and b) specific routines and guidelines are put in place to help referees enforce these rules. As it stands, there is effectively one referee who is asked to control what are often multiple players in a very chaotic penalty area, while players and teams are getting more and more sophisticated about the ways in which they play this psychological game.

A bigger question is, are these behaviours moral? One position is that mind games are OK as long as the rules issued by the governing body permit them – as they currently do, up to a point.[153] But should we be aiming to extinguish these behaviours altogether? After all, they are manipulative, exploitative and potentially psychologically harmful. Some of them are abusive, others border on being some form of bullying. Many would argue that these are not the kind of behaviours we want to condone and encourage in a sport.

However, on the other side of the argument, team games are a controlled conflict between two sides, where a psychological element is inevitable and essential. Penalty kicks, and particularly the penalty shootout, showcase performance under pressure in its most essential form, making this a psychological game more than anything else. An integral part of that game is the dynamic, intense and sometimes volatile cognitive and emotional duel between two combatants. Would we really want to neuter the conflict, emotionality and inter-personal drama around that contest? Aren't these behaviours quite simply part of what it means to compete?

I can see both points of view. But what cannot be disputed is that, in a penalty shootout, as in any other high-stakes competitive situation, there will be opponents provoking and exploiting the pressure, and always pushing the limits of what is allowed. And at the practical level, preparing for pressure involves preparing for what competitors will do, whether you approve of it or not.

Chapter 4

Uniting against the pressure

"Our sense of belonging constantly needs to be fuelled by signals of connection."

Dan Coyle, *The Culture Code*, 2018

Many players will tell you that the longest walk in football is the one from the centre circle to the penalty spot during a penalty shootout. That's not true. The longest walk in football is the one *back* to the centre circle after you have taken your penalty and missed. When Marcus Rashford failed to convert penalty number three for England in the shootout that decided the 2020 European Championships against Italy, he was clearly devastated as he headed back up the pitch. Returning to face your teammates, the people you have let down, the people whose dreams you have crushed along with your own, is probably the loneliest experience in sport. And that's before you factor in the live television audience – estimated at 328 million people on that occasion.[154]

The England team in this tournament had purportedly become a tight-knit group. This was reported by players such as Kieran Trippier ("We have a feeling of good team spirit. We fit well together and work hard for each other") and by the manager Gareth Southgate ("Many nations go out of the tournament because their team spirit is not like the one our guys have"). These were resounding words.

But to what extent did the team back each other up in their behaviour? What did Rashford's England teammates do while he embarked on the longest walk of his life? Nothing. They carried on holding onto each other in the centre circle and didn't move an inch until Rashford had arrived there with them. Why? Could it be that those players simply had too much respect for the laws of the game? "All eligible players, except the player taking the kick and the two goalkeepers, must remain within the centre circle," those laws state. However, even then, they could have walked to the edge of the circle and showed some support while remaining within the rules. But they did not. Bearing in mind Chris Markham's comments in Chapter 2 regarding what England spoke about prior to 2018, it could also be that the stoic reaction to a teammate missing was deliberate – an attempt to be and appear unfazed and process-oriented when faced with any kick outcome. There is a logic to that, and I suspect that this was on the mind of at least some of the players. Nevertheless, this does not match with the observation from the same shootout that several of the England players enthusiastically jumped up and down both when their own players scored and when their opponents missed. Nor does it match with the observation that there was one England player who, a couple of times, started moving towards Rashford, but stopped after glancing over his shoulder to see if anyone was coming with him, which nobody did. That player was Kalvin Phillips. If there was a collective plan to stay put after a miss, wouldn't Phillips have behaved differently?

Regardless of whether the static reaction to teammates missing was deliberate or not, this was a lost opportunity to show team spirit and belonging. Yes, holding onto each other at that point may communicate team unity, and it probably feels safe for the ones standing in the centre circle. But for the unlucky individual walking back to the team, that formation could send another signal: "We are a strong and connected group, and you are not a part of it."

Rashford was not the first player to miss in this shootout. When Italy's second penalty, taken by Andrea Belotti, was stopped by Jordan Pickford in the England goal, Belotti too had to embark on the long walk back to his group. However, that walk was cut short when Italy's captain, Giorgio Chiellini, and the defender Alessandro Florenzi broke free from the team's centre circle formation and walked towards Belotti, to get him back into the group again as soon as possible. This seemingly insignificant gesture carried a lot of meaning and it's plausible to think that it had a big impact. When you feel you have let everyone down and are at your loneliest, seeing your teammates approaching you lets you know very directly that you are still cared for and belong. And the rest of the team gets to pick up a reassuring message, too: "If you miss when it's your turn, this group is not turning away from you." That could dial down the pressure ever so slightly, and even be the difference between scoring or missing for the later kickers.

What about the England captain in this situation? Harry Kane had already scored his kick, England's first penalty, and as he no longer had an upcoming shot to think about, he was free to focus on leading and supporting the rest of the group. However, as Rashford made it back into the group, Kane remained standing still, hardly visible in certain photos, concealed behind the others. Although again, I suspect Kane might have followed a Team GB-inspired plan to not respond to failure, and the same with success. In any case, nobody stepped up to soften Rashford's pain and a chance to recover instantly as a group was lost. This docile collective reaction to the first penalty miss indirectly showed the likes of Jadon Sancho and Bukayo Saka that if they were to miss their later penalties, their teammates would be unlikely to be there for them either. Both Sancho and Saka did indeed later miss, and England once again failed to land a trophy.

In the 2022 World Cup, several teams responded swiftly and collectively to missed penalties, meeting their teammate on the way back and re-enfolding them into the group. Interestingly, some of the absolutely best players were the ones who stepped forward to do this. For example, in the final, Kylian Mbappé single-handedly took responsibility for approaching both of the French players who missed in the shootout, meeting them outside the centre circle. While in the quarter-final, Lionel Messi was the player who went out of his way to receive the returning Enzo Fernández after Argentina's solitary miss. Similarly, in the 2023 Women's World Cup, Wendie Renard, the French captain, moved far outside the centre circle to get Vicki Becho back to the group after her miss against Australia in the quarter-final.[155] The impact of this gesture of support is likely to be higher when a figure of high status in the group is the one extending it. This is leadership in actions, not just words.

Of the 93 penalty shootouts that have taken place in the combined history of the men's World Cup, the Euros and the Champions League/European Cup up to 2022, 49 (52.7%) have been won by a team who missed one or more of their penalties. More than half, then. This means that it is vitally important for a team to cope with and recover well from a miss. A miss is often just a temporary setback. What matters is how the team collectively responds to that setback. This is something I learned very thoroughly when I was a penalty kick consultant with Dutch national teams in the period 2005-2008.

In the fall of 2004, together with my colleagues from the

University of Groningen, I started speaking with the Dutch football association about doing that research project around penalty shootouts. After a few of those meetings, out of the blue, we suddenly got a phone call from Foppe de Haan, the U20/U21 coach. He was preparing his team to take part in the U20 World Cup that next summer, in 2005. His question was, would I be open to come to their training camp and talk to the players about how to cope with the stress of a penalty shootout?

Of course. What an opportunity. Now, I realised, obviously, that you cannot come barrelling out of a university environment and present dry, complex academic data at a football training camp without the risk of losing people's interest. So I spent a full six months gathering my information and preparing a presentation for the team, thinking always about the best means to condense it and communicate it in a smart and relevant way. Eventually my big day came. The presentation to the U20 side took place and I felt it went well.

My satisfaction at a job well done didn't last long.

In the round of 16 the U20s faced Nigeria in the quarter-finals. That game ended 1-1. Penalties.

Those days in late June were extremely warm in the Netherlands, and in my tiny one-bedroom apartment in downtown Groningen the heat was almost unbearable. I watched the game sitting on my couch, wearing nothing but boxer shorts. And it felt as if the room was getting hotter and hotter as the shootout progressed.

The shootout went to 24 penalty kicks – and the Dutch lost. They lost! I was crushed. And so, I figured, were my pretensions to any kind of practical, real-world expertise on the penalty shootout situation.

I was certainly convinced there would be no further collaboration with the Dutch FA, where my name, I was sure, was now mud. However, maybe something could be salvaged from this wreckage.

Over the next few weeks, I took trains around the Netherlands to meet with every one of the players at their clubs, to interview them about their penalty kicks and their preparation for them. Each of the interviews lasted for at least an hour, and I learned a lot about what to do when preparing for penalties, and even more about what *not* to do. More about that later.

Then, to my great surprise, about six months after this, the coach called again. He was preparing for a new tournament, this time the U21 Euros, and he asked if I could visit again, to meet with the team and teach them about penalties. After that, Marco van Basten called, which was something in itself: the great Ajax and Milan legend was managing the Netherlands at that time. The 2006 World Cup in Germany was coming up, and he invited me to come to their training camp and give a presentation for the squad. Meeting the Dutch senior team felt like the ultimate test. Would our observations about penalties make sense to truly elite players? That squad featured a golden generation of Dutch talent: Robin van Persie, Arjen Robben, Wesley Sneijder, Rafael van der Vaart, Ruud van Nistelrooy, Edwin van der Sar… I was, understandably, pretty excited in anticipation, and pretty nervous. But the presentation felt fine. After the talk, the two most experienced players with respect to penalty kicks, van Nistelrooy and van der Sar, came up to me and wanted to discuss more details. This is something I have experienced so many times since: the ones who approach you after a presentation are nearly always the ones who are already the most proficient. They are very good, but they want to be better. This is the mindset of so many high-achievers.

Unfortunately, the 2006 World Cup ended early for the Dutch team. They lost in the round of 16 to Portugal, in one of the ugliest battles in World Cup history, leading to four red cards, but not, alas, to a penalty shootout. That was the only time I did something with the Dutch senior team. However, I gave presentations to many other Dutch national teams over a period of four years; U20 in 2005, U21 in 2006 and 2007, the Olympic team in 2008. After that rough start in 2005, only one more of those teams ended up in a shootout – but that, too, was a shootout for the history books.

It happened in the semi-final of the 2007 U21 Euros, where the Netherlands played an England side that included many players who went on to have Premier League careers: James Milner, Ashley Young, Mark Noble, Scott Carson… The game was a home fixture for the Dutch – at the Abe Lenstra Stadion in Heerenveen. Two million people tuned in to watch on television, and the tension was palpable for everyone involved, including me – not least when the eventual penalty shootout ended up running to a massive 32 kicks. No other international shootout has ever gone on that long.[156] To my enormous pleasure and relief, the Dutch team won in the end. Gianni Zuiverloon scored the last and decisive penalty with an unreachable shot down to the left, and then very kindly gave me a mention in a post-match interview with *Algemeen Dagblad*, a Dutch newspaper: "Geir Jordet told me that you had to take time before taking the shot. Before the run-up, it is good to rest a second and take a breath. I did that and I knew exactly where I wanted to shoot the ball." After that tournament, it was clear that I had a proper research programme going, providing insights not just for publication in academic journals, but that could be put to the test in practice by coaches and players.

Did I do anything differently in 2007? There was one thing in particular. In 2005, I had the idea that the best way to build players' confidence ahead of a penalty shootout was to help them appreciate the moment and embrace what a penalty also is: a fantastic opportunity to score a goal. In short, I focused on feeling good about penalties and I wanted the players to "think positive", building optimism and positive expectations. Consequently, I made sure to speak only about scoring, and to show only video images of brilliant penalty goals.

This approach was naive, at best. Not that thinking positively is bad when performing under pressure. On the contrary, if players are able to do that, great for them. However, to make positive thinking the aim misses the mark. Performing under pressure is not about feeling good; it is about doing what is right and smart regardless of how one feels, and particularly when one feels bad. I fully understood this after I met with some of my colleagues at the University of Groningen who worked in the medical department. They were doing research on how doctors and nurses were behaving under extreme-stress situations, such as in an emergency room or the operating theatre. Given our obvious mutual interest in pressure situations, they invited me to come and speak with them about what we could learn from each other.

This was fascinating to me, and opened up a whole new world with respect to how people perform under real pressure. And the pressure *is* real in hospital settings because if people make mistakes, they don't just lose a game, a few points, or a trophy. They lose lives. These types of working environments – among which I would also include aviation, firefighting, nuclear power plants, aircraft carriers, oil platforms – are often called high-reliability organisations. These are places where failure is a strong possibility, where small events can make a big difference and where lives are at risk when things go wrong.[157] Research shows, for example, that 70% of aircraft accidents come from human error, and the causes of errors are often fatigue, fear, cognitive workload, bad communication and non-optimal decision making.[158] Interestingly, people working in aircraft, hospital emergency rooms and firefighting units make as many mistakes as people in other organisations, but they typically do not let the mistakes that arise incapacitate and stop them.[159] They have a system and a culture for responding to errors, with the logic that the response to the error is ultimately more important for safe task solution than the original error. They focus on quickly and carefully responding and coping with mistakes and on learning from them, rather than exclusively investing their efforts in initially avoiding them. The idea is to respond to threats mindfully, flexibly and dynamically, rather than automatically, habitually and rigidly. This error control is proactive, non-punitive and directed at the system, culture and communication, not just at the mistakes made by individuals.

I took all this on board ahead of my presentation to the Netherlands U21 team in 2007. I began by saying that it was likely that some of the players would miss their penalties in the shootout, so we would now spend some time talking about this. As I spoke, the players were clearly uncomfortable. They were really not so keen to discuss their worst fear in this area. I was on a mission, though, and continued: "The best players typically miss more shots than the others. Some players even panic under pressure." Following that, I showed a slide with the title "Missing penalties is natural!", where I quoted from players I had interviewed after the 2005 penalty loss against Nigeria.

After this, I had one more quote, which was accompanied by a video clip from that 2005 shootout: "The other guys received me well when I came back to the group." The video clip showed everyone welcoming and embracing a player who had missed. I then said: "We can do even better than this. Here is my suggestion. When one of us misses a shot, we ALL walk over to get that player back into the group again as soon as possible!" The players listened, but nobody commented on it, so I had no idea if this was something that they were prepared to do.

During that eventual 32-penalty shootout, several Dutch players missed. Every time, the whole group broke free from the centre circle and walked over to get the returning player back into the group, making the longest walk shorter. They then ended up winning the shootout. Afterwards, I had a student visit the players to interview them about the preparations that we had done.[160] The element they seemed to agree was most effective was the plan for picking up the players who had missed. This was something they understood and valued.

Human beings have a fundamental need to belong.[161] When we feel excluded, our body's alarm system fires. Indeed, exclusion activates the same neural and physiological alarm system that is involved in threats of physical harm.[162] In key moments of failure, such as having missed a shot in a penalty shootout and let everyone on the team down, the sound of the alarm is almost deafening. In this situation, receiving genuine hints that people still care, that one is still valued and is still part of the group, can have a significant positive impact.

The value of an inclusive gesture like this seems to have been clear to players in the past, when there were fewer conventions governing how one was supposed to act in a penalty shootout. The first shootout in any major international tournament was in November 1970, in the second round of the European Cup, when Everton beat Borussia Mönchengladbach 4-3 to go through to the quarter-finals. When you look back now at the body language in that shootout, the players appear extremely nervous. They all react swiftly to the referee's signal, with almost all players starting their run-up at the sound of the whistle. Most of the players turn their back on the goalkeeper after setting the ball down, as if determined to avoid looking at the stress-triggering figure in front of them. One player for Mönchengladbach, arguably the highest-profile player on the pitch, Günther Netzer, even turned his back on the whole penalty shootout by refusing, allegedly, to take a shot.

It starts badly for Everton. The goalkeeper for the West-German team, Wolfgang Kleff, saves the first shot from Joe Royle. This triggers a celebration as if Mönchengladbach have already won. Kleff is surrounded by teammates in tracksuits who come on to the pitch to congratulate him. Photojournalists in real suits also run on to take photos of him posing with a team flag draped around his shoulders – before the next shot has even been taken. Clearly these were different times. Everton's manager Harry Catterick had a point when he said after the game: "I still say these penalties to decide a match are like a circus."

It may seem like a spectacle, but it is actually incredibly fascinating: the shootout displays raw and uncontrolled individual and collective behaviours under extreme pressure. Royle is devastated after his miss and sinks to the ground on the six-yard line in anguish and shame. Then, impressively, his teammate Alan Ball, the world champion with England from 1966, who will be next up to shoot for Everton, puts his own fears aside and runs all the way over and into the penalty area to pick up his teammate. While the assistant referee tries his best to break this union up and get Ball back to the centre circle, Ball puts his arms around Royle, gives him a tap on the cheek and gestures to his own chin as if to say, "hold it up". He then escorts Royle back to the centre circle. When asked later about what Ball told him, Royle laughed and said: "We were great friends, but we said what we thought to each other. He was probably smiling and calling me a big – or something." The words don't matter much. It's about being there. Herbert Laumen later misses for Mönchengladbach and this is repeated, his teammates coming all the way to the penalty area to pick him up.

We saw earlier how Pierre Littbarski ran over to the penalty area to literally lift Uli Stielike off the ground in the 1982 World Cup semi-final penalty shootout. Further, in the same era, in the 1984 UEFA Cup final shootout between Tottenham and Anderlecht, when Danny Thomas missed kick number five for Spurs, which could have given them the cup, Graham Roberts and Steve Archibald ran a long way to console him and get him back into the group. Arnór Guðjohnsen then missed for Anderlecht and Tottenham won. Indeed, in these early shootouts, teammates can be variously seen running from the centre circle to the penalty area both to congratulate the players who score and to support those who miss. It seems a perfectly natural way to respond in both cases.

However, this is much rarer now. Nobody comes all the way over to the penalty area to fetch their teammate any more. So, why have players stopped doing this? There has been no rule change. The law was as clear in the 1970-1971 season as it is today that non-involved players are to remain within the centre circle, so why do players feel so firmly inclined to obey it now? My own impression is that teams stopped leaving the centre circle at the same time that they adopted the shoulder-to-shoulder formation all of them now use. This formation gives the impression of a team sticking together to support each other, and the physical touch and close proximity to teammates undoubtedly bring a sense of comfort and safety for the ones who stand there. There are good aspects of this formation, which I will come on to. However, if this formation prevents players from breaking free to approach and bring back to the group those who most need them, then surely this collective strategy backfires.

There is now much research showing that social support will reduce stress and anxiety when performing under pressure. One study revealed that just knowing that a person who is willing to offer support is available lowers physiological indicators of stress during a high-pressure task.[163] Thus, simply having spoken in advance about supporting each other could have an effect. Another study shows that receiving support prior to a high-pressure task significantly reduces stress, as indicated by cortisol responses, and if the support is offered by someone with whom one has a secure relationship, anxiety is at its lowest.[164] This suggests that groups need to work on their relationships and bonds with each other over a long time, to be able to offer social support most effectively when performing under pressure.

Nevertheless, there have also been some constructive movements with respect to the social aspect of penalty kicks. In the last few years, we have witnessed a revolution in how teams prepare for and execute their penalties. A penalty kick is no longer an isolated individual task, where everything is left to the penalty taker, with the others just watching. Nowadays, a penalty kick – both in-game and in shootouts – is better thought of as a collective team task, where several players play their part in making sure that the penalty taker is supported in every way possible in an attempt to increase the probability of that player being optimally prepared for success. Below I will describe some of the ways in which teams now go about this.

Protecting the penalty spot

In Brazil, the awarding of a penalty kick is nearly always the starting signal for an intense bout of on-field arguments between the two sides, all of which need to be resolved before the kick can be taken. This can be time-consuming: sometimes as much as four or five minutes will pass between the referee blowing for the offence and the player actually striking the ball off the spot. That's a long time for the penalty taker to be marinating in the pressure of the upcoming kick, and a huge window in which opposing players can do their very best to destabilise them. We saw earlier how scuffing up the penalty spot can complicate life for the taker both physically, by disrupting the surface, and psychologically, by injecting a small dose of intimidation in the build-up. Penalty takers might then consider it smart to take up a position over the penalty spot as quickly as possible in order to ward off any destructive forces.

The problem with this is that the penalty taker then assumes a place right at the centre of the pre-penalty chaos and becomes a sitting target for any other mind games and intimidations that the opposition have in mind. Is there a better way?

In July 2019, Filipe Luís returned to Brazil, joining Flamengo, in Rio de Janeiro, after spending 15 years in European football, most notably with Atlético Madrid. Luís has never taken a single official penalty kick in his whole adult career, yet he quickly became one of the most important players for Flamengo's penalty kicks.[165] Every time Flamengo were awarded a penalty, Luís would calmly walk over and take up position on top of the penalty spot, with one foot on either side of it. Often at this point, he would be the only Flamengo player in the penalty area, and surrounded by jostling opponents and the referee. Yet he would remain dutifully focused on his task, guarding his square of turf, gently pushing back any player who came near the penalty spot. Meanwhile, the actual penalty taker, typically Gabi Barbosa, would have collected the ball and be waiting somewhere on the edge of things, outside the area. When the referee had finally cleared the chaos around Luís, and all opponents had left, Luís himself would calmly leave too, his work here done, and Barbosa would come in to place the ball on the untouched penalty spot.

An elegant solution, then – supporting the penalty taker, allowing them to gather themselves away from the hustle and bustle, and protecting the spot itself from unhelpful boots. However, it can backfire.

In 2022, there was a widespread outbreak of penalty spot destruction. I and many others communicated about this on social media, and suggested ways to protect against it. Possibly as a result of increased attention around it, protecting the spot became a popular strategy with several teams in that year's World Cup and also in some of the European leagues. For example, in Qatar, every time Argentina had a penalty, several of their players would form a cordon around the spot, making sure no opponent got near it.

This, however, quickly exposed an unintended side effect. Unless the penalty spot protectors were smooth and subtle in the way they occupied that precious piece of territory, opponents would see their arrival in the penalty area as a direct and invasive confrontation. Or, alternatively, they would see their arrival as an opportunity to *create* a confrontation, which could actually work to their own advantage. And in some cases, those protective players actually broadened the scope for penalty spot destruction attempts.

Example 1: Argentina's penalty against Saudi Arabia. Lionel Messi places the ball on the spot and Lautaro Martínez stands next to it, on guard. A passing Saudi player touches the ball while passing the spot on his way to the referee. Three further Argentina players immediately swarm to the spot as back-up. Several Saudi players swarm in after the Argentinians. Suddenly, there's a whole push-and-shove battle scene going on around the spot, which Messi arguably doesn't need at this precise moment. He stands calmly to one side, though, and eventually converts the penalty.

Example 2: Portugal's penalty against Uruguay. The goalkeeper, in discussion with the referee, starts moving slowly towards the spot with, perhaps, evil intentions in his heart. Gonçalo Ramos of Portugal, seeing this, sprints in and jumps on top of the spot with his back to the goalkeeper. He is then instantly joined by three teammates, who position themselves around the spot as if it were a pile of gold. This, of course, sends the message to the opponents: we suspect you are up to no good. Again, multiple wrestling bouts ensue, and Uruguay's Matías Viña even gets a chance to poke his foot towards the penalty spot as he comes by. It's all highly chaotic, although, again, the penalty taker, Bruno Fernandes, stays calm and scores.

Example 3: Ghana's penalty against Uruguay. If Ghana win, they will qualify from the group stage and go into the knockout phase. While the referee is waiting for the VAR check to be complete, four Ghana players surround the penalty spot. Eventually, two more join them, making six, almost like some kind of ancient Roman shield wall. With André Ayew, the penalty taker, also standing nearby, that's seven Ghana players in the area, which the Uruguay players interpret as a provocation. Visibly irritated, some of those players now join the Ghana players in the area, multiple wrestling matches ensue, and Darwin Núñez attempts to break through the Roman wall with an attack making prominent use of his left foot, for which, after bitter Ghanaian protests, he earns a yellow card. Massive amounts of chaos all in all. And this time André Ayew's poor penalty is saved. Uruguay eventually win 2-0. Both teams have to go home.

Clearly the successful use of these collective counter-strategies requires finesse and delicate implementation. Indeed, following the mess outlined above, Argentina adapted their approach at the 2022 World Cup, staying back while monitoring the penalty spot and only jumping into action when required – as when Rodrigo De Paul moved in ahead of Messi's penalty against Croatia, and when Enzo Fernández and Leandro Paredes entered the area before

Messi's penalty against the Netherlands.

Perhaps the smoothest operator in this department that I have seen is Kieffer Moore of Bournemouth. In the 2022 World Cup, Moore featured for Wales in the opening game against the USA. The Americans were winning 1-0 when Wales were awarded an 82nd-minute penalty. Six US players went after the referee, trying to make him reverse the decision. Moore meanwhile first congratulated Gareth Bale, who had been fouled, and who would be the penalty taker, and then calmly walked over to the penalty spot, which had become the epicentre of the US protests. Most players in spot protection mode adopt a fixed position and try to appear as physically dominant as possible. Moore took a totally different approach. He appeared flexible, agile and friendly. He would gently, but firmly, push the opponents away, always with a comment and a smile. On several occasions, he would pass out hugs to the opponents, while keeping them away from the penalty spot and away from Bale. It was a classic piece of de-escalation. True, Moore towers 1.96 metres above the ground, which may have lent him some natural authority in this situation. But his poised, people-friendly attitude seemed to make the difference here. (And Bale calmly equalised.)

Maybe football has something to learn in this area from bouncers in bars. Even though the research clearly concludes that the strongest predictor of aggression in bars is the absence of doormen and security guards, multiple studies also show the unwanted side effects of employing aggressive and unreasonable bouncers, who end up *increasing* incidents of trouble.[166] Among the behaviours that reliably escalate conflicts are: appearing threatening, showing hostility, "squaring off", shouting and violating personal space.[167] Effective bouncers, on the other hand, were found to be firm but friendly,[168] have good verbal skills in dealing with problem patrons,[169] intervene early in conflicts, rely on teamwork and use physical force as the last resort.[170] Penalty spot protectors could do worse than take a leaf out of the good bouncers' book.

Protecting the penalty taker

In a Premier League match in 2021 against Aston Villa, Manchester United's Bruno Fernandes, waiting to take a penalty, found himself surrounded at the spot by no fewer than six Villa players, including our master manipulator from Argentina, the goalkeeper Emi Martínez. At that same moment, six Manchester United players could be seen with their backs to the penalty spot, walking away, seemingly oblivious to the fact that their penalty taker was outnumbered and getting harassed by opponents. After a few seconds, the Brazilian Fred turned his head around, saw what was happening and came running to assist. But the sluggishness of United's response on that occasion (and Fernandes eventually missed, by the way) reflects a standard idea that the penalty kick is an individual event – a situation that the kicker can be left to deal with on their own. It's a faulty assumption.

A couple of months later, it was Mo Salah, and Liverpool's turn to face Aston Villa, and Emi Martínez, with a penalty kick. They came prepared. First, when the penalty was given, Liverpool's captain, Jordan Henderson, escorted Salah out of the penalty area, beyond the toxic reach of Martínez. Second, when Martínez then came out from the goal line in pursuit of Salah, Henderson, accompanied by two teammates, confronted him, essentially erecting a screen between him and Salah. Third, once the chaos in the box calmed down, and the referee started getting some control, Henderson lingered behind, pretending to straighten his socks, making sure he was located in a direct line between Martínez and Salah, thereby maintaining the screen.

Fourth, when Martínez finally backed down and took up position on the goal line, Henderson remained with Salah to protect him against other threats. The Aston Villa players saw that Martínez was ineffective, so some of them, particularly Tyrone Mings, tried to get to Salah, but Henderson interfered and kept Salah isolated. Throughout this, two other Liverpool players were in another part of the penalty area, where Aston Villa players were engaging the referee in the obligatory protest rally. One never knows what will happen in a discussion like that, and it makes sense for the team who has been awarded the penalty to have some representation there. All in all, in addition to the penalty taker, five Liverpool players had functional roles in those couple of minutes leading up to the penalty. In other words, the penalty was a team event. And the kick itself? Salah struck it low, not very hard, but it went in even though Martínez almost had a hand on it.

Over the next couple of seasons, Liverpool continued, extended and expanded this territorial strategy of orchestrated support for the penalty taker. Sometimes, this would involve only Jordan Henderson, who would casually take up a guarding position behind Salah and the penalty spot. Other times, it would be more coordinated. For Fabinho's penalty against Watford in April 2022, three players offered comprehensive cover for the penalty taker: Henderson up front, screening Fabinho from the goalkeeper, Naby Keïta in behind and to the left, having Fabinho's back, and Andy Robertson on the other side, with his back to Fabinho on the lookout for additional threats. Jordan Henderson is the son of a policeman, and quite aware of what he can and cannot do on the football pitch: "I knew I could bring one quality to the table: I felt I could put everyone else before me."[171] With Henderson on the pitch, this protection strategy was always proactive, and concerted. Without Henderson, Liverpool seemed a little bit more reactive. In the 2022 Community Shield against Manchester City,

Henderson had been subbed off by the time Liverpool received a penalty in the 84th minute. Salah walked into the penalty area, and for a brief moment found himself alone with five City players, before Harvey Elliott and Thiago Alcântara came running to shield him. These two then split their duties, with Alcântara guarding against Ederson, City's goalkeeper, and Elliott covering Salah's back against the others.

Jordan Henderson is not a penalty taker. That is, he has taken two penalties in official senior games, one for Liverpool (scored) and one for England, in the 2018 World Cup penalty shootout against Colombia (missed).[172] His impact on other penalty takers cannot be understated, though. In the quarter-finals of the 2022 World Cup, when England were awarded the first of two in-game penalties against France, Henderson did what he does best. The instant the referee made his decision, Henderson grabbed the ball. He then handed it to Harry Kane while escorting him to the penalty area and offering some words of support, making sure no French players could get close enough to Kane to be able to communicate with him. Kane executed his normal routine to make it 1-1.

For England's second penalty, in the 84th minute, with France leading 2-1 and England's place in the tournament looking precarious, Henderson had just been subbed off. Consequently, for the first 30 seconds after the VAR review, Harry Kane was alone at the penalty spot, with only French players around, until Kane's teammates suddenly saw this and urgently stepped up. First Mason Mount, then Jude Bellingham got involved, ultimately escorting the particularly active Olivier Giroud out of the penalty area. All good, but it was reactive and executed with a vigour and intensity that seemed to attract, not repel, attention from the French players. Kane repeated his normal routine, but, for once, to no avail. He missed the penalty and England's hopes vanished.

It was interesting to note that the first players to reach Kane after the miss were all French, taking great delight in swarming joyfully around him and their goalkeeper, Hugo Lloris. Eventually, a lone England player reached Kane – Jude Bellingham, then just 19, who hugged him and spoke to him before running away to make energizing gestures to the other England players. But where were those other players? At the point at which the ball came back into play, not one of them had approached Kane in support. With the exception of Bellingham, they turned their backs on Kane, showing him support only after the final whistle. That was when Henderson was able to reach him, too. He got next to Kane and, in what seemed like a deliberate gesture, stayed next to him for the ensuing moments – literally standing by his teammate at that low moment and firmly broadcasting to anybody watching that football is a team game, even when it involves penalties. And perhaps especially then.

Teammates can fulfil many different roles in this situation, from functional help with practical issues (such as the ball and opponents) to straight-up emotional support to better cope with the pressure. When Maren Mjelde took her high-pressure penalty kick against Lyon in the 2023 Champions League, she received lots of help from the beginning. "I did not even have the ball," Mjelde told me, "but I was thinking, someone else has that. We have planned beforehand. And I had protectors out there. There are supposed to be two protectors, so you know that there should always be one on the pitch with that role. Just like we have two penalty takers."

Then, at the penalty spot: "I received the ball from one of these protectors, and just positioned myself, but I understood that there was a lot of commotion happening behind me. I am not listening, though. I am just standing there. The protector, my teammate next to me, Jess Carter, makes sure that nobody gets close to me."

Of course, what is being said, by whom, in what way will also be important here. "It's kind of funny with her, Jess, she is a good friend of mine, and she is really the perfect person to stand there with. She saw that I tried to prepare and focus, but she could say things like, 'This is dragging out, Maren, is there anything you want to talk about?' And I'm just, like, 'No, I'm in my own head.' But I think I also laugh a bit, because it is funny. And I am standing there with a lot of grass in my face, so she starts to remove it. And then she says, 'Wanna grab a coffee next week?' I hear all she's saying, but I am in my own head, thinking about my task. With that said, what Jess did will take down the seriousness of it all, for just a second or two. That can be such incredible help. Otherwise, one can just lock up completely."

The decoy penalty taker

The Covid-delayed 2021 FIFA Club World Cup final was played in Abu Dhabi in February 2022. Chelsea, representing Europe, faced Palmeiras of Brazil, representing South America. Going into the second half of extra time, the score was 1-1, and the prospect of a penalty shootout loomed. I was watching the game on my couch at home and, as always at this point in a match where I have no personal investment in either of the teams, I started getting my hopes up for penalties.

No such luck, unfortunately. Yet the match did produce something for keen students of the penalty – something genuinely innovative, in fact.

With about seven minutes remaining, Chelsea were awarded a penalty. Slightly disappointing for me, I must admit, and despite all my friends at Chelsea Football Club: one potentially game-deciding penalty is always nice, but no match for my default preference – an entire shootout.

So I guess I wasn't fully paying attention to what happened before the kick, because when Kai Havertz placed the ball on the penalty spot, I was slightly confused. Did I not see César Azpilicueta standing over the ball, just a few seconds before? Never mind. I would have another look at it later. Meanwhile, Havertz, seeming composed and focused despite the clear pressure of the moment, took a second's pause after the whistle, came in off a mid-length run-up and scored to the left. Goal. Chelsea were world champions.

Later that evening, still troubled by that Azpilicueta mystery, I watched it all again. But frustratingly, the TV production mostly kept its cameras on the Palmeiras players – one getting a yellow card for handling the ball in the incident that led to the penalty, and another getting cautioned for his part in the usual chaos around the penalty spot. However, the next morning, I went on YouTube, where multiple fans in the stands had posted their own videos of the event. And finally I could clearly see what had gone on. And it was brilliant!

After the VAR review confirmed the penalty, Azpilicueta, Chelsea's captain, walked with the referee towards the area, seemingly in discussion with him. Just before they got to the box, Azpilicueta seemed to look for someone behind him, and then resolutely grabbed the ball and walked towards the penalty spot, facing the goal, looking for all the world as if he was going to be the penalty taker. Inevitably, he attracted plenty of attention from the Palmeiras players. At one point, there were four of them clustered around him, talking to him, gesturing at him, clearly trying to get him off balance. Eduard Atuesta was so industrious in his efforts at this point that he earned himself a yellow card. The referee kept trying to shepherd the Palmeiras players out of the penalty area and away from Azpilicueta, but for a while it was a hopeless task. When one player left, another replaced him. All of this took a minute to unfold. Eventually, the referee had established control and cleared the area of its Palmeiras occupiers. At which point, Havertz, who had spent the chaos calmly waiting some yards away, entirely unnoticed and unbothered, walked into the area. Azpilicueta handed him the ball. Havertz set it on the spot, completely undisrupted, stepped back and scored the penalty that won Chelsea the FIFA Club World Cup.

Azpilicueta confirmed afterwards that the idea was to take pressure off the penalty taker. Chelsea had done their homework. At penalties earlier that season, Palmeiras had been forming an intimidating crowd around the ball and the referee. Indeed, Chelsea had been using the same crowding strategy themselves, swarming around the penalty taker. "It was a tactic," Azpilicueta said, "because I knew how they are, I knew they were coming for the penalty taker, so I took the ball. Kai knew that he was going to shoot so it was to release the pressure from him… I waited and listened to everything their players told me, and I think it worked, which is the most important thing."[173] We had been present at the birth of the decoy penalty taker. A true penalty kick innovation. Beautiful!

Since this match, many players and teams have copied the strategy, all over the world – from Norway (Bodø/Glimt v. Rosenborg, April 2022) to Costa Rica (Alajuelense v. Herediano, May 2022). Sweden used it against Slovenia in a UEFA Nations League tie in March 2022. And both USA national teams, women's and men's, have successfully carried out the ploy at pivotal moments – the women in the 2022 CONCACAF final against Canada in July that year, when Lindsay Horan drew all the attention before Alex Morgan stepped out of the shadows; the men in their crucial 2022 World Cup qualification game against Panama in March 2022, with Jesús Ferreira acting as decoy for Christian Pulisic. On that occasion, the USA went for maximum realism, with players acting as blockers to protect the decoy taker from the attentions of the Panama players, a very smart way to strengthen the illusion.

Of course, it helps when the penalty kicker is unknown to the opposition. In March 2023, there was a classic high-pressure penalty situation in the Premier League game between Newcastle and Nottingham Forest. The score was 1-1 when Newcastle got a penalty in the 91st minute. Newcastle's regular penalty taker, Callum Wilson, was on the bench, but Alexander Isak had taken their last penalty and would have been the logical choice this time. However, it was Kieran Trippier who took the ball and positioned himself at the spot, doing a magnificent impression of someone about to take a penalty: placing the ball on the spot, picking it up again when opponents approached, setting it back down again…

Sky Sports' producers were obviously convinced: they immediately screened a graphics bar showing Trippier's penalty stats. Even Newcastle's manager, Eddie Howe, said afterwards that he had been momentarily "confused". Forest's goalkeeper, Keylor Navas, did not fall for it though. He ignored Trippier and stepped outside the penalty area to engage with Isak. Isak said afterwards: "Sometimes, you might fool the opposition. The goalie, Keylor, kind of knew I was going to take it so he came straight to me and tried to get in my head. We did our best."[174] Isak scored the penalty and Newcastle won the game 2-1.

Arsenal may be the team at the highest level that has taken this strategy the furthest, albeit aided by the fact that it has for a while been extremely difficult to know or predict who would ultimately be their penalty taker. In the first half of the 2023-2024 season, seven penalties for Arsenal produced five different penalty takers: Bukayo Saka, Martin Ødegaard, Kai Havertz, Fabio Vieira and Jorginho. For five of those seven kicks, there was a decoy, where the initial ball holder ultimately handed over to the real penalty taker, but two times there was no decoy at all. Saka initially took the ball on four of those occasions, surrendered it on three of them and took the penalty himself on the other. Another time, Ødegaard took the ball, then gave it to Saka. With such variation, it becomes really hard for the opponents to know who they should be playing their mind games on, and also for the goalkeeper to prepare for the actual penalty. When I asked Martin Ødegaard about the way Arsenal does this, he explained how this is not an explicit strategy from the team, but something that has organically emerged between the players: "In the last few years, there have been more and more people and teams trying to play little mind games during matches. Scuffing up the penalty spot, speaking to the penalty taker and so forth. We haven't spoken about this really, it has just happened automatically. First we agree who will take the penalty. Then it is up to him what he needs. If he needs me to hold the ball and pretend that I will take the shot, I'll do that. If he needs to hold the ball and just focus on himself, he'll do that. It's really just making sure that whoever takes the shot will feel as much as possible in the zone."

As with any coping strategy, there are no guarantees that the decoy approach will yield a converted penalty, but, performed well, this team-led action can clearly soak up some of the threat from opponents, fight distraction with distraction and effectively dial down some of the pressure on the kicker. Perhaps equally impactful, this strategy is a way to obtain control of the situation and remain unpredictable for the opponent goalkeeper. Ødegaard: "For us, it's mostly about protecting the penalty taker, but there could be an effect with the goalkeeper as well. If I stand there with the ball, the keeper might think about analyses and go through scenarios with me, and if someone else suddenly appears, he needs to refocus."

Post-shot celebration

You are a penalty taker who has just scored. At this point you have two options. You can turn around and quietly jog back to the centre circle (assuming this is a shootout) or back to your own half (assuming this is mid-game). Or you can do something that might increase your team's chances of winning the game and the prize that lies beyond it: you can intensely celebrate your goal.

There is power in celebratory behaviours. Few probably remember the details of Megan Rapinoe's penalty in the 61st minute of the 2019 World Cup final against the Netherlands that gave the USA women's team their crucial 1-0 lead. But everyone remembers Rapinoe's celebratory pose after that goal: arms stretched wide, chest puffed, chin up, small smile. It became an iconic *Sports Illustrated* cover image. Moreover – and this could be the reason this image is so appealing – that exact expression is almost 100% consistent with what social psychologists would describe as the prototypical non-verbal expression of pride: expanded posture, head tilted slightly back, arms raised, and a small smile.[175]

Does celebration impact others? Can celebration affect the outcome of penalty shootouts? Consider the following moment in football history: Argentina face Italy in the semi-final of the 1990 World Cup at the Stadio San Paolo in Naples. Representing Argentina against the host nation is Diego Maradona, who also just happens to be a Napoli player – a Napoli legend, indeed, pivotal in the team's two recent Serie A titles. So Maradona is on his home ground here – yet playing for the away team. The game goes to penalties – as had Argentina's previous tie against Yugoslavia, during which Maradona had missed his kick. So, all in all, there's a lot going on as Maradona now steps forward to take penalty number four against Italy.

Deafening whistles accompany him all the way to the penalty

area and, if anything, intensify still further as he runs in. He makes his usual slight pause... and this time, his goalkeeper-dependent technique works. Italy's Walter Zenga goes early to the right, and Maradona rolls the ball just a metre to the left of the middle.

And with that, he's off – sprinting, picking up speed, extending his arms and roaring and turning in a wild display of exuberance. His destination is the Argentinian coaching staff on the sideline. Maradona jumps into their arms, celebrating as if he had won the World Cup itself. Bear in mind that he has not even won this *game* itself – the penalty shootout is ongoing. But not for long. Next up is Italy's Aldo Serena. An experienced forward, he is nevertheless affected by the moment: "I struggled to walk. My legs did not respond. They were no longer mine, they were someone else's, and they didn't do what I asked of them."[176] He goes for power, blasting the ball to his right. But Sergio Goycochea, the goalkeeper, reads it, saves it, and the hosts are out. Maradona's grandiose celebrations were prophetic. Argentina are in the final.

But were those celebrations prophetic, or was there something less mysterious going on? We conducted a study on the relationship between players' post-goal celebrations and the ultimate outcome of penalty shootouts.[177] The analysis was done with all kicks performed in penalty shootouts in the World Cup and the European Championships prior to 2008, but only included shots where the shootout was tied at the moment of the kick (thus, either no misses or an equal number of misses[178]). Even though the sample necessarily became quite small, there was a clear and significant relationship between post-goal celebration and team outcome in the shootout. Players who celebrated their goals elaborately were more likely to ultimately win the shootout. For example, 82% of the players whose post-goal celebrations involved extending both hands up or out from their bodies were on the team that won the shootout. Interestingly, this behaviour also significantly increased the chance that the next opponent would miss his shot, suggesting that opponents are negatively affected by a big display of post-shot affection. There was also a slight indication in the numbers that the next teammate was more likely to score after a big celebration.

Some of this has later been replicated under controlled conditions in a laboratory. Across four experiments, German and Dutch researchers found that simply observing penalty takers' expressions of pride had a strong effect on the observers' own anticipated emotions, thoughts and performance expectations.[179] Experienced goalkeepers, after observing opponent penalty takers showing pride, expected to feel less good, more stressed, less confident, and had lower performance expectations in a shootout compared with situations where they observed opponents with more neutral expressions. Similarly, experienced outfield players observing teammates expressing pride after penalty goals anticipated feeling better, being more confident, and having higher performance expectations in a penalty shootout than when observing teammates with a more neutral expression.

Put simply, puffing oneself up and putting one's hands in the air can potentially impact one's teammates positively and one's opponents negatively. I wouldn't necessarily recommend directly transferring this to non-sporting contexts: charging around the office with your arms outstretched after a making a good point in a meeting probably won't do much for your colleagues' collective esteem, nor your own reputation. Then again, I haven't actually tried it, so, maybe? But the general principle of celebrating small wins to strengthen collective confidence makes sense, also at the office.

In the context of a penalty shootout? Don't hold back, would seem to be the wisest advice.

Goalkeeper handoff

As we saw earlier, at the 2018 World Cup, England turned around their miserable history of penalty shootout failure following some unprecedentedly thorough work on penalty preparation. One of the key strategies that they prepared and trained was, wherever possible, for the England goalkeeper to take charge of the ball and hand it over to the next England kicker. This was clearly a way to take a measure of control over the situation. And it worked.

Except that, of course, the next time it didn't. At any rate, Jordan Pickford used the same goalkeeper handoff approach in the final of the 2020 European Championships against Italy, where three English penalty takers missed. As with all strategies, there are no guarantees. But that doesn't mean this particular strategy is without value.

Liverpool have been in a few penalty shootouts in the last few years and have generally been successful. Since they beat Leicester in the Carabao Cup quarter-final in December 2021, they have won every shootout they have taken part in – a four-shoot-out winning streak. This may be coincidence, but it may also be down to the deep preparation that Liverpool have conducted for penalties in recent times. Part of that preparation is work with the German neuroscience company Neuro 11, which has been publicly praised by Liverpool's players and manager for their role in this success. They help players develop their pre-performance routines and use objective feedback about brainwaves during training on the pitch to achieve optimal mental states under pressure. Over these past couple of years, I have had some contact with their founder and CEO, Dr Niklas Häusler. He told me he felt that their work with the Liverpool players has produced a "team-wide awareness to assess even psychologically very complex situations within the game more correctly and help others more efficiently". One of the details Liverpool has perfected in their preparation is the goalkeeper handoff. They employed this for the first time in the 2022 FA Cup final against Chelsea, when their goalkeeper, Alisson Becker, handed the ball to his next teammate penalty taker for every shot. The way Alisson does this is worth noticing. He takes up a position right outside the penalty area, on a straight line between the walking penalty taker and the middle of the goal. When he does this, what the approaching penalty takers see straight ahead of them is not the opposing goalkeeper, but their teammate. Then, as Alisson hands over the ball (and he always hands it directly, never throws it, and often adds an additional physical touch, perhaps a gloved pat on the head), he enters the penalty area alongside the taker. It's a smart way to be, in effect, two-against-one at the opening stage of the penalty contest and enables the taker to feel thoroughly supported. Regarding this strategy, Häusler states how crucial such a support structure is under pressure and adds: "The team has developed a brilliant dynamic of helping and understanding each other when it matters the most."

Adopting this support function even more noticeably was Australia's Andrew Redmayne in the 2022 World Cup play-off shootout against Peru. We have already noted Redmayne's dancing skills and his morally questionable water-bottle throwing; but we should take a further moment to note how thoroughly he adopted his role as chief protector of the penalty taker on the way to the spot. Not only was he there on the edge of the area to hand him the ball, and alongside him as he entered the area, it occasionally looked as though Redmayne was about to help the taker place the ball on the spot. At one point, Redmayne could even be seen in the area gesturing at the Peruvian goalkeeper to pipe down and/or back down.

Can the goalkeeper ever help too much in this situation? Well, maybe, but it depends. In the shootout between Sweden and the

USA in the round of 16 in the 2023 Women's World Cup, both goalkeepers handed the ball to their penalty takers ahead of each penalty kick. However, they substantially differed in *how* they performed the handoff. Alyssa Naeher, the US goalkeeper, waited with the ball between the penalty spot and the edge of the area, handed it over fairly swiftly, then jogged away. Rapid, effective, no sweat.

Zećira Mušović, the Swedish goalkeeper, had a completely different style. She approached each teammate with a big smile, engaged her in conversation, handed the ball over and then walked out of the penalty area slowly. For some of the Swedish penalty takers, their smiling, chatty goalkeeper triggered a smile, a laugh and a few words back. They seemed comfortable with the handoff style; perhaps it even helped them. A couple of the others seemed more serious, inwardly focused, less inclined to chat. Seventh up, and kicking to win the game, was Lina Hurtig, and she and Mušović had what looked like a joyful exchange as the ball was handed over. Asked about that exchange afterwards, Mušović said: "She asked me what happens if she scores. I didn't know if I dared to answer it, so I just said that she should shoot the f****** ball in the goal." She scored. Sweden won and progressed to the next round.

Mušović played an amazing game, stopped three American penalties and deservedly became the Swedish hero. She is so curious to learn. When she saw my tweets on this shootout, she reached out. In our conversations that followed, she admitted her style was not planned: "It was a spontaneous move that came naturally to me. In that pressure moment, the last thing I wanted my teammates to feel was that they were alone." However, it is legitimate to ask: does a smiling and talkative goalkeeper help or hinder a penalty taker in such high-pressure moments? Mušović said: "I changed my way of communicating based on which individual

I spoke to. Some of them I know really well, and I know that a more relaxed message is suitable, while with others I felt like a more serious and direct tone suited better." This is an important point. Some performers may perceive the friendly chat as helpful, while others may perceive it as disruptive, and others again may be entirely indifferent to it. It's an approach that needs careful tailoring.

Centre circle formation

As we have observed, in the 1970s and 1980s, the players in the centre circle would typically be randomly spread around, some standing and some sitting. Sometimes, they would mingle with players from the other team, and quite often, players from the two teams would be joined in the centre circle by coaches and other support staff. In the 1990s, teams would typically and gradually come together a little bit more, often on a line, although some players would still sit. From the late 1990s and going into the 2000s, teams sharpened up their formation, positioning themselves along the halfway line, standing closer to each other and interlocking their arms. Now, since around 2010, every single team will stand together in a tight and interlocked formation on the halfway line.

Does that interlocked formation have a function? Perhaps. A team is literally standing together in that shape, sending out signals of unity and cohesion. Plus, of course, contact can be comforting in a time of stress, as studies and our own experiences show.[180] With this said, I suspect that most teams assume this formation primarily because everyone else does it, without much further rationale behind it.

What are some of the alternative positions to assume in the

centre circle? First, there is no rule stating that teams have to stand on the halfway line, yet everyone stands there. I guess this is because the white on the pitch functions as a kind of a guideline: for teams lining up straight, it's the nearest straight line. However, a more progressive position would be to stand on the edge of the circle, which would be 8-9 metres closer to the goal. That would mean a shorter walk back and forth to the penalty area, and it would place the rest of the team closer to the penalty spot and the kicker. What's more, it would potentially put you nine metres ahead of the opposition, with your backs to them – at least until they noticed you and decided to join you in the same spot, which they most likely would do. But even then you would have forced them into a reactive role, which could be to your advantage psychologically.

The first time I suggested this progressive centre circle position to a team was when I was working with the Netherlands U21 players prior to the 2007 European Championships. The semi-final against England was, as I wrote earlier, the occasion of the record-breaking 32-penalty shootout. But, just as we had discussed a few weeks before the game, the Dutch players went and stood at the edge of the centre circle. As predicted, the English team immediately followed them, but the players later reported that it felt good to have taken the initiative and to see the other team react to that.

Another time I suggested this was with the Belgian team Zulte Waregem. I was invited to give a talk to the team about two weeks prior to their 2017 Belgian Cup final match against Oostende. The presentation was actually about team dynamics and cohesion in general and was planned before the management knew that they would end up in the cup final. However, leading up to the presentation, I was asked if I could also spend just a few minutes on penalties, so I decided to include some pointers, among them the suggestion about assuming a more progressive centre circle position.

It didn't seem an especially good omen when, on the day I turned up to give my presentation, there was a sudden power outage at the club's training facility. The meeting was postponed for a couple of hours and eventually moved from the nice, bright auditorium in the newly built training centre to an old, dark cafeteria in the stadium. Still, it seemed to go well and when the team duly ended up in a shootout at that cup final, they did all the things we had spoken about, including heading to the front of the circle, scored all their four penalties and saved two from the opposition. This gave them the trophy and qualification for the 2017-2018 Europa League.

Later that night, the players spoke to Belgian journalists about the Norwegian penalty specialist who had visited them, and soon after that my phone started ringing. I had to tell the journalists that the club was a client, as far as I was concerned, so I couldn't comment on what had happened. However, the club then called me and said they thought it would be good for them to get some attention regarding the detail of their planning and preparation around the penalty shootout, so I talked to the press – thereby earning myself 15 minutes of fame in Belgium, and also a wince-inducing misquote. One reporter had me saying: "I watched the final on a live stream, and at the moment the penalties began, I knew for sure: Zulte Waregem will win this!"[181]

Well, it's true that I watched the match on a live stream. But so far none of my work on penalties has granted me the superpower to see into the future and predict a shootout's outcome, regardless of how much I would love to be able to. And as for being confident when a shootout starts… in fact, I am never so nervous as when I watch a team I have worked with take part in a shootout. This was no exception. I was a mess.

Another team who used the progressive centre circle position was New York City FC. Under their manager, the Norwegian

Ronny Deila, to whom I had given presentations on this topic some years previously, they won their first ever MLS title in 2021, after winning on penalties in both the quarter-final, against New England Revolution, and the final, against Portland Timbers. On both occasions, the NY City players immediately took up an advanced position in the centre circle, which led both opposing teams to react and move up next to them.

Deila later spoke about the presentations he had attended with me and explained that their positioning was all calculated: "You're closer to the guy taking the kick. There's a shorter way to walk." In addition, the strategy had a more psychological purpose: "You're bossing the pitch. You're in charge."[182] There is a territorial competition in the centre circle, so why wouldn't you try to dominate that space? Martin Ødegaard told me about something similar: "Most teams just line up on the halfway line. I feel that this is about taking control. We want to stand here, so we are standing here. It's easy to be a little bit passive and let the situation, or others, take control." Case in point: Arsenal could be seen positioning themselves towards the front of the centre circle in the penalty shootout against Porto, in the round of 16 in the 2023-2024 Champions League.

Does it matter to what side of the circle, left or right, the team is positioned? Not necessarily, but it might. Standing to the side closest to the bench, with the coaches and the substitutes, will make it easier for coaches and players to communicate during the shootout, which could be advantageous. Psychologically, it could also be beneficial for the team to be close to their management and the rest of the squad – supported by their own people. With that said, there would be plenty of instances where players would feel more at ease with some *distance* from their coach. This is the same as in the regular game, where wingers and full backs can sometimes have profoundly different game experiences in the first and second halves of games, simply according to whether they perform with their supportive or over-controlling coach next to them or not.

It's also interesting to observe that there is nothing in the rules stating that the players in the centre circle have to stand still. Yet most of them tend to, as if forbidden from doing anything else. Physiologically, it does not make sense to play a football game for in excess of 120 minutes, and then all of a sudden freeze like a sculpture for 5-10 minutes right before you have to take what could be the most important kick of your whole life. Psychologically too, passively waiting with no task to occupy you can bring stress and pressure. Movement is smart, and it can be done in at least a couple of ways.

Why not, for instance, make the team formation a bit more dynamic, moving it around the centre circle during the shootout? The team could start at the front of the circle then, at pre-agreed points, move right to the back and then eventually right to the front again. Quite apart from getting the players moving a little, this could create a very unpredictable centre circle environment for the opposition, which would most likely aggravate them.

Alternatively, use the possibilities offered by goal celebration. This was another tip that was born with the Dutch U21 team back in 2007: breaking free from the team formation to celebrate individually after every scored goal, and after every opposition miss, too. This will not only loosen up stiff muscles, but also bring some fire and positive energy to one's own team. Again, it may also get to the opposition, it being well known how annoying it is when teams are perceived to be overly celebrating little victories. When New York City won that MLS final penalty shootout against Portland Timbers, the assistant referee had to reprimand the team for overly celebrating goals and saves, which suggests that players stuck to this part of the strategy as well as to the progressive centre circle positioning idea.

Again, though, I have to stress that there are no guarantees, and there are many examples of this celebration strategy not paying off. One thinks, for example, of the Netherlands in the 2022 World Cup penalty shootout against Argentina. The Dutch team consistently stood 1-2 metres ahead of the Argentinian team in the centre circle, intensely celebrated every single goal, and generally were moving around a lot throughout the shootout. However, the Argentina players never allowed themselves to be dominated, played the same game back, and ultimately won the match.

The "give and take" of penalty kicks

Erling Haaland is that rare type of football player who on the one hand is an extreme individualist, and on the other hand an extreme team player. His hunger for goals is world renowned. He always looks for goal-scoring opportunities, and this is an obsession for him. Thus, for him, a penalty kick is a much-desired chance to score a goal from a really favourable position. As such, taking a penalty is not a punishment; it is a privilege. Not a threat, but a treat, and so a valuable commodity that can be gifted and traded.

In October 2019, Haaland and Red Bull Salzburg played Rapid Wien at home. They got their first penalty after about half an hour of play, when Haaland powered into the area and was taken down by the goalkeeper. Haaland was the designated penalty taker, but when he came to his feet after the tackle, he instead gave the ball to the Hungarian Dominik Szoboszlai, our friend from Chapter 2 with the strong goalkeeper-independent shot. When this happened, another Red Bull player tried to interfere. South Korean Hwang Hee-chan seemed to also want the penalty kick.

But Szoboszlai held onto the ball.

At this point in the Austrian league, Haaland had already scored 11 goals in 11 games, while Szoboszlai had scored just three, and none in the last five. When Szoboszlai scored this penalty, with his trademark shot, hard to his left, Haaland was the first to arrive, grabbing him and shaking him ferociously, while screaming in the air like a madman. Szoboszlai first looked simply relieved that his goal drought had ended, but then he couldn't help but laugh at his generous and crazy-seeming teammate.

Less than two minutes after this, everything was repeated. Haaland galloped into the penalty area, was much quicker than the defender and was taken down. Another penalty. Again, Haaland gave it away. This one went to the previously denied Hwang. This time, the strategy backfired, though. Hwang's badly placed shot to his right was easy to stop. Again, Haaland was the first teammate over to the penalty taker, but now with a friendly and consoling pat on his shoulder.

Another four minutes after this, Haaland dashed into the area yet again, but this time he stayed on his feet and scored. After the game, Jesse Marsch, Salzburg's American manager, was not too happy about those penalties: Haaland was the designated penalty taker and should not have been giving them away. Marsch admitted this was no big deal because they had won, but added darkly: "It will be discussed in the future."[183] Later, after both Marsch and Haaland had moved on to other and bigger clubs, Marsch looked back on what he had experienced in this game and said about Haaland: "I haven't seen one selfish moment since I've known him in the last six months. We went through a time period where he was giving up penalties to his teammates, because he just felt like he wanted to share the positive energy with other guys in the team and I had to actually step in and say no, Erling is taking our penalties."

In his book *Give and Take*, the organisational psychologist Adam Grant divides people into takers, matchers or givers. Takers are the ones who try to get as much as they can from others; matchers are the ones who reciprocate whatever is done to them; and givers are those who are happy giving more to others than they get back. The ones who are most successful professionally are actually the givers. For example, studies of engineers, medical students and sales professionals show that the top performers are givers. However, curiously, it turns out that the bottom performers too, are givers. People who never stop indiscriminately giving end up exploited. They become pushovers or "doormats", and then underperform over time. So it's clearly important to be the right kind of giver.

Back to Haaland for a moment. In September 2020, Borussia Dortmund, the team Haaland joined from Salzburg, played the first league game of the new season against Borussia Mönchengladbach. After 53 minutes, Dortmund received a penalty and Jadon Sancho, who had scored a penalty in a cup game just a few days prior to this, grabbed the ball and started preparing. At this point, Haaland walked up to him, actively arguing some type of case, with his hand in front of his mouth. Sancho did not appear excited about the proposal put in front of him, but he could also not help smiling. There was a moment when Sancho clearly weighed his options, then he reluctantly gave up the ball, while looking down with a sheepish grin. Haaland had basically just stolen the penalty kick from him – but clearly in such a way that it was hard for Sancho to turn him down. Haaland then lined up the ball. A smart, well-executed goalkeeper-dependent kick. Goal.

Later in that second half, Haaland scored his second goal, assisted by Sancho. That goal was one of the most spectacular of his career, in my opinion. On a break after a corner, Haaland sprinted almost the entire length of the pitch at extraordinary speed in order to get in behind the defenders and receive Sancho's perfectly timed and delivered pass. In his celebration, he went straight to Sancho, almost tearing him apart in excitement about the goal the two of them had just created.

These stories show that Haaland is a pretty nice fit for Grant's model of the successful giver, the ones who give strategically. Haaland is a friendly giant. He is both altruistic and ambitious. He gives, both genuinely and generously, but also understands how to navigate people and relationships so others do not take advantage of him. When it is better for the team that he takes the penalty (as it may have been in the Sancho case), he does not hesitate but expresses his desire, perhaps even fights for it, and takes it. Also, in his role as a striker, as a goal scorer, he is completely dependent on his teammates to pass him the ball when he is in favourable positions. If they never get anything from him, they will pass the ball to him less. Hence, Haaland has to give in order to get back. Yet he is an authentic team player. When it is better for the team that he gives the penalty to someone else, he happily donates that opportunity to a teammate. In this way, Haaland is very intentional about his giving.

That does not mean his giving is always well received by everyone, though. A few years after the examples above, in May 2023, Haaland gave up another penalty. This time it was for Manchester City against Leeds United, in the 83rd minute, with City holding a relatively comfortable 2-0 lead. İlkay Gündoğan had scored City's two goals, and Haaland wanted to give him a chance to get his first ever senior hat-trick, with a third goal from that penalty. However, Gündoğan hit the post, and the opportunity was wasted. Pep Guardiola, City's manager, was furious, and could be clearly seen yelling at Haaland: "Erling, you have to take it!" To make matters worse, less than a minute later, Leeds United scored, to make it 1-2, and now suddenly there was a game. City held on to win in the end, but Guardiola was obviously asked about the penalty situation, and said: "It shows how nice and generous Erling is. But the game is not over. If it is 4-0 with 10 minutes left, OK. But at 2-0? Erling is the best penalty taker right now so he has to take it."

Interestingly, when Arsenal did something similar, in September 2023 in a match against Bournemouth, some people reacted against it strongly, even though it worked out. At 2-0 to Arsenal, the club's big signing for the season, Kai Havertz, was handed a penalty by his teammates Saka and Ødegaard, one of whom would normally have taken that shot. In 20 appearances, Havertz had yet to score and his first Arsenal goal would obviously mean a lot to him. He converted the penalty, making it 3-0, and his teammates and the Arsenal fans were as ecstatic as he was.

Yet Steve Nicol, formerly of Liverpool and now a pundit at ESPN, called it unprofessional, and his counter-advice took a more old-school, short-term view of this kind of situation. Referring to Saka and Ødegaard, he said: "*You* take the penalty, or *you* take the penalty. One of the two of you. Not, 'let's be nice and fuzzy and lovely and give it to Havertz'."[184]

Football is a complex social and psychological game, though, and played by real human beings. To get the most out of people, strategic gifts, such as the ones this current generation of players have found a space for, may not always look like the safest way to secure three points on a given day. But these gifts are more generous, more humane and, in the long run, more functional.

Chapter 5

Training for the pressure

"Normal is enough."

Ski-jumping coach Mika Kojonkoski

It's a beautiful Sunday morning, with a clear blue sky. Perfect flying conditions. You have clearance from the tower, and you're smoothly applying full throttle. The speed picks up, pushing you back into your seat in the cockpit and lifting the aircraft's nose off the runway while you carefully monitor the instruments. The climb rate looks good and you are clear of the runway, so you raise the landing gear. Rising to 500-feet altitude now, and all is smooth and easy and looking good for the two-hour flight ahead.

And then – *BANG!* There's a massive jolt and then a horrifying silence. You push hard at the throttle but it's dead in your hand. The engine is out. Out and unresponsive. Your heart rate surges. The aircraft is now in a glide – and, according to the altimeter, already descending. You try to fight the panic and check your options. What's out the window? Ahead of you are trees and hills – tricky terrain. Just behind you is the safety of the landing strip. But you need to act quickly because this plane is going down.

This is the critical moment. Fly on and look for a landing site? Or turn back? You have to decide, and now. You opt for the turn. After all, it's right there, isn't it, the runway? You should be able to turn, make it back and be on the ground again in no time.

You start to guide the aircraft around. Nice and easy. The plane starts to turn. But then suddenly it seems to develop a life of its own. And now the horizon isn't directly ahead of you but out the side-window to the left and the ground seems to be coming at you through the glass at a terrifying pace. You try to pull the craft up again, but there's no response. Just the ground getting closer and closer and alarms shrieking and the controls lighting up all across the panel in front of you while you grapple with the dead controls.

And then it all goes black.

At which point in your ear comes a calm voice. "Oops", says your instructor from his position outside the simulator. "A sharp turn with low power. Bad call. Never turn back below 1000 feet. You need to be flying on and looking for somewhere to put it down ahead of you."

And then the computer gets reset and you try it again.

In aviation, flight simulators have been an integral part of pilot training since before World War Two. Emergencies are prepared for. I'm sure all of us who fly as passengers are reassured to know that's the case. Similarly, medical training now routinely makes use of simulators, not least for complex surgery. Again, it's reassuring to know. Simulators are also used in the preparation of military operations and form a major part of astronaut training.

Pilots, surgeons, soldiers, astronauts... these people know that they work in environments where failure has real and irreversible consequences. They work under immense pressure and they train for that pressure in advance, in the belief that high-stress moments can be prepared for and mitigated. The ample experience of those professions is that you can usefully simulate the high-pressure conditions of a battle zone, or an operating theatre, or a module of the International Space Station, or the cockpit of a falling plane, and that the people who work in those situations will very much benefit.

Yet it remains one of football's fondest and most widely held beliefs that you can't possibly simulate the high-pressure conditions of a penalty shootout.

For example, here's Didier Deschamps, who captained France to the World Cup title in 1998 as a player, and then did the same as a manager in 2018. In 2016, Deschamps declared that he had never trained for penalties. His reasoning? "Because I believe that taking penalties in training in complete relaxation and in matches with enormous pressure has nothing to do with it."[185]

After France lost on penalties to Argentina in the 2022 World Cup final, Deschamps went into more detail about his thoughts in this area: "At training there is no one except you. You never manage to recreate the conditions of a match. If it's a final, the emotional side, the public, the positioning of the shooters, nothing can be prepared."

He did at least admit that some penalty kick practice at the end of a training session might have some value. But not much. "If the best shooters shoot one, two, three, four in training, why not? I'm not convinced that it does much, but that's just my opinion. This is why I don't do specific sessions. At the end of the session, it could happen that the offensive players stay to shoot, but that's it."[186]

Deschamps is by no means the only one of his countrymen who thinks this way. Mickaël Landreau, a former goalkeeper with 11 caps for France, also saw no point in training for penalties because "it's impossible to find yourself in the same circumstances as in a match. When you have 120 minutes in your legs, with crazy pressure, it has nothing to do with training."

Just for the record, France does not have a good recent record in penalty shootouts, having lost their last three (in 2006, 2016 and 2022) and won only three of eight in total (38% wins) since their first in the 1982 World Cup. Is it the lack of training? Or just bad luck?

Many esteemed coaches all over the world take the same position as Deschamps. When Carlo Ancelotti, one of the most accomplished managers of all time, was asked in January 2023 if his Real Madrid side had prepared for the possibility of a penalty shootout in a particular upcoming match, he admitted that they had not: "The truth is that we don't train penalties much. It's impossible to replicate the real-life atmosphere of an important penalty in training."[187]

The legendary Johan Cruyff felt the same: "I also don't think there is much point in training on penalties. It's not about whether you have the ability to shoot the ball – that's really not that difficult. No, it's all about whether you can do that in a full stadium, under enormous pressure. A situation that can never, ever be imitated on a training field."[188]

Ahead of the German Cup round of 16 match between Bayern Munich and Hertha Berlin in 2019, the Bayern manager, Niko Kovač, was equally clear: "You can't simulate that at all. In training, you'll make every shot, but when 40,000 or 50,000 whistle at you..."[189]

Other coaches seem to be open to their players doing some isolated penalty kick training, while offering the same opinion that it is impossible to simulate the pressure. Pep Guardiola, Cruyff's protégé: "Listen, we can train for the penalties, but you cannot replay the tension that happens in the real moments."[190]

And some coaches strongly believe in training penalty kicks, and make their players train a lot, while at the same time acknowledging that pressure itself cannot be prepared for. Luis Enrique, the Spain manager in the 2022 World Cup, expressed this in Qatar: "Over a year ago, in many national camps we told players, 'You have homework ahead of the World Cup. You must take at least 1000 penalties with the club.' I don't think it's a lottery. If you train often, then the way you take penalties improves. Obviously, you can't train the pressure and tension, but you can cope with it."[191]

However, even with 1000 repetitions, the Spanish men could not deliver in the World Cup. All three penalty takers, Pablo Sarabia, Carlos Soler and Sergio Busquets, missed their attempts and Spain lost the shootout to Morocco in the round of 16. Three thousand repetitions and not a single goal!

These are the claims that strongly reinforce the popular notion that a penalty shootout is a lottery. How could it be anything else when training seems not to help? How could it be anything else when some of the best coaches in the game resign themselves to going into shootouts fundamentally unprepared?

However, could all these profoundly experienced and highly intelligent managers be wrong about pressure training? Contrary to the widely received football wisdom, is it possible to simulate pressure to a degree that will positively impact players' ability to perform penalty kicks under pressure at the highest level?

Before we consider that question, take a moment to imagine that you are in a conversation with the surgeon who, the following day, is scheduled to perform a delicate procedure on you.

You: "You have practised for this, right?"

Surgeon: "Well, yeah, obviously I've done a few bits and pieces at the end of a work day. But in terms of training for the whole operation… well, you see, the thing is, you simply can't replicate the tension of that real-world scenario when the actual patient's on the table and the scalpel's in your hand. So there wouldn't be much point, would there?"

I may be wrong, but I think you'd hope your surgeon had practised. And I believe it is possible to derive benefits from simulation training for penalty shootouts just as it's possible to derive benefits from simulation training for medical surgery. And I'm pleased to see that at least the occasional coach agrees with me.

Here's Thomas Tuchel, who has managed at Chelsea, PSG and Bayern Munich: "We always practise penalties when we face a match where it's possible it could go to penalties. Can we simulate the pressure, the fatigue, the occasion, how it will feel tomorrow? No, we cannot. But still we believe we can take care about some patterns, and about a certain rhythm and certain habits during penalties."[192]

And here's Lionel Scaloni, the manager who has now won three major penalty shootouts in a row with Argentina, speaking about training, prior to the game (that ended with penalties) against the Netherlands: "We always kick penalties,"[193] and "We have been practising penalties, before and after training."[194]

After the World Cup, while acknowledging the difficulties around simulating pressure, Scaloni made clear that he still believed in the value of training: "When there are people behind the goal… and 80,000 in the stadium, it's not the same as kicking while in training. But I think that it counts for something. You feel the ball, you feel the strike."[195]

Further back in history, in 2002, Dutch manager Guus Hiddink coached South Korea in the World Cup in South Korea and Japan, and introduced a real penalty shootout training innovation. A few years ago, I went to Hiddink's townhouse in Amsterdam to speak to him. He's an impressive person with a unique international record, having coached in 10 countries and at some of the leading clubs in the world, including Real Madrid and Chelsea. Moreover, his cultural curiosity and the emphasis in his thinking on how players are first and foremost people make him a coach with much to offer in the way of psychological insight.[196] When he spoke about preparing South Korea for their World Cup quarter-final against Spain in 2002, penalties were a part of it.[197]

"The night before, we took penalties. I had each player take one. One. No repetition, none."

This was the opposite of Enrique and Spain's 1000 penalties. By having them take only one kick – Hiddink's theory was – there would be more pressure on that kick, which is closer to how it is in an actual shootout. The focus there was less on calibrating penalty mechanics over several attempts and more on finding a way to cope with the pressure of your one, single attempt, your one big moment.

Hiddink also created a special type of penalty shootout simulation: "While being watched by all the other players, the penalty takers had to walk across the entire pitch to take a penalty. That's a long way, if you have to walk 100 metres to take a penalty. A lot of thoughts will go through your head then."

Hiddink did not, then, just have the players walk from the halfway line on the training ground, as some teams sometimes do. He had them walk from the opposite penalty area, which exaggerates one specific aspect of the penalty shootout and, again, puts focus on the pressure more than the kick itself: "It was beautiful to see how their bodies reacted to the tension," Hiddink said, "where everyone had their own expressions, their own style of walking."

In this setting, there was no reward or punishment for scored or missed kicks: "If someone missed, we just acted as if nothing happened. Just go on with the other penalties."

How did it go the day after?

"The next day we indeed had to take penalties against Spain and all five shots went in. It was beautiful. Nobody wanted to take a kick, everyone scored."

With this, South Korea became the first Asian team ever to

reach the semi-final of a World Cup (where they ultimately lost to Germany, after a Ballack goal in the 75th minute).

So, taking off from Hiddink's approach, let's examine the concept of pressure training, the evidence for its effects, and finally set out how this mode of preparation can specifically be applied to penalty kicks in football.

Does pressure training work?

The core of pressure training is built on a quite simple idea: exposure to mild stress will enable performers to tolerate stress at a higher intensity.[198] Specifically, training with some form of pressure will increase one's capability to resist and thrive under greater magnitudes of pressure at some later point. The evidence for the value of such training comes from different sources.

Biological sciences, for example, show that when an organism is exposed to a low dose of stress, the survival of that organism is enhanced because mechanisms that protect against similar or more severe stress will be activated.[199] The most familiar example of this mechanism in action is vaccines. Inserting a micro-dose of a virus can be enough to trigger the immune system and create protection when the real virus arrives. Likewise, the thinking is, a small dose of stress produces resilience against a similar or higher dose of stress at a later point.

Maybe, then, we can think of pressure training as a kind of vaccination programme. By applying micro-doses of pressure, one is inoculated and protected against larger doses of pressure that one may be exposed to later. With this perspective, stress leads to post-traumatic growth, rather than enduring trauma – to an improvement in one's ability to cope with stress. The statistician and best-selling author Nassim Nicholas Taleb promoted the concept of "antifragility", to describe a system's ability to increase in capability and thrive as a result of stress.[200] In this line of thinking, stress actually benefits us.

Research with animals has yielded some findings consistent with this. Rodents and non-human primates that are exposed to moderate levels of stress, compared to those exposed to high/low stress, seem to display more adaptive neurobiological, neuroendocrinological, cognitive, affective and behavioural reactions to stressors later.[201] For example, a study shows that monkeys who are briefly separated from their mothers during early childhood not only experience lower anxiety and stress after nine months, but also exhibit higher cognitive control, more curiosity and larger brains later in life compared to a control group.[202]

Another line of studies suggests that the degree of control an animal has over the stress they are subjected to determines the outcome of the experience. If exposed to unavoidable and unpredictable shocks, for instance, an animal develops exaggerated fear, higher anxiety and ineffective coping, a phenomenon often called "learned helplessness". However, if animals are able to modify their behaviour to avoid the shock, they are much more in control, and enhanced resilience is the outcome.[203]

The principles observed in both biological systems and animals are also found in humans. Experiencing moderate doses of stress early in life is generally associated with a series of positive consequences later in life, such as lower stress, lower anxiety, better cognitive functioning and higher quality of life.[204] For example, in one study newlyweds who experienced moderate stress during the early months of marriage reported better marital adjustment following transition to parenthood, with all its extra stresses, than spouses who did not report early stress.[205]

More specifically for sport, a series of studies show that world class athletes are more likely to have experienced early-life adversity

Transcendent leadership: after misses in the 2022 World Cup final penalty shootout, Kylian Mbappé was first out of the centre circle to re-enfold his France teammates back into the group. Here with Kingsley Coman…

… and here, again, with Aurélien Tchouaméni.

Taking the high ground: on their way to the 2021 MLS title (via two shootouts in the playoff stages), New York City FC take up a position at the front of the centre circle rather than along the centre line, dominating the space and shortening the walk to and from the spot.

When Gareth Bale scored the late equalising penalty in Wales' 2022 World Cup match against USA, Kieffer Moore (no. 13) had been at work for several minutes, guarding the penalty spot, and Bale, from confrontational Americans.

Many teams now assign dedicated penalty taker protectors. Here, Chelsea's Jess Carter stays by Maren Mjelde's side ahead of the decisive penalty against Lyon in the 2022-23 Champions League quarter-final.

Birth of the decoy: César Azpilicueta does a convincing impression of the taker for Chelsea's late and potentially decisive penalty against Palmeiras in the 2021 Club World Cup final, drawing the heat from opponents trying to get into his head. Elsewhere Kai Havertz could prepare himself quietly, prior to stepping in at the last moment and scoring.

Arsenal are one of many teams to adopt the decoy strategy. Here, in a Champions League tie against Lens, Martin Ødegaard, his work done, leaves it to Jorginho.

Pride personified: the iconic *Sports Illustrated* cover showing Megan Rapinoe, exultant after scoring a penalty for the USA in the 2019 World Cup final.

A friendly hand: Liverpool's Alisson Becker gives the ball to teammate Trent Alexander-Arnold in the penalty shootout to decide the 2022 FA Cup final. The goalkeeper handoff ensures a friendly initiation for the penalty taker and prevents the opposition goalkeeper from acting disruptively.

In the 2023 World Cup, Sweden goalkeeper Zećira Mušović always handed the ball to teammates with an added smile and a little conversation. Here, Sweden's first penalty taker, Fridolina Rolfö, feels the warmth.

Erling Haaland gives: despite being Salzburg's designated penalty taker, the Norwegian donated a penalty he had won against Rapid Wien to Dominik Szoboszlai to restore his teammate's confidence after a string of goalless performances. Here, Haaland celebrates exuberantly after Szoboszlai scored.

Erling Haaland takes: desperate to get his tally for the season underway, Haaland tries to persuade Borussia Dortmund's designated taker, Jadon Sancho, to let him take a penalty against Borussia Mönchengladbach. He succeeded – and scored.

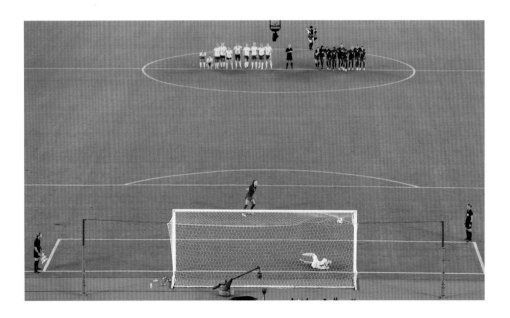

Julia Grosso scores with Canada's sixth penalty to clinch the 2020 Olympic Gold against Sweden. That win was the culmination of nearly nine years of penalty preparation and training.

The Norway women's team conducts a penalty shootout simulation at the Ulleval stadium in Oslo the day before departing for the 2023 World Cup in Australia and New Zealand. The author is standing to the left with his notebook in an attempt to increase the takers' perception of being scrutinised and more effectively simulate the pressure of the actual moment.

When Spain ended up in a penalty shootout against Morocco in the 2022 World Cup, their manager Luis Enrique nominated three penalty takers and then gave his list and a pen to the captain, Sergio Busquets, tasking him with selecting the remaining takers. Spain missed all their kicks and lost.

The Argentina manager, Lionel Scaloni, successfully piloted his team through two penalty shootout wins in the 2022 World Cup with a blend of preparation, connection with his players and effective communication.

or trauma than elite athletes at a lower level.[206] For example, researchers interviewed 32 former Great Britain athletes, of which 16 were multiple medallists at major championships, and 16 were elite athletes at a very high level, but not medallists.[207] Among the differences was that all 16 medallists had experienced an early significant negative critical event (such as the death of a significant family member, a parental divorce, an unstable home environment or being forcibly separated from their parents) while only four of the non-medallists had those kinds of experiences in their pasts. For 14 of the medallists, this negative event occurred shortly before a positive critical sport-related event (such as finding their sport, finding a significant coach or mentor, or experiencing an inspirational sporting moment), suggesting that sport somehow filled a gap or that perhaps the negative experience had stimulated these young athletes' motivation and focus on their sport. Regardless, experiencing the foundational traumatic event did not block the development of these athletes; if anything it helped them.

A version of this has been observed in football. A study of players at the famous Ajax academy in Amsterdam showed that those who ultimately became elite football players had more than three times as high a chance of having parents who had divorced compared with those who fell short of the elite level.[208] Overall, even though there are also studies which do not support these links between trauma and positive development,[209] some sport development researchers argue that talent needs trauma, and that trauma can be used as a development tool.[210] Now, this is obviously not an argument for indiscriminately exposing developing athletes to horrible things in order to reap the performance dividends. But let's switch the term "trauma" for the term "challenge" and then remove this to a purely sporting context. Small challenges that young aspiring athletes might helpfully be exposed to could include, say, competing at a level above the one they are used to at some sensible point, or warming up at a major senior event with senior players, or taking penalty kicks at half-time at well-attended senior events. Carefully administered and periodised, and with the athletes' coping needs vigilantly monitored, such challenges could provide an opportunity for athletes to mobilise, rehearse and hone ways to deal with higher stress loads, something that it might be valuable for any performer to learn early.

A team of researchers from the Free University of Amsterdam has conducted a series of experiments that quite elegantly show the impact of training under stress.[211] In one of them, 24 participants were randomly assigned to an experimental group and a control group. The experimental group practised throwing darts under artificially produced low doses of anxiety. That anxiety was induced in various ways. For example, the training sessions were recorded with a video camera and the participants were told that the videos would be used for a TV programme in which experts would analyse their behaviours. Or, more deviously, the participants were told that they had been paired up with another participant and that their combined scores would possibly yield a reward for each of them – but that their partner had already completed their throws, so it was now up to them to secure the prize for them both. In other tests, they were told that each sixth dart would earn double points, and that their scores would be circulated afterwards to everyone participating.

Self-report measurements showed that this training indeed produced mild anxiety levels in the participants. Afterwards, the participants were tested on dart throwing while standing on a tiny foothold four metres up in the air on an indoor climbing wall. The self-report and heart rate measurements confirmed that this test produced high anxiety levels for all participants. However, the participants who had undergone the training with mild anxiety were able to maintain their dart-throwing performance even under these conditions of high anxiety. The control group, who had trained under no-anxiety conditions, significantly underperformed in this more intensely pressured task.

This experiment shows something of utmost importance: it is not necessary to replicate perfectly the high stress levels of a test situation for the training to produce a significant impact. Rather, it can be sufficient to train with mild levels of stress. Although there is a need to replicate this study under much more realistic conditions, there are obvious implications here for our task of taking penalties in football, and for the thinking of those coaches who choose not to practise penalties because the pressure cannot be 100% replicated. Just as special forces soldiers spend months and years training military operations without ever being able to simulate perfectly the true stress of coming under live fire during war, footballers could engage in imperfect simulations of penalty shootouts and expect this to make them better prepared than those who do not practise at all.

What does other research say? A review of 47 studies on interventions designed to prevent choking under pressure found them generally to benefit performance.[212] The reviewed studies were in different categories, based on theoretical approaches to choking. Most relevant here, one category concerned tests using acclimatisation, that is, training under conditions that mimic pressure. A total of 10 studies in this area were reviewed, where training with self-consciousness and mild anxiety showed positive effects.

Another review of 23 studies on the efficacy of coping interventions for performance under pressure looked at various categories of intervention including education, consultancy, simulation and emotion regulation.[213] The most consistent finding was that simulation training that exposed individuals to pressure gave the largest improvements to performance by comparison with the control group. The researchers concluded that simulating performance under pressure provided context-specific competence and confidence, as well as an opportunity to develop coping skills in a controlled environment.

Finally, a meta-analysis was conducted with 14 studies on pressure simulation training across sport (10 studies) and policing (four studies).[214] Pressure in these tests was created using judgment (e.g. evaluation by coaches), reward (e.g. the offer of a cash prize) or forfeits (e.g. loser cleans the dressing room). The analysis found that the included studies showed a moderate-to-large positive effect on performance, suggesting that the performers who received pressure training performed better than those who did not receive it. This is very good news. Pressure training seems to work. It changes athletes' relationship to pressure. It enables them to think: "Yes, the pressure I am likely to experience in my role is uncomfortable, but it can be practised for, adjusted to and controlled."[215]

Pressure training can be done regularly with positive outcomes, but if it is done too often, its effects are blunted. Relatively rare high-pressure sessions, with occasional booster sessions (equivalent to booster vaccine shots, if you like), would appear to make the best sense.

However, there is a thin line between deliberately, temporarily and intermittently applying pressure to increase performers' capability in high-pressure situations, and straightforwardly abusing them.[216] It is easy to imagine coaches justifying excessively harsh practice regimens under the guise of pressure training, which cannot be condoned. People respond differently to pressure training. Based on age, experience and personality, some will benefit greatly from such training, others will benefit less and some will struggle with it, possibly even finding that it lowers their confidence, which is the exact opposite of the desired outcome.[217] Because of this, dosage and timing are critical.[218] And so is getting consent from those involved.[219]

Pressure training and penalties

José Mourinho, who coached penalty specialist Harry Kane at Tottenham from 2019 to 2021, said that "Harry decides before the game, a few days before, how he is going to take the penalty, and then spends 3-4 days practising that shot."[220] This approach is not unique to Kane.

All the competent penalty takers I have spoken to praise the value of practice for penalties. For example, when I asked Robert Lewandowski why he is so effective from the penalty spot, he simply responded: "Practice. Penalties after training a few times a week. All the time. The technique I am doing, I am always trying to find the best solution. To fix something or remember what I should do." Martin Ødegaard said something similar: "I take 1-3 penalty kicks in training, if not every day, it is often. On average, perhaps I take one penalty every day. Often after regular training ended. Against a goalkeeper." When Maren Mjelde told me about that decisive extra-time penalty against Lyon, she said: "The day before the match, I took five penalties in training, with five different types of shots to feel what I was most comfortable with. The penalty I ended up using, I also scored the day before in training." Celso Borges probably said it most concisely: "I haven't seen good penalty takers that don't practise." This is what they are used to. Players at this level are elite performers who build competence and confidence through daily training.

The big question, though, is: how do you build on this to train for the intense pressure experienced around penalties? In some ways, just conducting a replica shootout in training will produce a pressure stimulus. We did one such penalty shootout simulation with the Norway women's team when they prepared for the 2023 World Cup, prior to leaving for New Zealand. To increase pressure, we let the players know that their shots would be rigorously dissected and analysed to pieces by coaches and specialists. I, as a penalty kick specialist, took up position next to the penalty spot, in an attempt to trigger the players' feeling of being examined and judged as they prepared to take the kick. Maren Mjelde, the captain of this team, described it like this: "When you have a penalty shootout in training, your heart rate goes up, because it is a pretty uncomfortable situation with each player being put in the limelight. You do what you would have done in a match. Your decision. Your routines. Even if there is nobody in the stands and zero consequences, you must rehearse somewhere. I see the benefits of this. And a lot of teams who end up in this situation probably regret that they did not prepare better, that they did not rehearse it."

Some teams have started adopting highly sophisticated technology in this area. Liverpool's neurofeedback training consists of performing penalty kicks in training while being connected to equipment that measures brainwaves prior to and during the kick. Receiving continuous feedback about brainwaves, while on the pitch over the ball, allows players actively to work to achieve an optimal emotional state prior to their kicks, as Niklas Häusler says: "During our training, we help the players get into and stay in specific brain frequencies longer and deeper right before taking a penalty or a set piece." Another technology we are likely to see more of is augmented reality. In a recent study, penalty kick training was conducted with holographic goalkeepers to systematically train goalkeeper-dependent penalty kicks, with positive results.[221]

What about the penalty shootout, specifically? In 2012, we published a qualitative study documenting the subjective experience of taking a shot in a European Championship penalty shootout.[222] Building on these descriptions, researchers created a six-step protocol for simulating and recreating this type of pressure in a training environment, and then tested the extent to which 16 professional footballers were affected by that simulation compared to a low-pressure, control condition.[223]

Specifically, the high-pressure simulation involved 1) walking from the halfway line, and returning to the halfway line after a kick, 2) crowd noise, 3) announcing to the players they were in direct competition with each other, and that they would be ranked afterwards, 4) highlighting that the video of their performance would be evaluated by the coach afterwards, 5) showing the participants randomised targets to shoot at prior to each shot, and 6) announcing to the players that the goalkeeper would be informed about the shot direction for two of their shots. (In reality, direct competition and coach evaluation were "cover stories" and would not be carried out. For this test, what mattered was the experience of the potential, rather than the actual, consequences.)

The results showed that the players were indeed impacted by the high-pressure simulation. When taking a penalty under the induced-pressure conditions, the players rated the pressure significantly higher, had higher cognitive anxiety, lower self-confidence, were more distracted and recorded higher respiration rates than when they took it under low-pressure, control conditions. Overall, these results suggest that simulating a penalty shootout may indeed have a pronounced psychological impact on penalty takers, akin to the effects of taking part in a real shootout.

In other words, contrary to what the sceptics claim, you *can* replicate the pressure of a penalty shootout in training, at least up to a certain and probably beneficial point.

Training for penalties: the Canada story

The Canada women's national team was ranked number eight in the world going into the Covid-delayed 2020 Olympic football tournament in Tokyo. Although their manager, Bev Priestman, set the bar high ahead of the tournament by alluding to an appearance in the final as a natural aim, others' expectations were significantly more tempered. And with some reason: their last 11 games against top-10-ranked nations had produced eight losses and just one win.

In the group stage at the Olympics, they managed one win and two draws and crept into the knockout phase. The team seemed at least to possess resilience.

What this Canada team then produced was one of the greatest penalty kick accomplishments ever seen. First, they beat Brazil in the quarter-finals after a penalty shootout. Then, in the semi-finals, they met the big tournament favourites, the USA. In a very tight game, the score was 0-0 with 15 minutes to go, when Canada got a penalty. The 23-year-old Jessie Fleming stepped up. Goal. Final result: 1-0. They faced Sweden in the final and went behind in the first half. That remained the score until the 67th minute, when Canada received yet another penalty. Jessie Fleming again. 1-1. Thus, this match, too, ended up going to a penalty shootout. After a dramatic duel, with multiple misses on both sides, Canada ultimately became Olympic champions, thanks, in no small measure, to their ability at the penalty spot.

The Canadian women dominated everyone in the game of penalties. How did they do this? Was there a secret recipe? Or just luck?

There was probably some luck involved, particularly in the final, but there was indeed also a recipe. When I sat down to speak with the team's mental performance coach, Alex Hodgins, he told me that they had started penalty preparations a long time ago. "We always had what we would call a penalty shootout protocol," Hodgins explained. "Over eight or nine years, we developed this live document that we continued to update. We had a strategy for in-game penalty shots and penalty kick shootout scenarios.

And we had protocols for both."

Canada continued to refine the plan over the years, even though they did not experience many penalty shootouts.

"Before 2021, we had been in one penalty shootout in the nine years I worked with the team. That was a small tournament final, which didn't mean anything. But we always made sure we prepared just in case."

One of the aspects they focused on with their players was the time between the referee's whistle and the run-up.

"I loved the research on the whistle and the length of time to wait. I never liked players who went when the whistle went. We were trying to encourage our players to not just react to the whistle, but also not take too long. To really train that sweet spot."

They then proceeded to do a lot of work on the players' pre-performance routines.

"We provided information on routine. We looked at people like NFL kickers. They take a few steps back and a few steps to the side. No one had the same thing, but we wanted to make sure everyone had their own process. This is controllable in a very uncontrolled world."

Jessie Fleming, who played for Chelsea at the time, scored four penalty kicks in the Olympics, two in-game kicks and two in the shootouts. For each and every kick, her routine was identical.

"Jessie took three steps back. One step to the side. Then she took a breath, and she had an internal dialogue with herself. When the whistle went, which I love, she took another deep breath. I can imagine that that breath probably sets off goalies just a little bit, when they are used to penalty takers responding so quickly."

The focus and emphasis that the Canadian coaches put on the penalty takers' pre-shot waits and routines also seemed to help their own goalkeeper.

"What I thought was quite intelligent was that our goalkeeper took a lot of the information that we were giving to our penalty takers, like the time delays, and then reverse-engineered it. When the ball was on the penalty spot, she was standing right there and then slowly backing up, with this huge smile on her face. If I'd been a penalty taker, I'd have been so annoyed with her right out of the gate, and maybe that's distracting them from the job they had to do. She did a fantastic job. And she saved so many penalties."

This strategy also stretched into managing the team aspects of a penalty shootout.

"One of the things we did was we had a player who didn't want to take a kick, but she's like the heart and soul of the team, so she wanted to be the one to walk to meet the player that had taken a shot. Whether they scored or not, she went and met them halfway, so it didn't feel so lonely. Everyone always felt like they were part of something, not just by themselves, because that's a long walk to carry out in silence if you are by yourself."

With all of this said, some very small margins ultimately favoured the Canada team, particularly in the final. If Sweden had scored with their fifth penalty kick, they would have been Olympic champions. That kick was taken by an extraordinary footballer, Caroline Seger, the most capped European player ever, with 221 national team games for her country. Stephanie Labbé, Canada's goalkeeper, certainly tried to get into Seger's head by positioning herself on the edge of the goal area, then taking forever to back up to the goal line. When she saw Labbé's tricks, Seger turned her back on her after placing the ball on the penalty spot, walked back, and was then forced to wait more than 15 seconds for the whistle. That's an extraordinarily long interval in a penalty shootout. When the whistle came, Seger reacted quickly and drove the ball well over the crossbar. Miss. Canada were still in the game.

Seger later commented about that penalty: "I was fully sure I would score. The goalie doesn't even go in the right direction, but then the ball went up. After this, it feels more or less as if my whole life falls apart."[224]

After Seger in the shootout, Deanne Rose stepped up, having to score to keep Canada in the game. Rose, 22 years old, did the same distinctive walk back from the ball as Jessie Fleming, modelled on the approach of NFL kickers, with characteristically long steps, indicating a deliberate and rehearsed routine. Then a four-second wait after the whistle. Not too short, not too long. She then drilled the ball into the top right corner. This was probably the best-struck penalty in the tournament, under the most severe pressure. Even though the Swedish goalkeeper went early and to the correct side, no goalkeeper in the world, male or female, would have stopped that shot. The shootout was ultimately decided with the next two kicks in sudden death – a Swedish miss and a Canadian goal – but Rose's performance was perhaps Canada's greatest demonstration of the power of pre-performance routines. But it was also a huge testimony to the power of practice.

Because above all, what distinguished the Canadian approach to penalty preparation was the training that they did.

"Prior to the shootout in Tokyo, I would say, comfortably, we did four full dress rehearsals. Three before the tournament started. And then we did one right after the group stage ended."

And because this was conducted with many of the same players over many years, they could gather feedback, learn and adjust based on it.

"I would say the feedback was great. Before the 2019 World Cup, we had done a dress rehearsal where we were trying to distract the players. We had a couple of staff members behind the net banging things and chanting all sorts of random songs. We thought that was a good idea, to work on refocusing. Then one of the players came up and said: 'We get why you guys are doing that, but it's so quiet during a penalty shootout. It's almost silent.

So this is not really helpful.' That was great feedback. We stopped with the distracting sounds during training, and just allowed them that really long awkward silence."

This training also involved the coaches and the staff.

"We did a lot of dress rehearsals so the staff knew where they needed to stand, who was doing what, so the roles and responsibilities were clear."

All in all, the approach of the Canada team to that tournament in 2021 was the implementation of several of the themes from my research these past years, and which I have been relaying here in this book. But the main take-away message was that, contrary to so much prevalent thinking within football, penalties can indeed be trained for. And the Canada women's team have their Olympic gold medals to prove it.

Chapter 6

Managing the pressure

"Today in life it is essential to be a good person and care about the people you work with, because that brings them much closer; if not, it separates you from them. And now more than ever we need to have a lot of personal contact."

Lionel Scaloni, manager of Argentina

Born in Santa Fe, Argentina, in 1978, Lionel Scaloni had a decent playing career, mostly in Spain and Italy, with a brief loan spell in the Premier League with West Ham United. He was also a member of the Argentina squad that lost the penalty shootout to Germany in the 2006 World Cup quarter-finals, although he did not personally play in that game. His managing career started as an assistant for Jorge Sampaoli at the Spanish club Sevilla, who then brought Scaloni with him when he took over Argentina ahead of the 2018 World Cup in Russia. When Argentina disappointed in that World Cup, Scaloni and Pablo Aimar succeeded Sampaoli as caretaker managers, an arrangement that was extended at one point to include the 2019 Copa América. The decision did not go down terribly well in Argentina. Diego Maradona was one of the loudest in a chorus of voices who were not happy with the appointment of someone who had never been a great player.

"I don't want him for my team," Maradona said. "He couldn't even control traffic."[225]

A third place finish in that Copa América wasn't really enough to change the critics' minds, but Scaloni stayed on and the tide of opinion around him turned when he took Argentina to their first trophy in 28 years by winning the 2021 Copa América, defeating Brazil in the final. Now people seemed to be more interested in knowing who Scaloni really was as a person. The impression he gives in interviews is one of extreme humility, quite at odds with what one might expect from someone in his role. "The day I became confirmed coach of the national team," he once said, "they told me that from then on I was going to be the most important person in Argentina... crazy. I'm honestly not interested. Life happens outside of football. Enjoy family and friends. I don't think I'm more or less because I'm a national team coach. I am a coach of a group of players and nothing more than that."[226]

The 2022 World Cup started in the worst possible way for Scaloni's Argentina. In the opening match, they lost 2-1 to Saudi Arabia in a defeat labelled the greatest upset in World Cup history.[227] But things then turned. A video later emerged of Scaloni in a car right after that Saudi Arabia game, speaking, presumably, to one of his staff.

"We have to know that we can lose. Because, first of all, we haven't won anything for a lot of years. And second, it shapes our playing and it shapes our learning... If after receiving this blow, we recover... my friend, there will be no stopping us."[228]

Scaloni is a manager of people as much as he is a manager of players. One of his senior team members, Ángel Di María, describes him like this: "He's our father, the captain of this ship. He is a very affectionate person, very attached to the player." Leadership experts in Argentina call Scaloni "the peaceful leader".[229] Others refer to him as a "feminine" leader.[230] These are labels that are rarely applied to football managers. And perhaps in no place was the impact of his peaceful management style louder and clearer than in the final of that 2022 World Cup against France when he led his team through the severely pressured conditions of the penalty shootout.

When the whistle blew at the end of extra time, the Argentina players would have had good cause to feel deflated. Just moments before this, they had been on the verge of being crowned world champions – 3-2 up with three minutes of regulation time to go. Their hands were practically on the trophy. But then France broke into the Argentina penalty area, Mbappé firing in a cross. Handball. Penalty. Some Mbappé excellence from the spot. 3-3. And now Argentina would have to win it all over again in the penalty shootout.

For 30 seconds after the whistle, Scaloni remained seated on the bench, in conversation with an assistant. Then he rose and strode out onto the pitch, gesturing to the stragglers as they made their exhausted walks back to the sidelines: "Come! Hurry!" He then took up position in the midst of the earliest arrivals and bent down with his hands on his knees while the others gathered around him in a circle.

Some players drank water, some were hunched over with their eyes on the ground, others had placed a hand on a teammate's back in silent support. No one was talking. All were drained. Many of them were probably feeling the pressure beginning to rise. In just a couple of minutes, they would be returning to the field to take penalties with the World Cup on the line. They all knew – it doesn't get more extreme than this.

One player in the group looked particularly distraught: Gonzalo Montiel, the right-side defender. His body language at this point was that of a mourner at a funeral. Perhaps understandably so. It was Montiel who had committed the handball offence that gave France that last-gasp penalty. This whole situation, he must have felt, was because of him.

Scaloni spoke to his players for an extraordinarily short time – fewer than 10 seconds. No visible emotion. Then he got up and walked out of the huddle, leaving a moment for the players to reflect and compose themselves alone. As Scaloni walked away, Luis Martín, the fitness coach, who had been observing the group from the edge of the circle, immediately walked over to Scaloni and whispered a few words in his ear. Directly following this, Scaloni resolutely made his way back through the group of players, with his eyes locked on Gonzalo Montiel.

Montiel was positioned on the other side of the group, so it took Scaloni about 12 seconds to get to him. When he got there, he effectively body-tackled his own player, giving Montiel a robust bump with his shoulder. Scaloni then said one or two very quick words to him, got a minuscule nod in return and then walked away. The shoulder-bump didn't seem to have done much: Montiel was still clearly in a distressed state. Scaloni was not finished though. He paced around the group of players, constantly keeping an eye on Montiel. As he came full circle, after about 15 seconds, he leaned in to Montiel again, grabbed his shoulder, whispered a few words into his ear while covering his mouth with his other hand and gave him a supportive tap on the chest as he walked away again. It later became evident that Scaloni on both these occasions had asked Montiel if he was up for taking a penalty, to which Montiel, the second time, had responded with a yes.

Next, Scaloni immediately took up position in the middle of the circle, urged his players to lean in again, and delivered another short speech. This was more emotional than the first one, accompanied by a resolved face and several hand gestures. It was also slightly longer, but not much: it only lasted 15 seconds. And that was it for team talks. No more information was communicated to the group.

But, again, as Scaloni exited the circle, one of his assistants, this time Walter Samuel, caught him and whispered in his ear. Scaloni reacted swiftly, looking up and working his way through a knot of players to get to Emi Martínez, the goalkeeper. A hug, two or three last words of support, and he was good to go. The Argentina players then walked out to the centre circle and assumed their positions.

Before we unpack what was happening there, let's consider what was going on during this phase in the French camp. When the final whistle sounded, France had reason to be both relieved and disappointed. Relieved because they had been both 0-2 and 2-3 down, and Mbappé's penalties had kept them in contention when their World Cup dream appeared to be over. But also disappointed because after that, with just seconds left to play, only Emi Martínez's outstretched boot had prevented Randal Kolo Muani from completing an astonishing turnaround and stealing the trophy completely. Mbappé made his frustration plain. At the whistle, he put his hands to his head and swore from the bottom of his lungs: "Putain!" He then spent 10 seconds bent over with his hands on his knees, before the first teammate came over to him with a hand, and he slowly started walking towards the sideline.

When Mbappé reached the French group, Didier Deschamps, the manager, closely followed by Guy Stéphan, his assistant coach, immediately addressed him. Deschamps talked while hiding his mouth with his hand. The conversation lasted about 15 seconds before they parted. Mbappé would be penalty taker number one.

Deschamps and his assistant then walked over to Kingsley Coman, with Aurélien Tchouaméni standing just next to him. Deschamps did the talking, while Stéphan stayed within touching distance and kept copious records on a notepad. Coman was asked something: there was a quick back-and-forth, and a nod. Coman would be penalty taker number two.

While this happened, Tchouaméni stood next to Coman and drank from a bottle while looking out into the air. Deschamps stood just one foot away from Tchouaméni. Initially, he turned away from the player, then turned back and looked at him. Then he turned away through 180 degrees, said something to Stéphan and turned back to Tchouaméni, looking at him again. But apparently Deschamps was still not decided, so he now embarked on a full 360-degree pirouette, slowly casting an eye across the whole group of players, before he ultimately came back to Tchouaméni for the third time. Now, finally, he asked him. Tchouaméni would be penalty taker number three.

While this quiet but slightly painful drama unfolded, Kolo Muani was standing on the edge of the circle, across from the others, about seven metres away. Everyone in the circle seemed to be actively doing something – hugging their teammates, voicing some energising words, clapping their hands or looking around to find a way to help or support someone. Kolo Muani stood completely still, in silence. He did not say a word, just calmly gazed at some distant point high up in the stands – away from Deschamps, though occasionally moving his eyes in the direction of the manager, noticeably aware that a question might be coming his way and that he too would most likely be invited to take part in the extreme-pressure, destiny-deciding event that was about to unfold.

His hunch was right. After another exchange with Stéphan and his notes, Dechamps started walking in the direction of Kolo Muani, which the player sensed, shifting his full attention to his oncoming manager. However, it was a hesitant and undecided-looking walk that Deschamps made, heading for Kolo Muani but looking around him the whole time and scanning for other players. It took the manager seven seconds to cover five metres this way, during which time he conducted no fewer than seven visual scans for other players. Upon reaching Kolo Muani, Deschamps popped the question. A look, a nod, a few words, and that was it. Kolo Muani, like Tchouaméni before him, accepted the seemingly improvised, impersonal and possibly even, to all appearances, somewhat unconvinced proposal from his boss, and he would be penalty taker number four.

This whole business took almost two minutes from the final whistle. The French players seemed to be impatient, as they now formed a ring that rapidly closed around Deschamps and his assistant. The group was ripe for some last-second words from their boss, and Deschamps delivered. While continuously consulting with Stéphan, and the notepad, Deschamps hunkered down and gave a 30-second speech, replete with gestures and emotion. Then he stood up, some of the players clapped their hands, and the group broke away.

Deschamps had taken two and a half minutes to complete the final preparation of his team for the decisive phase of the biggest game in world football. Most of that time seemed to have been spent locating, approaching and confirming penalty takers. The contrast with Argentina's Scaloni was immense. Scaloni surely had a clear and pre-prepared plan so that very little information needed to be conveyed to his team at that pressure-filled moment, and communication was brief – just those two, short, almost staccato speeches. The players' roles appeared to be very quickly confirmed, if not known already. In fairness, Argentina, unlike France, had already taken part in a shootout in this tournament, in their quarter-final against the Netherlands, so that would have been a dress rehearsal to some extent. Nevertheless, with the crucial logistical matters taken care of in advance, Scaloni could focus his attention on two objectives: 1) getting across the necessary tactical information effectively, in short and engaging bursts, and 2) managing and supporting his players' psychological needs. In regard to the latter, he spent the bulk of his available time tending to Montiel, the player who probably needed his support the most at this point.

Moreover, the manager's assistants provided him with additional eyes and ears, also focusing on the emotional aspects: "This player needs support", "Have you spoken to this player?". So, there was delegation of tasks, but that delegation was about information gathering. The players heard only one voice, and that was from the person with the highest authority, the manager.

Scaloni has often spoken – as in the quotation at the head of this chapter – about how much the focus of his management style is on people. However, that principle is frequently easier to speak about than it is to practise. At that moment in the World Cup final, though, we saw Scaloni back his words with actions, and under some of the most severe pressure conditions that sport can produce. Indeed, those few post-match minutes with Scaloni in many ways offer a perfect real-world lesson in the exercise of leadership under intense pressure, and a checklist of the key practices for team management in conditions of extreme stress:

- Thorough preparation
- As many key decisions as possible made in advance, enabling the focus to fall on managing your own and your team's emotional readiness
- Concise and effective communication
- Receptivity to input
- The flexibility and the agility to communicate with whoever needs it most in the moment.

In the eventual shootout, Argentina scored all four of their penalties, and their goalkeeper, Emi Martínez, became a hero with his two saves. For France, Mbappé and Kolo Muani converted their kicks, while Coman and the much-deliberated-over Tchouaméni missed.

And what about the mortified Gonzalo Montiel, with whom Scaloni was so preoccupied between his two team talks? What about Montiel, the player from Buenos Aires who touched the ball with his hand to give France that equalising penalty, the one to whom Scaloni offered that shoulder-bump and those five seconds of private consultation at the lowest and tensest point in his career?

Montiel scored Argentina's fourth and final penalty and became the player whose shot will live on forever in football history as the one that delivered Argentina the 2022 World Cup, their first win since 1986.

Leadership under pressure

Penalty shootouts are not as rare as many seem to think. In the knockout stages of major tournaments, 20-30% of the (single-leg) games go to shootouts. From 2026, the teams in the final of the World Cup will be playing their fifth consecutive knockout game in that tournament. The chances of at least one of those games going to penalties are relatively high. When coaches then communicate before a knockout game that they have chosen not to prepare for penalties and instead have focused on winning the game in regulation time, this doesn't merely seem unprofessional; it flies in the face of the odds.

Researchers into leadership in extreme contexts (military or medical settings, law enforcement, firefighting, crisis response, etc.) define an extreme event as a "discrete episode or occurrence that may result in an extensive and intolerable magnitude of physical, psychological, or material consequences to organization members".[231] Sounds like a penalty shootout to me. Leaders play critical roles in ensuring that their organisations are prepared for such extreme events. Part of that preparation is overcoming the human tendency to think that "this can't happen to us". Leaders have to engage with the possibilities – to make sure they plan and prepare, even when the chance of something happening seems remote.

There is what I would call a "behaviour crisis" in the realm of academic psychology, where psychological research has largely ignored authentic behaviours in real-world settings.[232] This has been happening for decades, leaving us with a mountain of documentation regarding people's perceptions and memories of, and their beliefs about, high-pressure situations, but very little considered evidence of what people are actually *doing* in those situations. The same problem exists in leadership research. A recent review of 214 leadership behaviour studies shows that fewer than one in five studies include measures of what they purport to examine: actual leadership behaviours.[233] Moreover, as little as 3% of the examined variables in these studies are behavioural – the rest are typically about awareness and appraisals of behaviours. The same can be seen in sports research. A review of 610 studies on sports coaching showed that less than one fifth of them featured observation of actual behaviours as part of the methodology.[234] This essentially means that we have little evidence about what coaches actually do during training and competition in sport.

This knowledge gap also exists with penalty shootouts. There is not a single piece of published research on coach behaviours ahead of or during football penalty shootouts. In one way, this is not so surprising. Beyond the occasional cut-away, TV producers rarely focus on coaches and staff during penalty shootouts, so management behaviours are very difficult to study from broadcast video, leaving us with rare and inadequate publicly available documentation. This in turn means that pundits and fans, and even professionals, tend not to pay much attention to these areas.

I managed to access raw video material from each of the five penalty shootouts that were held in the 2022 World Cup. This footage showed everything that happened on the pitch from multiple uninterrupted video angles, including close-ups of players from both teams. This, at the very least, allowed me to make systematic observations about exactly what coaches are doing in those 2-3 minutes that they have to communicate with and support their teams right before the penalty shootout.[235]

What did I find?

Well, one thing leapt out of the video evidence straight away: nobody in a World Cup penalty shootout in the 21st century goes short of water. Bottles of it were in abundance every time, for every team. Ditto towels, energy supplements, massages... Herds of doctors, physical therapists and assistants seemed to be on hand instantly to furnish the players with everything their bodies needed. Elite football really does seem to have the physiological support thing nailed down.

Regarding psychological support, on the other hand... there there may be room for improvement.

Getting the message across

In the case of France v. Argentina, we saw how one manager took a relatively long time to make logistical and tactical decisions and then communicate them to his team (Deschamps), and how another manager communicated his plans and decisions to his team much more expeditiously (Scaloni).

Measuring the time it took each of the 10 managers involved in the 2022 World Cup penalty shootouts to complete their tactical and logistical instructions to their team revealed a very clear pattern (see diagram below). The teams who took the shortest time ended up winning the shootout. The teams who took the longest time lost. No exceptions. And the difference was quite pronounced, with the winning team who took the longest time (Morocco) still taking a shorter time than the losing team who took the shortest time (France).

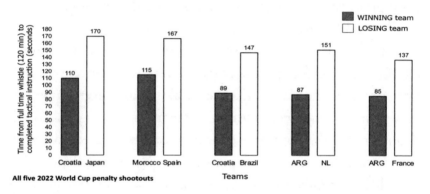

Time to complete collective tactical Instructions <u>after extra time</u>

One logical interpretation of these observations is that the teams who most swiftly delivered their plan to their members were also the teams who had prepared the most or best for the shootout. If you have made the majority of your decisions about player selection, shots and tactics before the game, it is easier to be succinct when the time comes. Related to this, note that Argentina clocked the two fastest times, with the time against France being number one on the list and the time against the Netherlands number two. Against France, Scaloni and Argentina had the luxury of having been through penalties previously in the tournament, which one would assume makes it easier to be effective the second time. This was also clearly the case with Croatia, who were more than 20 seconds faster the second time (against Brazil) compared with the first time (against Japan). One does not always get a penalty shoot-out to practise with, naturally, but the clear implication is that arranging practice games with penalty shootouts, or conducting realistic penalty shootout simulations that involve the manager and staff running through their communications, makes sense.

On the other hand, there were teams who seemed to have a pre-defined plan, but who took a longer time executing it. The Netherlands, who lost to Argentina, were one example. When the players came to the sideline, Louis van Gaal relatively speedily went from player to player asking/confirming that they would take a shot. Frans Hoek, the goalkeeper coach, seemed to have extra responsibility for penalty shootouts. When the group finally gathered in a huddle, Hoek visibly read off to the group 11 names from the note in his hand. This was most likely the order of all possible Dutch penalty takers – and very thorough, if so, because most teams will just have a plan for the first five, and at most six or seven. So far, so good.

However, an intense discussion then ensued between players and coaches: Frenkie de Jong and Davy Klaassen, most notably. Van Gaal voiced something also, to which both Hoek and Danny Blind, his assistant coach, seemed to object or have other views on. This led to a back-and-forth exchange with multiple voices that lasted for what seemed an eternity, 40 seconds, until they ended the huddle with players and staff sporadically urging each other on. It's tempting to speculate whether the typical (or stereotypical) Dutch management style of giving everyone a voice complicated player selection and tactics. The Dutch are known for a very flat structure, where status and titles are considered unnecessary, no one follows blindly, people speak directly and bluntly, and everyone wants to be involved.[236] Consequently, the discussion between players and coaches took up a lot of time. Meanwhile, Argentina were quickly done and dusted, which may in itself have induced a sense of competitive panic on the Netherlands side, because they would see Argentina next to them breaking up their huddle, making them rush to get finished themselves. Certainly van Gaal missed an opportunity to provide additional individual support to whomever needed it.

There are other potential benefits from keeping it short during last-minute tactical communications in situations of high pressure. Firstly, simplicity, clarity and a lack of ambiguity have their own virtues. No coach wants to overwhelm players with last-minute plans and instructions that might complicate, sow doubt, interfere with individual shot preparation processes and encourage overthinking.

Secondly, precise, succinct communications can help encourage the perception of control, giving players the reassuring impression of a robust plan and a clear strategy. Argentina is again a prime example here. During both their penalty shootouts, Scaloni was clearly running an incredibly smooth and well-oiled communications operation, where it must have seemed to everyone involved that the person in charge knew what he was doing. Even if this sense of control on Scaloni's part had been an illusion (which I don't believe it was), it would have been a helpful one; just the impression of order and control from the person in charge can have a positive impact on performers in a high-pressure situation.

And thirdly, quick communications free up time for other things, not least emotional support, as we saw in the exchanges between Scaloni and the distraught Montiel. Spend too long on the group-talk and there's no space for that.

Making the right choices

How do managers communicate to the team the line-up of penalty takers in a penalty shootout? Quite often, they combine the selection and the communication of the selection, by openly asking the group for volunteers. Several of the managers in the 2022 World Cup used such an approach, including two of the winning teams: Croatia and Morocco. In those cases, the managers, Zlatko Dalić and Walid Regragui respectively, had the groups around them in a huddle and must have posed a question like "Who wants to take one?", because you can see the players putting a hand or a finger in the air, one by one, and the coaches responding by consecutively raising their own fingers to indicate the kicker's position in the order. For these two teams, it is difficult to say whether this process was done without pre-consultation, or whether this was about repeating something that the involved players already knew to some extent. However, the players seemed at least pre-informed, as their hands went up fast, and at no point was there any visible confusion or disagreement. Rather, it all moved pretty efficiently.

Among the losing teams, this was also the chosen strategy for Japan. Their manager, Hajime Moriyasu, clearly asked the group for volunteers, and there was a moment of collective hesitation, to which Moriyasu responded by stretching his arms out to his sides, which could have been done in frustration with his non-volunteering players or to indicate that he was open to anyone. Or both. Takumi Minamino then put his hand up to become penalty taker number one, and a few seconds after Kaoru Mitoma did the same to become number two. After those two, the most high-status players in the team, it took some time for others to come forward, and in an awkward gap when nobody stepped up, one of the substitutes even pointed to a teammate, as if to nominate him.

Hence, for Japan the volunteer approach happened more slowly and fumblingly than for the two teams mentioned above. In the shootout, both Minamino and Mitoma missed, and so did Maya Yoshida, making it one goal in four attempts for Japan. After the World Cup, this "show of hands" nomination system was widely discussed in Japan, and Moriyasu announced he would do it differently next time: "Players who fail blame themselves and get hurt, so from now on I want to make the decisions myself."[237]

Spain, and their manager, Luis Enrique, also asked for volunteers, but in a very unusual way. Enrique chose the first three penalty takers, and then he left it up to the players, as a group, to identify the rest.[238] The captain on the day was Sergio Busquets, and after he was chosen by the manager to take shot number three, he was given the boss's paper and pen and tasked with figuring out who the other two players were going to be. That's quite a substantial extra job to hand a player who is about to take perhaps the most important kick of his life, particularly when that player is not an experienced penalty taker. (Busquets never takes in-game penalties, but had taken a shot in a big penalty shootout before, in the 2021 Euros, where he missed.) Furthermore, although Busquets is an experienced player for Spain, he couldn't be regarded as an experienced captain of the side, having first worn the armband for Spain in late October 2020. Anyway, Busquets accepted the somewhat uncharitable challenge, gathered the team in a new huddle and used the simplest method to complete the rota – asking for volunteers. Fortunately, Aymeric Laporte and Pedri González signed up pretty fast. Unfortunately, for Spain, all three players chosen by Enrique, including Busquets, missed their shots, so those two volunteer penalty takers never got a chance to show what they could do.

I have never seen many benefits of the volunteer approach, a point I have made in several previously published papers.[239]

Presumably, managers choose this path because they think it is important that penalty takers must *want* to take a penalty, and they believe this is a way to ensure that they have a full set of willing participants. I also suspect some managers do it this way because it is convenient and easy for them as managers. However, when the manager publicly, in front of the whole group, asks for volunteers, it creates a social situation that is practically fizzing with unintended, negative consequences:

1. The players the manager gets to volunteer will not necessarily be those who really want to take a penalty; one will get the players who think they should take the responsibility to volunteer. The players who think this, and dare to raise a hand, are not necessarily the best penalty takers.
2. A player who sticks up his hand also communicates, loud and clear: "I take responsibility for this shot!" Thus, when managers gets players to volunteer, they also effectively transfer responsibility (and pressure) to them. We know, from ample demonstrations in previous chapters in this book, that more pressure on players' shoulders results in fewer goals. The manager should be in the business of taking the pressure off the players, not adding to it.
3. When the manager asks for volunteers, it is clearly exposed and communicated that the manager and team have no master plan for the penalty shootout, beyond asking for volunteers.
4. To ask players to consider not only whether they are up for taking a shot, but also whether they should communicate this to the group and then put themselves ahead of other players in the queue, is to add significant weight to their cognitive loads at this crucial time. By posing this question, the manager creates a complex, unpredictable and uncer-

tain social situation, at a moment where players need simple and predictable direction.

5. When nobody volunteers (as seemed to be the case with Japan, for example), the situation is no longer just a logistical challenge; it is a deeper psychological one. Everyone sees that nobody wants to take a shot, and this can easily create a pessimistic, anxiety-driven and negative atmosphere in a group. There is evidence from other contexts that willingness to take risks is contagious,[240] and it is likely, conversely, that seeing teammates *not* accept the risk of a penalty kick will make others more risk-averse, possibly triggering avoidance motivation and anxiety.

Hope Powell, manager for the England women's team in the 2011 World Cup, went for a volunteer approach in the penalty shootout against France, but ran into this exact problem: "I had to ask three times for volunteers before a single player put their hand up. I was amazed. Where are you?"[241] Eventually, she would get her five players, but France ultimately won the shootout. When I spoke with Powell about this, she had completely revised her views on how to conduct the player selection and nomination for a penalty shootout: "Don't ask for volunteers! At a moment of pressure, don't think people are going to step up, they usually step back." Basically, she acknowledged that she had misread her players in 2011: "If putting myself into their position, I would step up. I assumed it would be easy for people to do so, which was wrong." She concluded that "I have to take responsibility for not preparing the players how they should have been prepared. I should not have asked for volunteers." If she were to lead a team in a new shootout, she would create a list with an order of penalty takers based on stats in training – "who scored the most and who didn't" – and have conversations with the players beforehand to see if they were feeling up to it: "You want the players to agree."

Often, managers do not openly ask for volunteers; instead, they identify and ask players one by one, in that public huddle immediately before the shootout. Posing this as an open question and waiting for the answer is only marginally better than taking the volunteer route. It will potentially produce all the consequences listed above. The manager takes responsibility off their own shoulders and effectively places it on the shoulders of the players who say yes. In addition, what happens if one or several players say no? From our interviews with players about penalty shootouts, we know that many players (up to 30%) turn down the offer from their manager in this situation.[242] Saying no is difficult for players, who may feel that they are abandoning their teammates, and it is also a difficult answer to hear for the other players, who may be affected by the anxieties underpinning the refusal and start to doubt their own capability as well. Besides, shootouts sometimes go to more than five kicks, so even players who in this meeting before the shootout overtly express unwillingness to take a shot may at some point in the shootout still have to take one. At that point, having to take a shot anyway, after thinking it through, committing to not taking one and making that decision known to everyone else, could make the penalty so much harder.

That does not mean that managers should not find out how their players think and feel about taking penalties. The question can be asked, but, as Powell said, it should be asked beforehand and probably privately. Scaloni said that his players were asked how they felt about taking a kick: "When we went around to see who wanted to take a penalty, we had two players too many."[243] But this was clearly done beforehand. Thus, the recommendation for managers would be: well in advance of a game that could go to penalties, ask all the players in the squad about their attitude to taking part in a shootout. This should be an open-ended question, and not just whether they want to or not, because nobody really wants to. Ask about how confident they would be, their experiences in the past and about details of their technique and pre-shot routines. Based on how this conversation goes, managers can form an impression of where the player is with respect to this task, which can then be one of the several pieces of information that they use to inform and support their ultimate decision.

One challenge managers will always face is that they do not know beforehand who will be on the pitch after 120 minutes, and inevitably this complicates drawing up a complete list of kickers in advance. This was something Deschamps spoke about after the World Cup final: "All the planned shooters were no longer on the field." This problem can be mitigated in a few ways. First, managers and teams need to plan for the eventuality of penalties in a completely different manner than most of them currently do. Just as most managers spend vast amounts of time reflecting on who should start a match, they need to spend almost as long thinking about who should end a match. It is of course impossible to control all match events; for example, substitutions will be made based on the match context, injuries and standing between the teams. Yet managers still need to plan with the end in mind, which involves thinking about who they would want to be on the pitch in the event of the match going to penalties. In addition, based on all the information that is gathered before the match, managers should have a ranked list of penalty takers, so that after 120 minutes, they can take a few seconds simply to check who is present against the list. There will still be factors about the current situation to take into account, but a best five for the occasion can still be fairly quickly arrived at, and in an informed way. I suspect this is how Scaloni and his team did it.

The manager's decisions in this area should ideally be communicated beforehand. I believe the overall benefits of predictability outweigh the overall risk of the selected players dreading their penalties in advance. It could be communicated to players that they will always retain the right to opt out of a penalty kick, if for some reason they do not feel ready on the day. But the manager should emphasise that the reason the player has been picked to take a penalty is that they are likely to do a good job under extremely difficult circumstances. If they don't score, the manager then takes responsibility for that outcome, and will communicate as much to the press after the game.

In general, the manager's perhaps most important task is to dial down the pressure on their players. Sometimes it's amazing how simply this can be achieved. When Norway were in the 2019 Women's World Cup, the manager, Martin Sjögren, said this to the players right before they faced penalties in the round of 16 against Australia: "It doesn't matter what you do, I am super proud of you regardless." The Norway and Barcelona player, Caroline Graham Hansen, said afterwards that, with those words, "just like that, all the pressure was gone". Norway then scored with all their kicks and went through.

Top-down management

In leadership research, it is typically argued that under tight time constraints, members of a team are unusually receptive to direction from their manager.[244] Moreover, under pressure conditions, teams are frequently said to respond better to solo decision making from a leader than to delegation.[245] A leader who is dominant, even aggressive, may be positive in these situations.[246] Some classic studies suggest that in extreme conditions, authoritative leaders are more likely to be followed.[247] These studies are quite old, though, and people's perception of effective leadership may have changed since they were published. However, a more recent German study also shows that in severely pressured emergency contexts (fire-fighting, for instance), when immediate actions are required, auto-cratic leadership behaviours create more trust among staff than democratic behaviours.[248] By contrast, when decision making takes place in a less urgent setting, democratic leadership behaviours create more trust. By extension, then, trust formed with people prior to extreme events is critical to how those people ultimately perform when the extreme event happens.[249] Or, to put it another way: weak leadership in peace time leads to even weaker leadership in war time. Thus, the smart leaders build a stock of trust away from these high-pressure situations, which they can access when the pressure is on.

Consider Scaloni again. In the pre-shootout huddle, he made all the decisions, he did all the talking with the players, and most of his communications seemed to consist of direct commands. However, he clearly had invited his staff to give input, which he also received in that moment and instantly accommodated and acted upon. This was all consistent with thoughts that Scaloni has publicly expressed on player management. "For me, imposition is not a thing, period," he once said. "I cannot tell a player to do something that he is not convinced of doing. It is impossible. It's worse for the team, and it's worse for him. Many times, when we finish doing a tactical exercise, I ask them, how do they see it, if they are comfortable and convinced of doing it [this way]. 'Imposing' doesn't suit me. You have to be authentic with what you do, and I feel better that way. It is essential that the player believes you."[250] Accordingly, it's interesting to note that of the eight managers who were involved in a penalty shootout in the 2022 World Cup, the manager who was the most authoritative and direct in the huddle before the penalty shootout (Scaloni) may also be the manager who is the most democratic in other areas of his work. This is logical. When you spend each working day investing in your players' opinions and experiences, you gain the opportunity to be more direct when a situation occurs that calls for authority, speed and crisp messages.

What's clear is that, immediately ahead of a high-pressure situation, such as a penalty shootout, management gains from speaking with one voice. Those last few minutes before the players step into the centre circle should be led by the manager, not by other staff. Just as that's the wrong time to delegate responsibility to the players, it's also not the time to delegate responsibility to assistant coaches.

All the managers on the winning sides in the 2022 World Cup penalty shootouts adhered closely to this principle. With no exceptions. The Argentina, Croatia and Morocco managers handled the entirety of the pre-shootout speech personally and theirs was the only voice the players heard directly. The managers on the losing teams did not adhere to the principle. With no exceptions. The losing manager who was closest to taking full responsibility in the pre-shootout phase was France's Deschamps. He was the one who addressed the players individually and gave the speech to the team. But he was closely shadowed and supplemented by his assistant, Stéphan, and on a few occasions Stéphan also shared information with players. How about the others? Japan's manager, Hajime Moriyasu, conducted the selection process, but when he finished, an assistant took over, conveying more technical information to the players from his pad. With Spain, manager Enrique gave a speech to the team, but then the player and captain, Busquets, was given a key role in both penalty-taker selection and motivational-speech making, while Enrique was speaking with the referees or hanging out over by the bench. With the Netherlands, manager van Gaal approached some of the players individually and gave some of the speech to the team, but then the goalkeeper coach,

Hoek, took over, communicating the player selection, and by the end of the team meeting other assistant coaches and players had also mingled in.

Finally, for Brazil, the manager, Tite, removed himself completely from the process, leaving everything to his assistants. While they were addressing the team, Tite was walking around nervously, standing 20 metres away by the bench and at one point even sitting down, looking anxious and partly paralysed by the situation. But there were reasons for this seemingly bizarre behaviour by the team's leader. Back in 1986, Tite had been part of a Guarani team that faced Sao Paolo in the finals of the Campeonato Brasileiro Serie A. The second leg finished 3-3 and went to penalties, which Guarani lost. Tite did not take a penalty but understandably, he was affected. That night, unable to sleep, he and his wife decided to leave the hotel in the early-morning hours and drive home. As Tite recalled: "We got in the car and drove to Caxias. Halfway there, I skidded on the road. The car went round. We went down a ravine. We could have lost our lives there at that moment. So I got traumatised, big time."[251]

For this reason, it seems, Tite's assistant, Cléber Xavier, was in charge of penalties with Brazil. Xavier explained, "I make a list of the best penalty takers. In the training sessions and in general, and I share that list with the staff. With the exception of Tite. Tite does not deal with penalties."[252]

With all this taken into account, the Brazil team meeting appeared by far the least structured briefing held by any of the 2022 teams. At no point did Xavier have the players' undivided attention. Rather, he seemed to be conducting a loosely structured collective brainstorming around the theme of who would take which penalty kick. Some players, such as Neymar, Marquinhos and Antony, would regularly disengage from the group. That the manager was roaming around in the background may also have contributed to the players' manifestly patchy focus at that moment.

To me, it makes sense for top management to be heavily involved in both preparing and conducting a penalty shootout. If the manager gets involved at the planning stage, the topic gets prioritised. Having the manager lead the communication before the shootout conveys this priority to players, and also makes it more likely that players will fully engage and commit. When the pressure is on, the psychological impact of having the manager personally communicating with you can be profound. That opportunity should not be wasted.

Making connections

We all know how important eye contact is for communication. And if we don't, there's always the neuropsychological research to show us: direct eye contact facilitates faster connection, more durable connection and more emotional connection.[253] So one would think managers would be eager to seize this basic communications tool in the high-pressure build-up to a penalty shootout. Surprisingly, though, some of them instead rely on props that effectively grab the players' attention, and remove the direct connection that can be established when we communicate face to face.

Notepads, tablets, pieces of paper – these items frequently seem to proliferate in the moments prior to a shootout, and not always helpfully. I repeat that there are no absolutes with respect to probabilities for the future, but it is at least interesting to observe that not one of the winning sides in the 2022 World Cup shootouts was using props of any kind in their final organisational moment with the players, and all of the losing sides were.

Thus, in the case of the losers, we saw the use of a piece of paper with a list of penalty takers (Enrique/Spain, Hoek/Netherlands,

Stéphan/France), a list of players where numbers would be added to indicate penalty takers (Xavier/Brazil) and a tablet showing data on opponent penalty takers and goalkeepers (Japan). Where paper and tablets were being wielded, at least some of the players' attention, inevitably, would go to the prop, and eye contact, and possibly connection, with the speaker would suffer. The winning teams, by contrast, were all about looking straight at each other and using non-verbal behaviours – gestures, touches – to back up the messages, with not a piece of paper or a tablet to be seen anywhere. All winning managers appeared fully present, giving the players their undivided attention without any external device in sight to loosen the connection.

Can the presence or absence of a bit of paper in a crucial moment really affect the outcome of a penalty shootout and a football match? I'm aware that it might sound unlikely. But think about what it does to a conversation if the person you're having it with is constantly on their phone. At the same time, let us consider what happened to Brazil's players after they walked off the pitch at the end of regulation time against Croatia, and how they spent the approximately two minutes they had together with their staff on the sideline, before they walked back out to the centre circle. Firstly, they had to wait 15-20 seconds for the two assistant coaches, Cléber Xavier and Matheus Bachi, to finish their private meeting. This was potentially a time when the manager, Tite, could have communicated with the team, but, for his own reasons, he spent that period standing alone in the tactical area around the Brazil bench. When the assistant coaches finished, Xavier walked into the loosely shaped formation of players, with a notebook in one hand and a pen in the other. He then spent 20-30 seconds asking some of the players whether they wanted to take a kick. When he got an answer, he jotted something down in the notebook. Very soon, this book seemed to take on magnetic properties. It became the centre piece of the occasion, and several players now leaned in to try to see what was being scribbled in it. Some players, such as Thiago Silva, ended up staring at the notebook for more than a minute. The majority of the players looked at it over the next 40 seconds or so – or *tried* to have a look, because obviously the notebook had generated quite a crowd. Finally, Xavier put the notebook down and the team quickly moved closer to each other, ending the gathering with a 15-second huddle led by some of the players, most notably Neymar. In total, the players spent almost half of the available time reading, or trying to read, names and numbers on a piece of paper. Is this the ideal cognitive activity right before taking a penalty kick? I would suggest it probably wasn't. But what's for sure is that this minute spent reading precluded any other helpful connection and interaction that could have taken place at that time.

I'm not suggesting that it isn't perfectly possible to win a penalty shootout even if there is a note in the coach's hand or, for that matter, an entire book of notes. But props can come with a cost. In some cases, the lack of eye contact risks compromising the vital connection between coach and players, and might even negatively impact the players' mental readiness for the shootout. At the very least, managers need to think about the props they take into these high-pressure briefings and ask themselves whether it might be better to leave them on the bench.

Not forgetting the goalkeeper

To what extent were the goalkeepers included in the coaches' communication prior to each shootout? Goalkeeper is a unique position, normally with its own separate coaching staff, and we get used to seeing these players treated separately from the rest of the squad. However, in a penalty shootout, the goalkeeper is the team's most important player, the only one with a role to play for every other shot. Yet my analysis of the 2022 World Cup shootouts showed that there was only one manager who at any point in the pre-shootout huddle personally addressed the goalkeeper. Yes, you guessed it – Lionel Scaloni for Argentina. None of the other managers did so. The only one to come close was Luis Enrique for Spain, who shook hands with each of his players when they initially walked off the pitch after 120 minutes, including his goalkeeper, Unai Simón, but at no point after this was there any contact between the two. The other managers interacted not one little bit with their goalkeepers, and a couple of times (I'm thinking of Croatia's Zlatko Dalić here) it almost seemed as if the manager went out of his way to *ignore* his goalkeeper. The goalkeepers' teammates behaved differently. Across the teams, scores of them came over to deliver a hug and few words, which seems the natural and human thing to do when your friend and colleague is about to play a leading and potentially decisive role in a hypertense event. The managers could maybe have learned from their players when it comes to this.

The revolution still to come

There are some deeper lessons about leadership and communication at play here. A wonderful video shows Scaloni's immediate reaction when Montiel scores the penalty that wins the World Cup for Argentina. He literally just became world champion, with his country. But you would not be able to tell. There is no bravado. No leaping or fist-pumping. Nothing macho. Before the ball goes in, Scaloni's facial expression is focused and calm. When the ball goes in, his expression continues to be calm, but now with the very slightest of smiles, and over the next 30 seconds, a very small tear forming in the corner of his eye. I have seen few images in football more expressive of the power of vulnerability.

Since the year 2000, football has undergone a few revolutions. The game itself has evolved tremendously, led by a series of pioneering, and some might say revolutionary managers, who have changed the way it is played with their tactical sophistication. There has been a physical revolution, in which teams have embraced sports science and fitness training to an unprecedented degree. And more recently, there has been an analytics revolution, in which teams rely more and more on data to make or support tactical decisions on the pitch. But what of the fourth revolution that some, including Arsène Wenger, predicted – the psychology revolution?

Speaking at a conference in London in 2010, Wenger said: "In the last 10-15 years, we have been in the physical and in the technical area. The next 10-15 years, we will certainly move forward in more mental areas. Not only linked to the desire to win, but linked to vision, to speed of understanding the game, and that is certainly the new area of development for our sport."

As yet, though, there is little sign of this. Steps, certainly, have been taken, and many players nowadays see the value for performance of using mental coaches. But in the main, football management remains stuck where it always has been. The psychology revolution is still to come. Or in Wenger's words, when I spoke about this with him again in 2024: "On the mental side, yes, we have moved forward, but we still have a lot to discover. Has there been progress with respect to performing under pressure? I don't think so."

The penalty shootout displays the wider problem in microcosm. For many managers, assuming they get beyond the "lottery" mindset, a penalty shootout is a mostly technical matter – one where analytics fuel decisions on shots and saves and in which the final and potentially vital minutes for communication get eaten up by basic logistics rather than support for the selected players. Whereas, as I hope I have made clear in the pages of this book, managing a penalty shootout is ultimately about managing not just footballers, but people. People who just happen to be potentially on the verge of delivering the most important kick of their lives.

Or as Lionel Scaloni puts it: "The distance between the football player and people should not be there. In the end, the footballer is just a football player, and he is still a human being."[254]

Epilogue

"Are you able to speak with me about preparing for penalty shootouts?"

I get these requests frequently. Sometimes they're from people working for football teams, sometimes from journalists. This particular email was from the assistant coach for a national team, someone I knew but hadn't spoken to for a while. The unusual thing about it was the timing. It was early evening, on the day before his team was due to play in a World Cup quarter-final.

One appreciates that football exists substantially in the here and now. Teams prepare for the next match. "We're just taking it one game at a time" is, for better or worse, a footballing mantra. People reach out to me when they suddenly realise that their next match could go to penalties. Grateful to be asked, and happy to help, of course. But the *night before* a World Cup quarter-final? Might it have been helpful to think about this just a little earlier?

Then there was the email that said: "Hi Geir, are you free sometime next week for a chat?" The sender worked for a club that was playing in the Champions League that season. And on this occasion the timing was good. The competition's knockout stages were a few months away; enough time to put into practice whatever we spoke about, if they chose to.

At the appointed time for the chat, I logged onto the Teams

link and briefly saw the face of my friend who had reached out to me. However, before I even had the chance to say hello, he excused himself and the screen went blank. After a few confusing moments, the screen came back up, and he briefly panned the camera across the room he was in. It was full of people. "We have all the first team coaches present," he told me, "and they want to know everything there is to know about penalties. What can you tell us? We have 45 minutes."

So much for our personal chat. Afterwards, my friend apologised. He hadn't known that the coaches all wanted to take part until five minutes before the meeting. He then asked me to send an invoice for my time.

That wasn't the first time this kind of thing had happened. A few years earlier, I had met the academy director at a club for a "chat" and he had cheerfully walked me into a room rammed with people, sat me down and opened with the terrifying line: "Show us what you got!"

And then there was the time a meeting was set up between me and one of the national team coaches at the impressive headquarters of a major European football association. The coach was late, so I waited. He then strode in and briskly announced that he could only spare me 30 minutes. Not ideal, but I knew he was busy, and there was still time enough to get something across. He then said he wanted to start by explaining his own thoughts on penalties. Naturally, I obliged, and he proceeded to talk. And talk. After 28 minutes, the coach had presented his whole philosophy, in detail. Wrapping up, he asked, "What do you think about this?"

There wasn't much time to say anything, really, but I thanked him for his presentation, and the meeting ended there. There was no further contact between us.

Those stories give some flavour of the attitudes still prevalent in football, even now, to the idea of preparing for penalties. Football is chaotic, volatile and short-term focused. Priority is always on what is perceived critical to win the next match – everything else is postponed, including penalty kicks. The sport is a multi-billion-pound industry, but around this potentially crucial aspect of the game it remains oddly unstructured, improvised and reactive. This lack of priority and structure can also be interpreted as fundamental avoidance. There are exceptions, several of which have been referred to in this book. But overall, directors, coaches and other decision makers around football teams have never embraced speaking about and preparing for penalties. The subject gets avoided or ignored.

This is a problem. Obviously, when teams do not put time or effort into preparing any task, performance will suffer. But the bigger problem is that many of those who are selected to take a shot in penalty shootouts never receive proper training or support. Thus, not treating the penalty shootout seriously ultimately exposes, harms and sacrifices the players. It is not that performing in penalty shootouts is too tough, nor that players will miss. Penalty shootouts are extremely demanding, and someone will fail to score – that is natural. Rather, the problem is that players are required to perform under this severe pressure without help. Too many players have not learned proper coping techniques for this situation, have not received pressure training and have certainly not been appropriately supported by their managers and coaches in the minutes leading up to the event. These players are being sent into the lion's den unprepared and unprotected.

It would be easy to blame the coaches. The likes of Didier Deschamps, Luis Enrique and Hajime Moriyasu put their players in difficult spots, seemingly armed with very little to combat the pressure they then encountered. However, these coaches were themselves not taught what to do in these situations. When they were players, this is how it was. No one showed them effective ways to train, comprehensively prepare and optimally support players going into a penalty shootout. The problem is not individual coaches, any more than it is individual players. The problem is the culture. Football is characteristically traditionalist and conservative. For the longest time, the attitude has been that players either have the confidence and the courage for this task or they don't. The concrete tools to acquire, improve and apply that confidence have not been a part of the conversation. We need to break this cycle.

Historically, football's focus has been elsewhere. That's not to say that things haven't evolved at all since those raw, wild, instinctive early penalty shootouts of the 70s and 80s discussed at the start of this book. What clearly solidified in the beginning was a sense of this uniquely pressured contest's gravity and terror – and, with that, a feeling that it was beyond preparing for. Players rapidly understood that missing a penalty kick was potentially legacy defining. Failing to deliver could hurt you for eternity. And yet skill alone might not save you. The biggest superstars of the game missed penalty shots on the biggest stages – Michel Platini and Zico in the 1986 World Cup, Diego Maradona in the 1990 World Cup, Marco van Basten in the 1992 Euros, Franco Baresi and Roberto Baggio in the 1994 World Cup, Paolo Maldini and the entire Dutch team (almost) in the 2000 Euros, to name only a handful. Because the very best players frequently and spectacularly flopped,[255] with devastating consequences, the lesson to everyone was obvious: a penalty shootout was something that nobody could control. It was a lottery. You either coped, or you didn't.

Small wonder that those initial decades were a time of collective escapism. Going into shootouts, and seeking to manage the immense stress, the players by and large would choose the simplest route and opt for avoidance – the "just get it over with" mentality. Even the sport itself seemed to be in some kind of denial about the penalty shootout, seeking for a long time to avoid it by the most radical means – by trying to get rid of it entirely. Sepp Blatter, who was FIFA general secretary from 1981 to 1998 and FIFA president from 1998 to 2015, was never a fan of the shootout. "Football is a team sport," he once said, "and penalties are not about a team, they are about individuals." True, that is a normal way to view penalties, although I beg to differ: a penalty kick is a team event. Then Blatter took a breath and called it how he saw it: "When it comes to the World Cup final it is passion, and when it goes to extra time it is a drama. But when it comes to penalty kicks it is a tragedy."[256]

Throughout Blatter's tenure, he campaigned assiduously to replace the shootout as football's official tie-breaker. Thus, in 1993, FIFA introduced the "golden goal", where the first goal scored in extra time would immediately end the game. The format was used in the men's Euros in 1996 and 2000, as well as the men's World Cup in 1998 and 2002. The 2003 Women's World Cup final was decided with a golden goal in the 98th minute. But overall, the system seemed to be paralysing play in extra time and introducing extreme caution rather than opening the game up, and the format was abandoned, with no particular complaints from fans.

Still, with this insistent message coming from football's governing body that shootouts were inherently the wrong way to decide games – and possibly only with us on a temporary basis – it is hardly surprising that the teams of this era did not embrace penalties more completely than they did. Well into the 2000s, most coaches did what they could to avoid thinking about and planning for penalties. It was even felt that speaking with players about penalties would create a bigger problem than it solved and simply increase their already enormous anxiety about them.

Yet by the turn of the century, penalty shootouts had become a regular feature of the game's top competitions, with many of the biggest matches decided this way. They became unignorable.

And there were some performance patterns, obvious for everyone to see: Germany tended to win on penalties, while England, the Netherlands and, to some extent, Spain, tended to lose. Consequently, penalties now started attracting interest also from scientists, analysts, and authors. Studies were conducted and books were written. The scientific research at the time mainly focused on goalkeepers' ability to anticipate the kick. There was a preoccupation with the shots themselves – left/right/middle; power or precision – and the quest to identify the perfect penalty. On my bookshelf are six books about penalties published between 1998 and 2005 alone.[257] What researchers and authors had in common was the strong belief, sometimes confrontationally argued,[258] that penalties are not a lottery, and that training will benefit both penalty takers and goalkeepers.

This is still the consensus, not least among self-proclaimed football intellectuals. However, this unconditional rejection of the uncontrollable facet of penalties is a mixed blessing. While the contrarian conviction that penalties are *not* a lottery helpfully underscores the value of skill and puts the emphasis back on preparation, it indirectly neglects the equally correct perception that parts of the penalty kick are, indeed, beyond a player's ability to control. Chance plays a larger role for the outcome of a penalty kick than it does for the outcome of a whole game, and unless one is at the proficiency level of the very best penalty takers, one can do most things right with a penalty kick and still miss. Of course, for penalty takers, standing over the ball, it is beneficial to have 100% belief in oneself and one's skill, completely rejecting the operation of chance. Nevertheless, with respect to preparation and training, we need to acknowledge the chance element and the perception of low control that could sneak in, to help players better cope with and prepare for the psychological aspect of penalty kicks. In addition, those coaches who use the "lottery metaphor" after a lost penalty shootout, where one or several of their players failed from the penalty spot, at least do something to protect their players. They were not able to protect them leading up to the shootout (which of course they should have taken more responsibility for), but they do what they can to remove responsibility from the players who missed. Although this perpetuates the perception that penalties are uncontrollable, at least someone stood up for the players.

The data revolution that has swept through professional sports over the last decade or so has brought another spate of published research and books on penalty kicks.[259] This too has undoubtedly impacted practice in such areas as shot placement, goalkeeper positioning and penalty taker-goalkeeper dynamics (game theory). But such analyses tend to provide the numbers without the contextual and psychological understanding. Ironically, in my experience, some of the most outspoken promoters of data and analytics with respect to penalties are even more biased in their thinking than those stuck in the previous "penalties are a lottery" era. This is, I guess, normal and human, and the key will always be to acknowledge one's biases and act with them in mind (as I have tried to do in the course of this book with some of my own biases; for example my fascination with behaviour analysis, which could lead me to attribute meaning to behaviours that actually are arbitrary).

For a clear demonstration of the peril of adopting purely data-driven analysis, consider the game-wide take-up of the concept of "first-mover advantage", a notion originally conceived by the Spanish economist Ignacio Palacios-Huerta. He discovered that 61% of teams shooting first in a penalty shootout win, and since the publication of that finding in 2010, very few team captains will choose *not* to go first if they win the coin toss. Furthermore, this research almost produced a penalty shootout format change, where it was argued that it would be fairer to replace alternating kicks (the AB format) with an ABBA format, where, after the first kick, teams take consecutive pairs of penalties. However, when studies from larger and updated data samples were published, the first-mover advantage has progressively and dramatically shrunk, with one study showing 55% wins[260] for those going first, another 51%[261] and the third, which is the largest one, with most recent data, 49%.[262] There is no longer an advantage in going first. Teams in practice seem to have found a way to compensate for and eliminate the impact of first-mover effect and to neutralise the luck of the draw. The format change has quietly been taken off the table. Human beings are never as simple as the numbers coming out of statistical software. People adopt and adapt, with higher velocity now than before. Thus, what were pivotal discoveries a few years ago are not necessarily observable at all any more. Old observations become dated very fast, and data constantly needs to be updated and conclusions revised. My research is no exception. I welcome researchers with better data sets, sharper analyses and more sophisticated statistical tools than mine to challenge and replicate the observations provided in this book. I expect some findings and principles to survive, but others will not.

With this said, psychology has now hesitantly made its entry on the scene. Some of the penalty takers these days focus on more than just the mechanics of their shots. They have figured out ways to achieve a sense and feeling of control at the penalty spot. Meanwhile, goalkeepers have identified methods to manipulate and disrupt opponents in a manner that – as we saw – Machiavelli would rise from his grave to take note of. Players, in turn, have discovered ingenious ways to protect their teammates from those Machiavellian tactics. Many European top teams now draw up not just a list of prioritised penalty takers (which most teams have done for a while), but also a list of two or three designated penalty-taker protectors. Some pioneering managers have invented methods to simulate pressure in training, and they have found ways to communicate optimally when sending their players into the war zone of a penalty shootout. Teams and organisations have been able to integrate research into practice, inform their players with appropriate dosages and execute the whole package for maximum impact.

The time is ripe, though, for extending and expanding this new, more considered psychological approach to the shootout. This does not mean taking away the pressure or the intensity of the competitive duel between penalty taker and goalkeeper. Nor does it mean reaching a place where players stop missing penalty shots altogether. The psychological game is more about accepting being vulnerable and exposed under this type of pressure, and then taking the necessary steps to cope with and perform under it. This involves skill development, control strategies, teamwork, quality pressure training and sensitive coach communication and support. Fortunately, the new generation of elite football players and young progressive coaches are well equipped for this development. They have a level of access to online resources, game footage and best practices which is unlike that of any previous generations. They're passionate students of the game. And so are the best organisations. Just as some teams in the past decade have substantially raised their set-piece game (corners, free kicks, throw-ins) to new levels of sophistication and impact by hiring specialist coaches and spending time on quality practice, I believe we will now see something similar with penalty kicks.

Psychology will play an ever-more important role in all of this. We will come to appreciate more fully how a penalty shootout is about so much more than just a set of kicks: how it's also about pre-shot behaviours, body language, relationships with teammates, communication – how it's an entire cognitive, emotional and social event. The current elite players are much more comfortable with psychology than the previous generation. They do not mind showing their own vulnerability and are therefore open to what psychology can show and teach them in this area. As we saw, when Erling Haaland speaks about taking important penalty kicks, he does not shy away from explaining how nervous he is. This ease about expressing his own anxiety would have been unthinkable for the leading forwards of previous generations.

But this, too, cuts to a truth about the penalty shootout – and perhaps one of the key reasons this spectacle speaks to us as profoundly as it does. In a high-stakes drama where everything is on the line, penalty takers leave their teammates and stand alone over the ball. At that moment, we see them as, first and foremost, human beings – people put under pressure, subject to the full range of emotions that people under pressure are subject to, and doing their best to cope and get through to the other side. And we can all intimately relate to that. Their pressure is our pressure.

Endnotes

Full details for all references recorded in brief here can be found
in the bibliography on p254

1   FIFA (2023)
2   Tartaglione (2022)
3   Based on study of 6853 matches in 6 top European competitions (Premier League, Serie A, Bundesliga, Eredivisie, La Liga, Champions League) from five seasons (2015-2016 until 2019-2020), Veldkamp & Koning (2023)
4   Edgar (2022)
5   MrFrandefoot (2009)
6   FIFA (2022)
7   Wilbert-Lampen et al. (2008)
8   Witte et al. (2000)
9   See meta-analysis of 13 studies by Lin et al. (2019) and meta-analysis of 19 studies by Wang et al. (2020)
10   Pearce (2000), p. 3
11   Jordet & Elferink-Gemser (2012)
12   Russell & Lightman (2019); Rohleder et al. (2007)
13   Rogers et al. (2003)
14   Jafari et al. (2017); Stephenson et al. (2022)
15   Shields et al. (2016)
16   Stephenson et al. (2022); Balk et al. (2013)
17   Jordet et al. (2008)
18   Jordet & Elferink-Gemser (2012)
19   Martens et al. (1990)
20   Guardian Sport (2021)
21   Rashford & Anka (2021)
22   She did pause longer for the last penalty kick prior to the World Cup against Louisville – 7.5 seconds. However, for that shot, she was rearranging her shorts when the referee blew the whistle and finished doing that before starting the run-up. Because the purpose with showing these pause times is to display the cognitive preparation, not the time to get clothing and equipment in order, that penalty was excluded from the diagram.
23   There are several names for these theories, such as "turning toward theories", explicit monitoring or conscious processing (Gray, 2020). For simplicity, I will refer to these theories as simply overthinking.
24   Baumeister (1984)
25   Beilock et al. (2002)
26   Slutter et al. (2021)
27   Interview with Dutch player after the penalty shootout between the Netherlands and Nigeria in the 2005 U20 World Cup.
28   Wegner et al. (1998)
29   Bakker et al. (2006); Binsch et al. (2010)

30 Vickers (1996)

31 Lebeau et al. (2016)

32 Giancamelli et al. (2022)

33 Brimmell et al. (2019); Moore et al. (2013)

34 Eysenck et al. (2007); Wilson et al. (2009)

35 Hayes et al. (1996); Gardner & Moore (2004)

36 Watzlawick et al. (1967)

37 FIFA (2022)

38 Jordet & Hartman (2008)

39 Jordet (2009a)

40 Furley et al. (2012), Furley et al. (2012), Greenlees et al. (2008); Laurin & Pellet (2023)

41 Bijlstra et al. (2020)

42 FIFA (2022)

43 Both defenders and midfielders score more with approach looking, but not significantly so.

44 Furley & Roth (2021)

45 Jordet, Hartman, & Sigmundstad (2009)

46 Lonsdale & Tam (2008)

47 Jackson (2003)

48 WorldRugby (2021)

49 Stein (1997), p. 1

50 Southgate et al. (2003), p. 191

51 Gerrard (2006), p. 420

52 Gucciardi et al. (2010); Hill et al. (2010)

53 Berns et al. (2006); Mischel et al (1969)

54 Story (2014)

55 Jordet et al. (2009)

56 Men: 2020 European Championships, 2020 Olympics, 2021 Copa América, 2022 AFCON, 2022 World Cup. Women: 2020 Olympics, 2022 Euro, 2023 World Cup.

57 Soccer Illustrated (1994). However, because of the measurement methods used in the 1990s, the real number may have been considerably lower.

58 Baggio (2022)

59 Arrondel et al. (2019)

60 Vollmer et al. (2023)

61 First published by Jordet & Hartman (2008), updated with all the penalty shootouts in the same tournaments until 2023.

62 Teams tend to put their five best penalty takers up first and accordingly it seems reasonable to assume that it's the less skilled penalty takers that are frequently facing the negative shots, there being a greater preponderance of those in a shootout from shot number six onwards, which would skew these numbers. Well, on the contrary, when we repeat the analysis using the first five shots only, there is an even stronger relationship between shot type and performance (negative 58%, neutral 72% and positive 87%), where the difference between negative and neutral shots is also significant.

63 Arrondel et al. (2019)

64 Vollmer et al. (2023)

65 Sky Sports (2009)
66 AFP (2022)
67 Lyttleton (2021)
68 White & Murphy (2023)
69 Ball & Shaw (1996), p. 178
70 Navia et al. (2019)
71 Jordet et al. (2006).
72 CIES Football Observatory (2022)
73 Deux-Zero (2023)
74 Data obtained from transfermarkt.com
75 This and the following conversion rates are from transfermarkt.com
76 Jordet (2009b)
77 Almeida & Volossovitch (2023)
78 Brinkschulte et al. (2023)
79 Wunderlich et al. (2020)
80 Horn et al. (2021); Almeida & Volossovitch (2023)
81 Bar-Eli et al. (2007)
82 Farkas (2023)
83 The quotes from Lewandowski in this book never made it to the finished film, but are published here with permission from the film's producers and from Lewandowski himself.
84 Interestingly, the goalkeepers only went correctly on seven of these shots (33%). This could indicate that Lewandowski got a bit lucky with them, and that his conversion rate for goalkeeper-independent shots is somewhat inflated.
85 Mukherjee (2022)
86 HaytersTV (2018)
87 Cotterill, (2010); Perry & Katz (2015); Hill et al. (2010); Hazell et al. (2014); Cohn et al. (1990)
88 Rupprecht et al. (2021)
89 Jordet et al. (2009)
90 Hustad (2018)
91 Horsinek & Barth (2019)
92 Logically, as he is often standing by the ball when the whistle signal is given, and it takes time to walk back.
93 Robazza et al. (1998). However, the physical demands of prolonged tensing of the bow may have contributed to these effects.
94 60 Minutes (2023)
95 Balban et al. (2023)
96 Honigstein (2021)
97 From conversations with Rachel Vickery, a breathing coach, and a mental performance consultant for elite teams in different sports, such as Golden State Warriors in NBA basketball.
98 The word was actually not "incredibly", but "grævla", which is a local power phrase, or swear word, really only used in the area of Norway Erling Haaland is from, Bryne and Jæren.
99 The expression "shit nervous" is pretty much directly translated from the Norwegian word he used: "Dritnervøs".

100 Based on words by Mark Twain, Heshmat (2022)

101 Rotella & Lerner (1993), p. 536

102 60 Minutes (2023)

103 Jackson & Delehanty (1995)

104 Jordet (2009a). Note that similar tendencies were found for players on other teams with a preceding history of penalty shootout losses (Jordet et al. 2011).

105 Jordet & Elferink-Gemser (2012)

106 Ahmed (2017)

107 The award presented by France Football to the best performing goalkeeper of the year.

108 Maheshwari (2021)

109 Vignolo (2023)

110 Ben & Gabe (2023)

111 To be fair, the Dutch team took an active part in these mind-games, and they may even have started it, when their goalkeeper Andries Noppert engaged with Messi for Argentina's first kick. However, the bad blood between the teams started much earlier than that, with intense confrontations during the game and offensive remarks in the pre-game press conferences.

112 Vignolo (2023)

113 LFC History (2023)

114 LFC History (2023)

115 FIFA (2022)

116 Geleit (2022)

117 Wood & Wilson (2010)

118 Furley et al. (2017)

119 This difference was just not statistically significant (p=.056). A more sensitive and nuanced test of goalkeeper performance (based on Dicks et al. 2010) showed a significant difference (p=.029). However, this suggests that the observed difference is not a strong one.

120 Ramsdale against Manchester United, December 2, 2021 and Gabriel against Manchester City, January 1, 2022

121 Against Liverpool, August 28, 2021

122 Against West Ham, October 20, 2022

123 Against Brighton, April 23, 2023 (in the penalty shootout)

124 Against Brentford, September 18, 2021

125 Guus Hiddink nearly beat van Gaal to it when he prepared to perform a goalkeeper switch for Australia in the decisive 2006 World Cup playoff against Uruguay. Australia's backup goalkeeper, Zeljko Kalac, who stood an impressive 2.02 meters above ground and would have been an intimidating opponent on a penalty kick, was warming up in the second half of extra time, ready to come on, when an injury forced Hiddink to make another late substitution and he had to scratch his plan. It worked out in the end for Hiddink: his original goalkeeper Mark Schwarzer saved two shots, and Australia went through to the World Cup.

126 Roth et al. (2019)

127 Conmy (2005); McDermott & Lachlan (2021)

128 Svenson (1981)

129 Conmy et al. (2013)

130 Yip et al. (2018)
131 Based on 29 goals in 33 attempts prior to the two penalties that will be described here.
132 Van de Vooren (2006)
133 Budgen (2022)
134 Original study conducted by Masters et al. (2007); then replicated by Weigelt et al. (2012), Weigelt & Memmert (2012), Noel et al. (2016), and Noel et al. (2015).
135 My recommendation based on an interpretation of the studies referred to above as well as Memmert et al. (2020).
136 Masters et al. (2010)
137 Brinkschulte et al. (2023)
138 Engber (2005)
139 Sports Illustrated (2012)
140 Engber (2015)
141 Wolfers (2015)
142 Benz (2019.
143 Eventually, they did the coin toss. When Ferdinand won it, he seemed to hesitate for a moment, then turned to his team and shouted: "Gaffer, hey, do we shoot first?". He repeated the question three more times while Terry impatiently started to pull Ferdinand's shirt, in an attempt to make him reach a faster decision.
144 Jordet et al. (2009)
145 Berry & Wood (2004)
146 Goldschmied et al. (2010)
147 Hsu et al. (2019)
148 Veldkamp & Koning (2023)
149 Eysenck et al. (2007); Hsu et al. (2008)
150 Wilson & Richards (2011)
151 Oettingen et al. (2012)
152 IFAB (2023)
153 Kerchnar (2015); Kerchnar (2018); Johnson & Taylor (2018)
154 UEFA (2021)
155 Renard did not offer the same support for the two French players who had missed previously, and with Becho it was too late – Australia scored their next shot to win the shootout.
156 It took 48 penalties to settle the 2005 Namibian Cup Final between KK Palace and Civics, with some players on both sides having to take three penalties and the shootout lasting almost as long as the match. This held the record for shootout duration until 2022 when the English non-league sides Washington and Bedlington shared 54 penalties (49 converted) to decide a first round Memorial Cup tie.
157 Weick & Sutcliffe (2007)
158 Helmreich (2000)
159 Weick & Sutcliffe (2007); Reason (2000)
160 We were able to interview eight of the 10 players who took part in the penalty shootout.
161 Baumeister & Leary (1995)
162 Eisenberger & Cole (2012)
163 Uchino & Garvey (1997)

164 Ditzen et al. 2008
165 The first time Luis took this role was August 20, 2020, when Flamengo received a penalty in the 86th minute at home to Gremio, when the score was 0-1. Barbosa equalized and Flamengo got a draw.
166 Roberts (2009)
167 Graham et al. (2005)
168 Fox and Sobol (2000)
169 Hobbs et al. (2002)
170 Graham (2000)
171 Henderson (2022), p.4
172 Coincidentally, both Henderson's kicks were against the same goalkeeper, David Ospina.
173 Chelsea FC (2022)
174 Kelly (2023)
175 Tracy et al. (2023)
176 FIFA (2022)
177 Moll et al. (2010)
178 Note that Maradona's kick above was not included following these criteria, as Argentina were ahead in the game at the time of his kick.
179 Furley et al. (2015)
180 Morrison (2016)
181 Doms (2017)
182 Crooks (2022)
183 Sky Sport Austria (2019)
184 Nicol (2023)
185 Ricotta (2016)
186 Pardon (2023)
187 McTear (2023)
188 Cruyff (2012)
189 NTV (2019)
190 Purewal (2021)
191 Nair (2022)
192 Purewal (2021)
193 Victor (2022)
194 GetFootball (2022)
195 Inside FIFA (2023)
196 For more on this conversation, see Hiddink & Jordet (2019)
197 Van den Nieuwenhof (2006), p.145
198 Long (1980); Fletcher & Arnold (2021)
199 Calabrese et al. (2007)
200 Taleb (2012); Kiefer et al. (2018
201 Russo et al. (2012); Fletcher & Arnold (2021)
202 Parker et al. (2004); Parker et al. (2005); Lyons & Parker (2007)
203 Krishnan et al. (2007); Berton et al. (2007); Greenwood & Fleshner (2008)
204 Fletcher & Arnold (2021)
205 Neff & Broady (2011)
206 Collins et al. (2016); Hardy et al. (2017); Howells & Fletcher (2015); Sarkar et al.

(2015); Savage et al. (2017); van Yperen (2009)

207 Hardy et al. (2017)

208 Van Yperen (2009)

209 Collins et al. (2016)

210 Collins & MacNamara (2012)

211 Oudejans & Pijpers (2009); Oudejans & Pijpers (2010)

212 Gröpel & Mesagno (2017)

213 Kent et al. (2018)

214 Low et al. (2021)

215 Fletcher & Arnold (2021)

216 Owusu-Sekyere & Gervis (2016)

217 Fletcher & Arnold (2021)

218 Stoker et al. (2016)

219 Fletcher & Arnold (2021)

220 Talk SPORT (2021)

221 Bloechle et al. (2024)

222 Jordet & Elferink-Gemser (2012)

223 Ellis & Ward (2022)

224 Berander et al. (2021)

225 Tribuna (2019)

226 Noticias & Protagonistas (2022)

227 Phillips (2022)

228 All About Argentina (2024)

229 Noticias & Protagonistas (2022)

230 Chiatorrini (2022)

231 Hannah et al. (2009)

232 Baumeister et al. (2007); Dolinski (2018)

233 Banks et al. (2023)

234 Gilbert & Trudel (2004)

235 Managing and communicating with people is exceptionally complex, of course, and I'm under no illusion that I'm about to identify a one-size-fits-all style of management under pressure that will work with all managers and groups, across all levels, cultures, and situations. Besides, the sample is restrictively small (five shootouts, but only eight different managers and teams, because Argentina and Croatia took part in two each).

236 Crossculture2go (2024)

237 Yomiuri (2023)

238 Quaile (2022)

239 Jordet & Elferink-Gemser (2012); Furley et al. (2020)

240 Mavletova & Witte (2016)

241 Powell (2016)

242 Jordet & Elferink-Gemser (2012)

243 Tembah (2023)

244 James & Wooten (2010)

245 Vroom & Yetton (1973)

246 Fodor (1978)

247 Mulder et al. (1986)

248 Rosing et al. (2022)

249 Hannah et al. (2009)

250 New Paradigm (2022)

251 Gilberto (2020)

252 Gilberto (2020)

253 Senju & Johnson (2009)

254 Noticias & Protagonistas (2022)

255 Highly profiled players miss more shots than players with comparable skill levels, but with lower public profile (Jordet, 2009b)

256 Doyle (2006)

257 In English: "He always puts it to the right: A history of the penalty kick" (by Clark Miller, who sadly passed while completing the last chapter, published in 1998), "On penalties" (Andrew Anthony, 2000) and "How to take a penalty: The hidden mathematics of sport" (Rob Eastaway & John Haigh, 2005); in Dutch: "De straf-schop: Zoektocht naar de ultieme penalty" (Gyuri Vergouw, 2000) and "Penalty: Het trauma van Oranje" (Henri van der Steen, 2004); in German: "Elfmeter: Kleine Geschichte einer standardsituation" (René Martens, 2003).

258 Nobody more than the Dutch author, Gyuri Vergouw.

259 In English: "Twelve Yards: The art and psychology of the perfect penalty" (by Ben Lyttleton, 2014) and "Beautiful game theory: How soccer can help economics" (Ignacio Palacios-Huerta, 2014; a book not entirely about penalties, but with prominent sections on them); in Dutch: "Duel in de zestien: De penalty wetenschappelijke ontleed" (Geert Savelsbergh & John van der Kamp, 2014); in German: "Elfmeter: Die psychologie de strafstosses" (Daniel Memmert & Benjamiin Noël, 2017).

260 Rudi et al. (2020)

261 Santos (2023)

262 Vollmer et al. (2023)

Bibliography

60 Minutes (2023, December 11). "Even though there is no physical contact in tennis, there's still a lot of eye contact," says Novak Djokovic. He" [...]. [Tweet]. X. https://twitter.com/60Minutes/status/1734022929141158153?s=20

Ahmed, M. (2017, March 17). How to save a penalty: The truth about football's toughest shot. *Financial Times*. https://www.ft.com/penalties

AFP (2022, December 10). "Van Gaal says World Cup exit on penalties 'incredibly painful'." *New Straits Times*. https://www.nst.com.my/sports/football/2022/12/859466/van-gaal-says-world-cup-exit-penalties-incredibly-painful

All About Argentina (2024, January 22). Unedited video of Lionel Scaloni right after the loss against Saudi Arabia with English subtitles. You can't [...]. [Tweet]. X. https://twitter.com/AlbicelesteTalk/status/1749326028433186832?s=20

Almeida, C. H., & Volossovitch, A. (2023). Multifactorial analysis of football penalty kicks in the Portuguese First League: A replication study. *International Journal of Sports Science & Coaching*, 18(1), 160-175. https://doi.org/10.1177/17479541221075722

Anthony, A. (2000). *On penalties*. Yellow Jersey Press.

Arrondel, L., Duhautois, R., & Laslier, J.-F. (2019). Decision under psychological pressure: The shooter's anxiety at the penalty kick. *Journal Of Economic Psychology*, 70, 22–35. https://doi.org/10.1016/j.joep.2018.10.008

Baggio, R. (2002, May 19). My penalty miss cost Italy the World Cup? *The Guardian*. https://www.theguardian.com/sport/2002/may/19/worldcupfootball2002.football

Bakker, F. C., Oudejans, R. R. D., Binsch, O., & Kamp, J. V. D. (2006). Penalty shooting and gaze behavior: Unwanted effects of the wish not to miss. *International Journal of Sport Psychology*, 37(2-3), 265–280.

Balban, M. Y., Neri, E., Kogon, M. M., Weed, L., Jo, B., Holl, G., Zeitzer, J. M., Spiegel, J. M., & Huberman, A. D. (2023). Brief structured respiration practices enhances mood and reduce physiological arousal. *Cell Reports Medicine*, 4(1). DOI:https://doi.org/10.1016/j.xcrm.2022.100895

Balk, Y. A., Adriaanse, M. A., de Ridder, D. T., & Evers, C. (2013). Coping under pressure: Employing emotion regulation strategies to enhance performance under pressure. *Journal of Sport & Exercise Psychology*, 35(4), 408-418. https://doi.org/10.1123/jsep.35.4.408

Ball, P. & Shaw, P. (1996). *The Umbro book of football quotations*. Ebury.

Banks, G. C., Woznyj, H. M., & Mansfield, C. A. (2023). Where is "behavior" in organizational behavior? A call for a revolution in leadership research and beyond.

The Leadership Quarterly, 34(6), 101581.

Bar-Eli, M., Azar, O. H., Ritov, I., Keidar-Levin, Y., & Schein, G. (2007). Action bias among elite soccer goalkeepers: The case of penalty kicks. *Journal of Economic Psychology*, 28(5), 606–621. https://doi.org/10.1016/j.joep.2006.12.001

Baumeister R. F. (1984). Choking under pressure: Self-consciousness and paradoxical effects of incentives on skillful performance. *Journal of Personality and Social Psychology*, 46(3), 610–620. https://doi.org/10.1037//0022-3514.46.3.610

Baumeister, R. F., & Leary, M. R. (1995). The need to belong: Desire for interpersonal attachments as a fundamental human motivation. *Psychological Bulletin*, 117(3), 497–529.

Baumeister, R. F., Vohs, K. D., & Funder, D. C. (2007). Psychology as the science of self-reports and finger movements: Whatever happened to actual behavior? *Perspectives on Psychological Science*, 2(4).

Beilock, S. L., Carr, T. H., MacMahon, C., & Starkes, J. L. (2002). When paying attention becomes counterproductive: Impact of divided versus skill-focused attention on novice and experienced performance of sensorimotor skills. *Journal of Experimental Psychology: Applied*, 8(1), 6–16. https://doi.org/10.1037//1076-898x.8.1.6

Ben, T., & Gabe, T. (Producers) (2023, December 30). *Captains of the world.* [TV-series], Netflix.

Benz, L. (2019, December 26). Does Arizona State's curtain of distraction work? Luke Benz. https://lukebenz.com/post/asu_curtain/#:~:text=Conclusion,-doesn't%20necessarily%20contradict%20i

Berander, M., Rydén, A., & Asahara, A. (2021, August 6). Segers besvikelse efter OS-silvret:

"Allt är brutalt". Aftonbladet. https://www.aftonbladet.se/sportbladet/fotboll/a/jaBdmw/segers-besvikelse-efter-os-silvret-allt-ar-brutalt

Berns, G. S., Chappelow, J., Cekic, M., Zink, C. F., Pagnoni, G., & Martin-Skurski, M. E. (2006). Neurobiological substrates of dread. *Science*, 312(5774), 754–758. https://doi.org/10.1126/science.1123721

Berry, S. M., Column Edi, & Wood, C. (2004). A statistician reads the sports pages: The cold-foot effect. *Chance*, 17(4), 47–51. https://doi.org/10.1080/09332480.2004.10554926

Berton, O., Covington 3rd, H. E., Ebner, K., Tsankova, N. M., Carle, T. L., Ulery, P., Bhonsle, A., Barot, M., Krishnan, V., Singewald, G. M., Singewald, N., Birnbaum, S., Neve, R. L., & Nestler, E. J. (2007). Induction of FosB in the periaqueductal gray by stress promotes active coping responses. *Neuron*, 55, 289-300.

Bijlstra, G., Furley P., & Nieuwenhuys, A. (2020). The power of nonverbal behavior: Penalty-takers' body language influences impression formation and anticipation performance in goalkeepers in a simulated soccer penalty task. *Psychology of Sport and Exercise*, 21(2), 137-151.

Binsch, O., Oudejans, R. R. D., Bakker, F. C., Hoozemans, M. J. M., & Savelsberg, R. A. H. (2010). Ironic effects in a penalty shooting task: Is the negative wording in the instruction essential? *International Journal of Sport Psychology*, 41, 118-133.

Bloechle, J.-l., Audiffren, J., Le Naour, T., Alli, A., Simoni, D., Wüthrich, G., & Bresciani, J.-P. (2024). It's not all in your feet: Improving penalty kick performance with human-avatar interaction and machine learning. *The Innovation*, 5. https://doi.org/10.1016/j.xinn.2024.100584

Brimmell J., Parker J., Wilson M. R., Vine S. J., Moore L. J. (2019) Challenge and threat states, performance, and attentional control during a pressurized soccer penalty task. *Sport, Exercise, and Performance Psychology*, 8(1), 63–79.

Brinkschulte, M., Wunderlich, F., Furley, P., & Memmert, D. (2023). The obligation to succeed when it matters the most: The influence of skill and pressure on the success in football penalty kicks. *Psychology of Sport and Exercise*, 65. https://doi.org/10.1016/j.psychsport.2022.102369 (88, 152)

Budgen, S. (2022, June 17). Hero Socceroos goalkeeper Andrew Redmayne reveals the toll throwing away Peruvian goalkeeper's water bottle took on him: 'It goes against every moral fibre in my body'. *Daily Mail*. https://www.dailymail.co.uk/sport/football/article-10925559/Andrew-Redmayne-reveals-throwing-away-Peruvian-goalkeepers-water-bottle-took-huge-toll-him.html

Calabrese, E. J., Bachmann, K. A., Bailer, A. J., Bolger, P. M., Borak, J., Cai, L., Cedergreen, N., Cherian, M. G., Chiueh, C. C., Clarkson, T. W., Cook, R. R., Diamond, D. M., Doolittle, D. J., Dorato, M. A., Duke, S. O., Feinendegen, L., Gardner, D. E., Hart, R. W., Hastings, K. L., … Mattson, M. P. (2007). Biological stress response terminology: Integrating the concepts of adaptive response and preconditioning stress within a hormetic dose-response framework. *Toxicology and Applied Pharmacology*, 222(1), 122–128. https://doi.org/10.1016/j.taap.2007.02.015

Chelsea FC (2022, February 13). Azpilicueta reveals how he helped Havertz and expresses pride at completing the set. Chelsea FC. https://www.chelseafc.com/en/news/article/azpi-reveals-how-he-helped-havertz-and-expresses-pride-at-comple

Chitarroni, C. (2022, December 15). Scaloni´s leadership. Rosario Nuestro. https://rosarionuestro.com/el-liderazgo-de-scaloni-2/?_x_tr_sl&_x_tr_tl&_x_tr_hl

CIES Football Observatory (2022). Penalty stats across Europe: Manchester United stands out. CIES. https://football-observatory.com/IMG/sites/b5wp/2021/wp364/en/

Cohn, P. J. (1990). Preperformance routines in sport: Theoretical support and practical applications. *The Sport Psychologist*, 4(3), 301-312. https://doi.

org/10.1123/tsp.4.3.301

Collins, D., & MacNamara, Á. (2012). The rocky road to the top: Why talent needs trauma. *Sports Medicine*, 42, 907-914.

Collins, D., MacNamara, Á., & McCarthy, N. (2016). Super champions, champions, and almosts: Important differences and commonalities on the rocky road. *Frontiers in Psychology*, 6, 171615.

Conmy, O. B. (2005). Investigating a conceptual framework for trash talk: Cognitive and affective states [Unpublished master's thesis]. Florida State University.

Conmy, B., Tenenbaum, G., Eklund, R., Roehrig, A., & Filho, E. (2013). Trash talk in a competitive setting: Impact on self-efficacy and affect. *Journal of Applied Social Psychology*, 43(5), 1002–1014. https://doi.org/10.1111/jasp.12064

Cotterill, S. (2010). Pre-performance routines in sport: Current understanding and future directions. *International Review of Sport and Exercise Psychology*, 3(2), 132–153. https://doi.org/10.1080/1750984X.2010.488269

Coyle, D. (2018). *The culture code: The secrets of highly successful groups*. Bantam.

Crooks, G. (2022, February 3). Ronny Deila learned it 10 yrs ago when he was at

@godset & it helped #NYCFC win #MLS Cup. [Tweet]. X. https://twitter.com/GlennCrooks/status/1489305722684907521?s=20

Crossculture2go (2024). Country guide Netherlands. https://crossculture2go.com/leadership-in-the-netherlands/#:~:text=Managers%20always%20involve%20all%20team,eye%20level%20with%20each%20other.

Cruyff, J. (2012). *Voetbal.* Schuyt Nederland.

Deux-Zero (2023). *Penalties - Classement des tireurs de la saison.* Deux Zero. https://www.deux-zero.com/ligue-1/penalties-tireurs-epreuve/edition/2022-2023

Dicks, M., Button, C., & Davids, K. (2010). Examination of gaze behaviors under in situ and video simulation task constraints reveals differences in information pickup for perception and action. *Attention, Perception, & Psychophysics*, 72, 706-720.

Ditzen, B., Schmidt, S., Strauss, B., Nater, U. M., Ehlert, U., & Heinrichs, M. (2008). Adult attachment and social support interact to reduce psychological but not cortisol responses to stress. *Journal of Psychosomatic Research*, 64(5), 479-486. doi: 10.1016/j.jpsychores.2007.11.011.

Dolinski, D. (2018). Is psychology still a science of behavior? *Social Psychology Bulletin*, 13(2).

Doms, K. (2017). ESSEVEE bedankt noorse psycholoog voor bekerwinst. HLN. https://www.hln.be/zulte-waregem/essevee-bedankt-noorse-psycholoog-voor-bekerwinst-a214a366/?referrer=https%3A%2F%2Fwww.google.com%2F

Doyle, P. (2006, September 27). Blatter suggests scrapping shoot-outs. *The Guardian*. https://www.theguardian.com/football/2006/sep/27/newsstory.sport3

Eastaway, R., & Haigh, J. (2005). *The Hidden Mathematics of Sport*. Robson.

Edgar, B. (2022). A history of scorelines in English football: 95 different results in 203 229 matches. *The Times*. https://www.thetimes.co.uk/article/a-history-of-scorelines-in-english-football-95-different-results-in- 203-329-matches-3gsllqcj8

Eisenberger, N. I., & Cole, S. W. (2012). Social neuroscience and health: Neurophysiological mechanisms linking social ties with physical health. *Nature Neuroscience*, 15(5), 669–674. https://doi.org/10.1038/nn.3086

Ellis, L., & Ward, P. (2022). The effect of a high-pressure protocol on penalty shooting performance, psychological, and psychophysiological response in professional football: A mixed methods study. *Journal of Sports Sciences*, 40(1), 3-15.

Engber, D. (2005, January 6). How a Slate scientist changed the NBA forever—or at least a week. Slate. https://slate.com/culture/2005/01/how-a-slate-scientist-changed-the-nba-forever.html

Engber, D. (2015, February 17). Is ASU's bizarre new technique the holy grail of free-throw distraction? Slate. https://slate.com/culture/2015/02/asu-curtain-of-distraction-has-arizona-state-university-discovered-the-holy-grail-of-free-throw-distraction.html

Eysenck, M. W., Derakshan, N., Santos, R., & Calvo, M. G. (2007). Anxiety and cognitive performance: Attentional control theory. *Emotion*, 7(2), 336–353. https://doi.org/10.1037/1528-3542.7.2.336

Farkas, F. (2023, July 4). Liverpool: Dominik Szoboszlai's secret weapon revealed, proving Neymar wrong. ClutchPoints. https://clutchpoints.com/liverpool-news-dominik-szoboszlai-secret-weapon-neymar-wrong

FIFA (2023). One Month On: 5 billion engaged with the FIFA World Cup Qatar 2022™. FIFA. https://www.fifa.com/tournaments/mens/worldcup/qatar2022/news/one-month-on-5-billion-engaged-with-the-fifa-world-cup-qatar-2022-tm

FIFA (2022). *The long walk*. [TV-series]. FIFA plus. https://www.plus.fifa.com/en/content/the-long-walk/cfb1f47c-42aa-4c9c-a906-766ae87afe69

Fletcher, D., & Arnold, R. (2021). Stress and pressure training. In R. Arnold, & D. Fletcher (Eds.), *Stress, well-being, and performance in sport*. Routledge.

Fodor, E. M. (1978). Simulated work climate as an influence on choice of leadership style. *Personality and Social Psychology Bulletin*, 99, 20-35.

Fox, J. G., & Sobol, J. J. (2000). drinking patterns, social interaction, and barroom behavior: A routine activities approach. *Deviant Behavior*, 21(5), 429–450. https://doi.org/10.1080/01639620050085834

Furley, P., Dicks, M., & Jordet, G. (2020). The psychology of penalty kicks: The influence of emotions on penalty taker and goalkeeper performance. In J. G. Dixon, J. B. Barker, R. C. Thelwell, & I. Mitchell (Eds.), *The Psychology of Soccer* (pp. 29-43). Routledge.

Furley, P., Dicks, M., & Memmert, D. (2012). Nonverbal behavior in soccer: The influence of dominant and submissive body language on the impression of success of soccer players. *Journal of Sport & Exercise Psychology*, 34(1), 61–82.

Furley, P., Dicks, M., Stendtke, F., & Memmert, D. (2012). Get it out the way. The wait's killing me: Hastening and hiding during soccer penalty kicks. *Psychology of Sport and Exercise*, 13(4), 454-465. https://doi.org/10.1016/j.psychsport.2012.01.009

Furley, P., Moll, T., & Memmert, D. (2015). "Put your hands up in the air"? The interpersonal effects of pride and shame expressions on opponents and teammates. *Frontiers in Psychology*, 6, 1361. https://doi.org/10.3389/fpsyg.2015.01361

Furley, P., Noël, B., & Memmert, D. (2017). Attention towards the goalkeeper and distraction during penalty shootouts in association football: A retrospective analysis of penalty shootouts from 1984 to 2012. *Journal of Sports Sciences*, 35(9), 873–879. https://doi.org/10.1080/02640414.2016.1195912

Furley, P., & Roth, A. (2021). Coding body language in sports: The nonverbal behavior coding system for soccer penalties. *Journal of Sport & Exercise Psychology*, 43(2), 140-154. https://doi.org/10.1123/jsep.2020-0066

Gardner, F. L., & Moore, Z. E. (2004). A mindfulness-acceptance-commitment-based approach to athletic performance enhancement: Theoretical considerations. *Behavior Therapy*, 35(4), 707–723. https://doi.org/10.1016/S0005-7894(04)80016-9

Geleit, L. (2022). "It was discussed weeks prior": Aussie hero Redmayne opens up on water bottel tactic. Sen. https://www.sen.com.au/news/2022/06/16/it-was-discussed-weeks-prior-redmayne-opens-up-on-water-bottle-tactic/

Gerrard, S. (2006). *Gerrard: My autobiography*. Bantam Press.

GetFootball (2022, December 8). Argentina coach: "We're ready for penalties, all 8 teams are good enough for the final." GetFootball. https://getfootball.eu/argentina-coach-were-ready-for-penalties-all-8-teams-are-good-enough-for-the-final/

Giancamilli, F., Galli, F., Chirico, A., Chirico, A., Fegatelli, D., Mallia, L., Palombi, T., Cordone, S., Alivernini, F., Mandolesi, L., & Lucidi, F. (2022). When the going gets tough, what happens to quiet eye? The role of time pressure and performance pressure during basketball free throws. *Psychology of Sport and Exercise*, 58.

Gilbert, W. D., & Trudel, P. (2004). Analysis of coaching science research published from 1970–2001. *Research Quarterly for Exercise and Sport*, 75(4), 388-399.

Gilberto, T. (Producer). (2020). All or nothing: Brazil national team. [TV-series]. Amazon. https://www.primevideo.com/region/eu/detail/0G58NJZZOX5C-9CUYK7L5YJF8TI/ref=atv_sr_fle_c_Tn74RA_1_1_1?sr=1-1&pageTypeId-

Source=ASIN&pageTypeId=B083STCJ5C&qid=1710409262024

Goldschmied, N., Nankin, M., & Cafri, G. (2010). Pressure kicks in the NFL: An archival exploration into the deployment of TOs and other environmental correlates. *The Sport Psychologist*, 24(3), 300-312.

Graham, K. (2000). Preventive interventions for on-premise drinking: A promising but underresearched area of prevention. *Contemporary Drug Problems*, 27, 593-668.

Graham, K., Bernards, S., Osgood, W., Homel, R., & Purcell, J. (2005). Guardians and handlers: The role of bar staff in preventing and managing aggression. *Addiction*, 100(6), 755-766.

Gray, R. (2020). Attentional theories of choking under pressure revisited. In G. Tenenbaum, & R. C. Eklund (Eds.), *Handbook of Sport Psychology* (pp. 595–610). John Wiley & Sons.

Greenlees, I., Leyland, A., Thelwell, R., & Filby, W. (2008). Soccer penalty takers' uniform colour and pre-penalty kick gaze affect the impressions formed of them by opposing goalkeepers. *Journal of Sports Sciences*, 26(6), 569–576. https://doi.org/10.1080/02640410701744446

Greenwood, B. N., & Fleshner, M. (2008). Exercise, learned helplessness, and the stress-resistant brain. *NeuroMolecular Medicine*, 10(2), 81-98.

Gröpel, P., & Mesagno, C. (2017). Choking interventions in sports: A systematic review. *International Review of Sport and Exercise Psychology*, 12(1), 176-201. https://doi.org/10.1080/1750984X.2017.1408134

Guardian Sport (2021). Marcus Rashford sorry for penalty but says 'I will never apologise for who I am'. *The Guardian*. https://www.theguardian.com/football/2021/jul/12/marcus-rashford-sorry-for-penalty-but-says-i-will-never-apologise-for-who-i-am

Gucciardi, D. F., Longbottom, J. L., Jackson, B., & Dimmock, J. A. (2010). Experienced golfers' perspectives on choking under pressure. *Journal of Sport & Exercise Psychology*, 32(1), 61–83. https://doi.org/10.1123/jsep.32.1.61

Hannah, S. T., Uhl-Bien, M., Avolio, B. J., & Cavarretta, F. L. (2009). A framework for examining leadership in extreme contexts. *The Leadership Quarterly*, 20(6), 897-919.

Hardy, L., Barlow, M., Evans, L., Rees, T., Woodman, T., & Warr, C. (2017). Great British medalists: Psychosocial biographies of super-elite and elite athletes from Olympic sports. *Progress in Brain Research*, 232, 1-119.

Hayes, S. C., Wilson, K. G., Gifford, E. V., Follette, V. M., & Strosahl, K. (1996). Experimental avoidance and behavioral disorders: a functional dimensional approach to diagnosis and treatment. *Journal of Consulting and Clinical Psychology*, 64(6), 1152–1168. https://doi.org/10.1037//0022-006x.64.6.1152

HaytersTV (2018, June 25). Harry Kane | How to take the perfect penalty -

England v Belgium. [Video]. YouTube. https://www.youtube.com/watch?v=b-jsw0Khan7E

Hazell, J., Cotterill, S. T., & Hill, D. M. (2014). An exploration of pre-performance routines, self-efficacy, anxiety and performance in semi-professional soccer. *European Journal of Sport Science*, 14(6), 603–610. https://doi.org/10.1080/17461 391.2014.888484

Helmreich R. L. (2000). On error management: lessons from aviation. *BMJ*, 320(7237), 781–785. https://doi.org/10.1136/bmj.320.7237.781

Henderson, J. (2022). *Jordan Henderson: The autobiography*. Michael Joseph Ltd.

Heshmat, S. (2022). 10 Sources of a Courageous Mindset: Courage is an antidote to anxious mind. *Psychology Today*. https://www.psychologytoday.com/intl/blog/science-choice/202207/10-sources-courageous-mindset

Hiddink, G., & Jordet, G. (2019). The coach nomad. In D. Collins, A. Cruick-shank, & G. Jordet (Eds.), *Routledge handbook of elite sport performance*. London: Routledge.

Hill, D. M., Hanton, S., Matthews, N., & Fleming, S. (2010). A qualitative exploration of choking in elite golf. *Journal of Clinical Sport Psychology*, 4(3), 221–240. https://doi.org/10.1123/jcsp.4.3.221

Hobbs, D., Hadfield, P., Lister, S., & Winslow, S. (2002). 'Door lore'. The art and economics of intimidation. *The British Journal of Criminology*, 42(2), 352–370. https://doi.org/10.1093/bjc/42.2.352

Honigstein, R. (2021, August 19). Robert Lewandowski: My game in my words. *The Athletic*. https://theathletic.com/2775337/2021/08/19/robert-lewandowski-my-game-in-my-words/

Horn, M., de Waal, S., & Kraak, W. (2021). In-match penalty kick analysis of the 2009/10 to 2018/19 English Premier League competition. *International Journal of Performance Analysis in Sport*, 21(1), 139–155. https://doi.org/10.1080/24748668 .2020.1855052

Horsinek, J., & Barth, J.C. (2019). Emil (20) var den siste som reddet en Haaland-straffe. TV2. https://www.tv2.no/sport/fotball/emil-20-var-den-siste-som-reddet-en-haaland-straffe/10972183/

Howells, K., & Fletcher, D. (2015). Sink or swim: Adversity-and growth-related experiences in Olympic swimming champions. *Psychology of Sport and Exercise*, 16, 37-48.

Hsu, K. E., Man, F. Y., Gizicki, R. A., Feldman, L. S., & Fried, G. M. (2008). Experienced surgeons can do more than one thing at a time: Effect of distraction on performance of a simple laparoscopic and cognitive task by experienced and novice surgeons. *Surgical Endoscopy*, 22(1), 196–201. https://doi.org/10.1007/s00464-007-9452-0

Hsu, N. W., Liu, K. S., & Chang, S. C. (2019). Choking under the pressure of competition: A complete statistical investigation of pressure kicks in the NFL, 2000-2017. PLOS ONE, 14(4), e0214096. https://doi.org/10.1371/journal.pone.0214096

Hustad, T. (2018, April 15). Haaland tok ballen fra Aursnes: Jeg er best på straffespark. *Aftenposten*. https://www.aftenposten.no/sport/fotball/i/xPJ0dj/haaland-tok-ballen-fra-aursnes-jeg-er-best-paa-straffespark

IFAB (2023). Law Changes 23/24. IFAB. https://www.theifab.com/law-changes/latest/

Inside FIFA (2023, May 9). Argentina coach Lionel Scaloni talks to Coaches Forum about FIFA World Cup™ campaign. InsideFIFA. https://www.fifa.com/technical/news/argentina-coach-lionel-scaloni-talks-to-coaches-forum-about-fifa-world-cup-campaign

Jackson, P., & Delehanty, H. (1995). *Sacred hoops: Spiritual lessons of a hardwood warrior*. Hachette Books.

Jackson R. C. (2003). Pre-performance routine consistency: Temporal analysis of goal kicking in the Rugby Union World Cup. *Journal of Sports Sciences*, 21(10), 803–814. https://doi.org/10.1080/0264041031000140301

Jafari, Z., Kolb, B. E., & Mohajerani, M. H. (2017). Effect of acute stress on auditory processing: A systematic review of human studies. *Reviews in the Neurosciences*, 28(1), 1-13. https://doi.org/10.1515/revneuro-2016-0043

James, E. H., & Wooten, L. P. (2010). *Leading under pressure. From surviving to thriving before, during and after a crisis*. Routledge.

Johnson, C., & Taylor, J. (2020). More than bullshit: Trash talk and other psychological tests of sporting excellence. *Sport, Ethics, and Philosophy*, 14(1), 47-61.

Jordet, G. (2009a). Why do English players fail in soccer penalty shootouts? A study of team status, self-regulation, and choking under pressure. *Journal of Sports Sciences*, 27(2), 97–106. https://doi.org/10.1080/02640410802509144

Jordet, G. (2009b). When superstars flop: Public status and choking under pressure in international soccer penalty shootouts. *Journal of Applied Sport Psychology*, 21(2), 125–130. https://doi.org/10.1080/10413200902777263

Jordet, G., & Elferink-Gemser, M. T. (2012). Stress, coping, and emotions on the world stage: The experience of participating in a major soccer tournament penalty shootout. *Journal of Applied Sport Psychology*, 24(1), 73-91. https://doi.org/10.1080/10413200.2011.619000

Jordet, G., Elferink-Gemser, M. T., Lemmink, K. A. P. M., & Visscher, C. (2006). The "Russian roulette" of soccer?: Perceived control and anxiety in a major tournament penalty shootout. *International Journal of Sport Psychology*, 37(2-3), 281–298.

Jordet, G., Elferink-Gemser, M. T., Lemmink, K. A. P. M., & Visscher, C.

Bibliography

(2008). Emotions at the penalty mark: An analysis of elite players performing in an international penalty shootout. In T. Reilly, & F. Korkusuz (Eds.), *Science and football VI: The proceedings of the sixth world congress on science and football.* London: Routledge.

Jordet, G., & Hartman, E. (2008). Avoidance motivation and choking under pressure in soccer penalty shootouts. *Journal of Sport & Exercise Psychology*, 30(4), 450-457.

Jordet, G., Hartman, E., & Vuijk, P. J. (2011). Team history and choking under pressure in major soccer penalty shootouts. *British Journal of Psychology*, 103(2), 268-283. https://doi.org/10.1111/j.2044-8295.2011.02071.x

Jordet, G., Hartman, E., & Sigmundstad, E. (2009). Temporal links to performing under pressure in international soccer penalty shootouts. *Psychology of Sport and Exercise.* 10(6), 621-627.

Kelly, C. (2023, March 21). Keylor Navas penalty twist revealed as he fails to get in yet another Newcastle player's head. Chronicle Live. https://www.chroniclelive.co.uk/sport/football/football-news/newcastle-penalty-keylor-navas-twist-26519563

Kent, S., Devonport, T. J., Lane, A.M., Nicholls, W., & Friesen, A. P. (2018). The effects of coping interventions on ability to perform under pressure. *Journal of Sport Science and Medicine*, 17, 40-55.

Kershnar, S. (2015). The moral rules of trash talking: Morality and ownership. *Sport, Ethics and Philosophy*, 9(3): 303–323. doi:10.1080/17511321.2015.1099117

Kershnar, S. (2018). For ownership theory: A response to Nicholas Dixon. *Sport, Ethics and Philosophy*, 12(2): 226–235. doi:10.1080/17511321.2018.1428148

Kiefer, A. W., Silva, P. L., Harrison, H. S., & Araújo, D. (2018). Antifragility in sport: Leveraging adversity to enhance performance. *Sport, Exercise, and Performance Psychology*, 7(4), 342– 350. https://doi.org/10.1037/spy0000130

Krishnan, V., Han, M.-H., Graham, D.L., Berton, O., Renthal, W., Russo, S.J., LaPlant, Q., Graham, A., Lutter, M., Lagace, D.C., Ghose, S., Reister, R., Tanous, P., Green, T.A., Neve, R.L., Chakravarty, S., Kumar, A., Eisch, A.J., Self, D.W., … Nestler, E.J., (2007). Molecular adaptations underlying susceptibility and resistance to social defeat in brain reward regions. *Cell, 131*, 391-404.

Laurin, R., & Pellet, J. (2024). Affective responses mediate the body language of penalty taker - decision-making relationship from soccer goalkeepers. *Research Quarterly for Exercise and Sport*, 95(1), 227–234. https://doi.org/10.1080/02701367.2023.2189466

Lebeau, J. C., Liu, S., Sáenz-Moncaleano, C., Sanduvete-Chaves, S., Chacón-Moscoso, S., Becker, B. J., & Tenenbaum, G. (2016). Quiet eye and performance in sport: A meta-analysis. *Journal of Sport & Exercise Psychology*, 38(5),

441–457. https://doi.org/10.1123/jsep.2015-0123

LFC History (2023). *Dynasty: The Joe Fagan years 1983-1985 (based on Paul Tomkins' book Dynasty)*. LFC history. https://www.lfchistory.net/Articles/Article/898/2

Lin, L.- L., Gu, H. -Y., Yao, Y. -Y., Zhu, J., Niu, Y. -M., Luo, J., & Zhang, C. (2019). The association between watching football matches and the risk of cardiovascular events: A meta-analysis. *Journal of Sports Sciences, 37*(24), 2826-2834.

Long, B. C. (1980). Stress management for the athlete: A cognitive-behavioral model. In C. H. Nadeau, W. R. Halliwell, K. M. Newell, & G. C. Roberts (Eds.), *Psychology of motor behaviour and sport—1979* (pp. 73–83). Human Kinetics.

Lonsdale, C., & Tam, T. M. J. (2008). On the temporal and behavioural consistency of pre-performance routines: An intra-individual analysis of elite basketball players' free throw shooting accuracy. *Journal of Sports Sciences, 26*(3), 259-266. 10.1080/02640410701473962

Low, W. R., Sandercock, G. R. H., Freeman, P., Winter, M. E., Butt, J., & Maynard, I. (2021). Pressure training for performance domains: A meta-analysis. *Sport, Exercise, and Performance Psychology, 10*, 149-163.

Lyons, D., & Parker, K. J. (2007). Stress inoculation-induced indications of resilience in monkeys. *Journal of Traumatic Stress, 20*(4), 423-433.

Lyttleton, B. (2014). *Twelve yards: The art and psychology of the perfect penalty*. Bantham Press.

Lyttleton, B. (2021, July 14). *Frank de Boer and Dutch penalty trauma*. Twelve Yards. https://twelveyards.substack.com/p/frank-de-boer-and-dutch-penalty-trauma

Maheshwari, A. (2021, July 8) How Emiliano Martinez resorted to dirty mind games during penalties against Columbia | Watch. India.com. https://www.india.com/sports/copa-america-how-emiliano-martinez-resorted-to-dirty-mind-games-during-penalties-against-columbia-watch-4797671/

Martens, R. (2003). *Elfmeter: kleine Geschichte einer Standardsituation*. Eichborn.

Martens, R., Burton, D., Vealey, R. S., Bump, L.A., & Smith, D. E. (1990) Development and validation of the Competitive State Anxiety Inventory-2 (CSAI-2). In R. Martens, R. S. Vealey, & D. Burton (Eds.), *Competitive anxiety in sport* (pp. 117-190). Human Kinetics.

Masters, R. S., van der Kamp, J., & Jackson, R. C. (2007). Imperceptibly off-center goalkeepers influence penalty-kick direction in soccer. *Psychological Science, 18*(3), 222–223. https://doi.org/10.1111/j.1467-9280.2007.01878.x

Masters, R., Poolton, J., & van der Kamp, J. (2010). Regard and perceptions of size in soccer: Better is bigger. *Perception, 39*(9), 1290–1295. https://doi.org/10.1068/p6746

Mavletova, A., & Witte, J. (2016). Is the willingness to take risks contagious? A comparison of immigrants and native-born in the United States. *Journal of Risk Research,* 20(7), 827-845.

McDermott, K. C. P., & Lachlan, K. A. (2021). Emotional manipulation and task distraction as strategy: The effects of insulting trash talk on motivation and performance in a competitive setting. *Communication Studies,* 72(5), 915–936. https://doi.org/10.1080/10510974.2021.1975139

McTear, E. (2023, January 10). Ancelotti: "We have things to work on, but we don't have training time to work on them". Managing Madrid. https://www.man-agingmadrid.com/2023/1/10/23548250/ancelotti-press-conference-valencia-su-per-cup

Memmert, D., & Noel, B. (2017). *Elfmeter: Die psychologie des strafstoßes.* Hogrefe.

Memmert, D., Noël, B., Machlitt, D., van der Kamp, J., & Weigelt, M. (2020). The role of different directions of attention on the extent of implicit perception in soccer penalty kicking. *Human movement science,* 70, 102586. https://doi.org/10.1016/j.humov.2020.102586

Miller, C. (1998). *He always puts it to the right: A history of the penalty kick.* Orion.

Mischel, W., Grusec, J., & Masters, J.C. (1969). Effects of expected delay time on the subjective value of rewards and punishments. *Journal of Personality and Social Psychology,* 11, 363-373.

Moll, T., Jordet, G., & Pepping, G.-J. (2010). Emotional contagion in soccer penalty shootouts: Celebration of individual success is associated with ultimate team success. *Journal of Sports Sciences,* 28(9), 983–992. https://doi.org/10.1080/02640414.2010.484068

Moore, L. J., Vine, S. J., Freeman, P., & Wilson, M. R. (2013). Quiet eye training promotes challenge appraisals and aids performance under elevated anxiety. *International Journal of Sport and Exercise Psychology,* 11(2), 169–183. https://doi.org/10.1080/1612197X.2013.773688

Morrison, I. (2016). Keep calm and cuddle on: Social touch as a stress buffer. *Adaptive Human Behavior and Physiology,* 2(4), 344–362. https://doi.org/10.1007/s40750-016-0052-x

MrFandefoot (2009, November 23). C2: Finale 1980: Valence - Arsenal: 0-0 Pen. [Video]. YouTube. https://www.youtube.com/watch?v=C_DBNAc4FdE

Mulder, M., de Jong, R. D., Koppelaar, L., & Verhage, J. (1986). Power, situation, and leaders' effectiveness: An organizational field study. *Journal of Applied Psychology,* 71, 566-570.

Mukherjee, S. (2022, April 10). What is Diego Maradona's record in penalties? Goal. https://www.goal.com/en/news/what-is-diego-maradona-s-record-in-penal-ties/blt8308abdd6b4e890b

Nair, R. (2022, December 5). I told my players to take 1000 penalties- Spain's Luis Enrique. Reuters. https://www.reuters.com/lifestyle/sports/i-told-my-players-take-1000-penalties-spains-luis-enrique-2022-12-05/

Navia, J. A., van der Kamp, J., Avilés, C., & Aceituno, J. (2019). Self-control in aiming supports coping with psychological pressure in soccer penalty kicks. *Frontiers in Psychology*, 10, 1438. https://doi.org/10.3389/fpsyg.2019.01438

Neff, L. A., & Broady, E. F. (2011). Stress resilience in early marriage: Can practice make perfect?. *Journal of Personality and Social Psychology*, 101(5), 1050.

New Paradigm (2022). Leaders and leading a team. https://presscoaching-com. translate.goog/los-lideres-y-la-conduccion-de-un-equipo/?_x_tr_sl=es&_x_tr_tl=en&_x_tr_hl=en&_x_tr_pto=sc

Nicol, S. (2023). Video on X. https://x.com/adamkeys_/status/1708885240108740934?s=20

Noël, B., van der Kamp, J., & Memmert, D. (2015). Implicit goalkeeper influences on goal side selection in representative penalty kicking tasks. *PLOS ONE*. https://doi.org/10.1371/journal.pone.0135423

Noël, B., van der Kamp, J., Masters, R., & Memmert, D. (2016). Scan direction influences explicit but not implicit perception of a goalkeeper's position. *Attention, Perception & Psychophysics*, 78(8), 2494–2499. https://doi.org/10.3758/s13414-016-1196-2

Noticias & Protagonistas (2022, December 11). Lionel Scaloni: the peaceful leader. https://noticiasyprotagonistas.com/editoriales/lionel-scaloni-el-lider-pacifico/?_x_tr_sl&_x_tr_tl&_x_tr_hl

NTV (2019, February 6). Pokal-krimis: Antwort auf Kovac "Druck beim elfmeter kann man simulieren". NTV. https://www.n-tv.de/sport/fussball/Druck-beim-Elfmeter-kann-man-simulieren-article20845498.html

Oettingen, G., Marquardt, M. K., & Gollwitzer, P. M. (2012). Mental contrasting turns positive feedback on creative potential into successful performance. *Journal of Experimental Social Psychology*, 48(5), 990–996. https://doi.org/10.1016/j.jesp.2012.03.008

Oudejans, R. R., & Pijpers, J. R. (2009). Training with anxiety has a positive effect on expert perceptual–motor performance under pressure. *Quarterly Journal of Experimental Psychology*, 62(8), 1631-1647.

Oudejans, R. R., & Pijpers, J. R. (2010). Training with mild anxiety may prevent choking under higher levels of anxiety. *Psychology of Sport and Exercise*, 11(1), 44-50.

Owusu-Sekyere, F., & Gervis, M. (2016). In the pursuit of mental toughness: Is creating mentally tough players a disguise for emotional abuse?. *International*

Journal of Coaching Science, 10(1).

Pardon, J. (2023, November 30). EdF: Didier Deschamps ne compte toujours pas travailler les tirs au but. Footmercato. https://www.footmercato.net/a67887497451950944769-edf-didier-deschamps-ne-compte-toujours-pas-travailler-les-tirs-au-but

Palacios-Huerta, I. (2014). *Beautiful game theory: How soccer can help economics.* Princeton University Press.

Parker, K. J., Buckmaster, C. L., Justus, K. R., Schatzberg, A. F., & Lyons, D. M. (2005). Mild early life stress enhances prefrontal-dependent response inhibition in monkeys. *Biological Psychiatry*, 57, 848-855.

Parker, K. J., Buckmaster, C. L., Schatzberg, A. F., & Lyons, D. M. (2004). Prospective investigation of stress inoculation in young monkeys. *Archives of General Psychiatry*, 61, 933-941.

Pearce, S. (2000). *Psycho: The autobiography of Stuart Pearce.* Headline.

Perry, I. S., & Katz, Y. J. (2015). Pre-performance routines, accuracy in athletic performance and self-control. *Athens Journal of Sports*, 2(3), 137–151. https://doi.org/10.30958/ajspo.2-3-1

Phillips, M. (2022). Saudi Arabia win is statistically biggest World Cup shock, say Gracenote. Reuters. https://www.reuters.com/lifestyle/sports/saudi-arabia-win-is-statistically-biggest-world-cup-shock-say-gracenote-2022-11-22/

Powell, H. (2016). *Hope: My life in football.* Bloomsbury Sport.

Purewal, N. (2021, May 29). Pep Guardiola and Thomas Tuchel prepared for penalties in Champions League final. Breaking news.ie. https://www.breakingnews.ie/sport/pep-guardiola-and-thomas-tuchel-prepared-for-penalties-in-champions-league-final-1134792.html

Quaile, K. (2022, December 6). Luis Enrique: "I chose the first three penalty takers and the rest were decided by the players.". Get football news spain. https://getfootballnewsspain.com/luis-enrique-i-chose-the-first-three-penalty-takers-and-the-rest-were-decided-by-the-players/?expand_article=1

Rashford, M., & Anka, C. (2021). *You Are a Champion - How to Be the Best You Can Be.* Macmillan Children's Books.

Reason, J. (2000). Human error: Models and management. *BMJ*, 320(7237), 768–770. https://doi.org/10.1136/bmj.320.7237.768

Ricotta, J. (2016, July 6). Euro 2016: ne pas s'entraîner aux tirs au but, une erreur des Bleus? Europe1. https://www.europe1.fr/sport/euro-2016-ne-pas-sentrainer-aux-tirs-au-but-une-erreur-des-bleus-2791987

Robazza, C., Bortoli, L., & Nougier, V. (1998). Physiological arounsal and performance in elite archers: A field study. *European Psychologist*, 3(4), 263-270.

Roberts, J. C. (2009). Bouncers and barroom aggression: A review of the research. *Aggression and Violent Behavior*, 14(1), 59–68. https://doi.org/10.1016/j.avb.2008.10.002

Rogers, T.J., Alderman, B.L., & Landers, D.M. (2003). Effects of life-event stress and hardiness on peripheral vision in a real-life stress situation. *Behavioral Medicine*, 29(1), 21-26.

Rohleder, N., Beulen, S. E., Chen, E., Wolf, J. M., & Kirschbaum, C. (2007). Stress on the dance floor: The cortisol stress response to social-evaluative threat in competitive ballroom dancers. *Personality and Social Psychology Bulletin*, 33(1), 69-84. https://doi.org/10.1177/0146167206293986

Rosing, F., & Boer, D. (2022). When timing is key: How autocratic and democratic leadership relate to follower trust in emergency contexts. *Frontiers in Psychology*, 13, 904605

Rotella, R. J., & Lerner, J. D. (1993). Responding to competitive pressure. In R. N. Singer, M. Murphy, & L. K. Tennant (Eds.), *Handbook of research on sport psychology*. (pp. 528-541). Macmillan.

Roth, A.M., Reig, S., Bhatt, U., Shulgach, J., Amin, T., Doryab, A., Fang, F., & Veloso, M. (2019). A robot's expressive language affects human strategy and perceptions in a competitive game. *IEEE International Workshop on Robot and Human Communication* (ROMAN).

Rupprecht, A. G. O., Tran, U. S., & Gröpel, P. (2021). The effectiveness of pre-performance routines in sports: A meta-analysis. *International Review of Sport and Exercise Psychology*. https://doi.org/10.1080/1750984X.2021.1944271

Rudi, N., Olivares, M., & Shetty, A. (2020). Ordering sequential competitions to reduce order relevance: Soccer penalty shootouts. *PLOS ONE*. https://doi.org/10.1371/journal.pone.0243786

Russell, G., & Lightman, S. (2019). The human stress response. *Nature Reviews Endocrinology*, 15(9), 525-534. https://doi.org/10.1038/s41574-019-0228-0

Russo, S. J., Murrough, J. W., Han, M. H., Charney, D. S., & Nestler, E. J. (2012). Neurobiology of resilience. *Nature Neuroscience*, 15(11), 1475–1484. https://doi.org/10.1038/nn.3234

Santos, R. M. (2023). Effects of psychological pressure on first-mover advantage in competitive environments: Evidence from penalty shootouts. *Contemporary Economic Policy*, 41(2), 354-369.

Sarkar, M., Fletcher, D., & Brown, D. J. (2015). What doesn't kill me…: Adversity-related experiences are vital in the development of superior Olympic performance. *Journal of Science and Medicine in Sport*, 18(4), 475-479.

Savage, J., Collins, D., & Cruickshank, A. (2017). Exploring traumas in the development of talent: What are they, what do they do, and what do they require? *Journal of Applied Sport Psychology*, 29(1), 101-117.

Senju, A., & Johnson, M. H. (2009). The eye contact effect: mechanisms and development. *Trends in Cognitive Sciences*, 13(3), 127-134.

Shields, G. S., Sazma, M. A., & Yonelinas, A. P. (2016). The effects of acute stress on core executive functions: A meta-analysis and comparison with cortisol. *Neuroscience and Biobehavioral Reviews*, 68, 651-668. https://doi.org/10.1016/j.neubiorev.2016.06.038

Sky Sports (2009, December 23). Capello knows penalty takers. Sky Sports. https://www.skysports.com/football/news/12016/5794402/capello-knows-penalty-takers

Sky Sport Austria (2019, October 28). Salzburg holte gegen Rapid „ganz wichtige" drei Punkte. Skysportaustria. https://www.skysportaustria.at/salzburg-holte-gegen-rapid-ganz-wichtige-drei-punkte/

Slutter, M. W., Thammasan, N., & Poel, M. (2021). Exploring the brain activity related to missing penalty kicks: an fNIRS study. *Frontiers in Computer Science*, 3(32). https://doi.org/10.3389/fcomp.2021.661466

Soccer Illustrated (1994). 1994 FIFA World Cup... by the numbers. *Soccer Illustrated*. https://www.rsssf.org/wk94/numbers.html

Southgate, G., Woodman, A., & Walsh, D. (2003). *Woody and Nord: A football friendship*. Michael Joseph.

Sports Illustrated (2012, February 13). Fine art of the free throw distraction. *Sports Illustrated*. https://www.si.com/college/2012/02/13/13fine-art-of-the-free-throw-distraction#gid=ci0255c94190042515&pid=utah-state-fans

Stein, M. (1997). *Chris Waddle: The authorised biography*. Simon & Schuster.

Stephenson, M. D., Schram, B., Canetti, E. F. D., & Orr, R. (2022). Effects of acute stress on psychophysiology in armed tactical occupations: A narrative review. *International Journal of Environmental Research and Public Health* 19, 1802. doi: 10.3390/ijerph19031802

Stoker, M., Lindsay, P., Butt, J., Bawden, M. & Maynard, I. (2016). Elite coaches' experiences of creating pressure training environments for performance enhancement. *International Journal of Sport Psychology*, 47(3), 262-281.

Story, G. (2014). Anticipating pain is worse than feeling it. *Harvard Business Review*.

Svenson, O. (1981). Are we all less risky and more skillful than our fellow drivers? *Acta Psychologica*, 47(2), 143–148. https://doi.org/10.1016/0001-6918(81)90005-6

Talk SPORT (2021, June 29). José Mourinho REVEALS the secrets behind Harry Kane's penalty technique. [Video]. YouTube. https://www.youtube.com/

watch?v=5wPZmXQ8lwY

Taleb, N. N. (2012). *Antifragile: Things that gain from disorder.* Allen Lane.

Tartaglione, N. (2022). *World Cup ratings: Epic final sets all-time viewing record in France.* Deadline. https://deadline.com/2022/12/world-cup-ratings-final-all-time-viewing-record-france-tf1-1235202220/

Tembah (2023, May 10). Argentina coach Scaloni reveals the change in Argentina's style! https://tembah.net/en/news?nid=32126

Tracy, J. L., Mercadante, E., & Hohm, I. (2023). Pride: The emotional foundation of social rank attainment. *Annual Review of Psychology*, 74(1), 519–545. https://doi.org/10.1146/annurev-psych-032720-040321

Tribuna (2019). Maradona fumes about Argentina coach Scaloni: Messi's return comforts me, but where's Aguero? https://tribuna.com/en/news/fcbarcelona-2020-03-06-maradona-fumes-about-argentina-coach-scaloni-messis-return-comforts-me-but-wheres-aguero/?utm_source=copy

Uchino, B. N., & Garvey, T. S. (1997). The availability of social support reduces cardiovascular reactivity to acute psychological stress. *Journal of Behavioral Medicine*, 20(1), 15–27. https://doi.org/10.1023/A:1025583012283

UEFA (2021). UEFA EURO 2020 impresses with 5.2 billion cumulative global live audience. UEFA. https://www.uefa.com/insideuefa/news/026d-132519672495-56a014558e80-1000--uefa-euro-2020-impresses-with-5-2-billion-cumulative-globa/

Van de Vooren, J. (2006). Het verbrande penaltyboekje van Reker. https://www.nu.nl/jurryt/769085/het-verbrande-penaltyboekje-van-reker.html

Van den Nieuwenhof, F. (2006). *Hiddink: Dit is mijn wereld.* Eindhoven DeBoeken Makers.

Van der Kamp, J., & Savelsbergh, G. J. P. (2014). *Duel in de zestien. De penalty wetenschappelijk ontleed.* 2010 Uitgevers.

Van der Steen, H. (2004). *Penalty. Het trauma van Oranje.*

Van Yperen, N. W. (2009). Why some make it and others do not: Identifying psychological factors that predict career success in professional adult soccer. *The Sport Psychologist*, 23(3), 317-329.

Veldkamp, J., & Koning, R. H. (2023). Waiting to score. Conversion probability and the video assistant referee (VAR) in football penalty kicks. *Journal of Sports Sciences*, 41(18), 1692-1700. https://doi.org/10.1080/02640414.2023.2292893

Vergouw, G. S. (2000). *De strafschop: zoektocht naar de ultieme penalty.* Funsultancy.

Vickers J. N. (1996). Visual control when aiming at a far target. *Journal of Experimental Psychology.* Human perception and performance, 22(2), 342–354. https://

doi.org/10.1037//0096-1523.22.2.342

Victor, J.M. (2022, December 8). Scaloni: "¿Pensar ahora en penales? Eso es de mediocres". ArgentinaAS. https://argentina.as.com/futbol/scaloni-pensar-ahora-en-penales-eso-es-de-mediocres-n/

Vignolo, S.(Producer). (2023). *Campeones, un año después* [TV-series]. Star+.

Vollmer, S., Schoch, D., & Brandes, U. (2023). Penalty shootouts are tough, but the alternating order is fair. *Arxiv.* https://doi.org/10.48550/arXiv.2310.04797

Vroom, V. H., & Yetton, P. W. (1973). *Leadership and decision-making* (Vol. 110). University of Pittsburgh Press.

Wang, H., Liang, L., Cai, P., Zhao, J., Guo, L., & Ma, H. (2020). Associations of cardiovascular disease morbidity and mortality in the populations watching major football tournaments: A systematic review and meta-analysis of observational studies. *Medicine, 99*(12).

Watzlawick, P., Beavin, J. H., & Jackson, D. D. (1967). *Pragmatics of human communication: Study of interactional patterns, pathologies and paradoxes.* WW Norton.

Wegner, D. M., Ansfield, M., & Pilloff, D. (1998). The putt and the pendulum: Ironic effects of mental control in action. *Psychological Science, 9*(3), 196-199.

Weick, K. E., & Sutcliffe, K. M. (2007). *Managing the unexpected: Resilient performance in an age of uncertainty* (2nd ed.). Jossey-Bass.

Weigelt, M., & Memmert, D. (2012). Goal-side selection in soccer penalty kicking when viewing natural scenes. *Frontiers in Psychology, 3,* 312. https://doi.org/10.3389/fpsyg.2012.00312

Weigelt, M., Memmert, D., & Schack, T. (2012). Kick it like Ballack: The effects of goalkeeping gestures on goal-side selection in experienced soccer players and soccer novices. *Journal of Cognitive Psychology, 24*(8), 942–956. https://doi.org/10.1080/20445911.2012.719494

White, J., & Murphy, D. (2023). talkSport. [Radio]. talkSPORT. https://twitter.com/talkSPORT/status/1414533241835458568?s=20

Wilbert-Lampen, U., Leistner, D., Greven, S., Pohl, T., Sper, S., Völker, C., Güthlin, D., Plasse, A., Knez, A., Küchenhoff, H., & Steinbeck, G. (2008). Cardiovascular events during World Cup soccer. *The New England Journal of Medicine, 358*(5), 475-483. https://doi.org/10.1056/NEJMoa0707427

Wilson, M. R., & Richards, H. (2011). Putting it together: Skills for pressure performance. In D. Collins, A. Button, & H. Richards (Eds.), *Performance psychology: A practitioner's guide* (pp.337-360). Churchill.

Wilson, M. R., Vine, S. J., & Wood, G. (2009). The influence of anxiety on visual attentional control in basketball free throw shooting. *Journal of Sport & Exercise Psychology, 31*(2), 152–168. https://doi.org/10.1123/jsep.31.2.152

Witte, D. R., Bots, M. L., Hoes, W. W., & Grobbee, D. E. (2000), Cardiovascular mortality in Dutch men during 1996 European football championship: Longitudinal population study. *British Medical Journal*, 321, 1552-1554.

Wolfers, J. (2015, February 13). How Arizona State reinvented free-throw distraction. *The New York Times*. https://www.nytimes.com/2015/02/14/upshot/how-arizona-state-reinvented-free-throw-distraction.html

Wood, G., & Wilson, M. R. (2010). A moving goalkeeper distracts penalty takers and impairs shooting accuracy. *Journal of Sports Sciences*, 28(9), 937–946. https://doi.org/10.1080/02640414.2010.495995

WorldRugby (2021). Amazing and nail biting World Cup conversions! [Video]. Youtube. https://www.youtube.com/watch?v=nJheKNA8C8M

Wunderlich, F., Berge, F., Memmert, D., & Rein, R. (2020). Almost a lottery: The influence of team strength on success in penalty shootouts. *International Journal of Performance Analysis in Sport*, 20(5).

Yip, J. A., Schweitzer, M. E., & Nurmohamed, S. (2018). Trash-talking: Competitive incivility motivates rivalry, performance, and unethical behavior. *Organizational Behavior and Human Decision Processes*, 144, 125–144. https://doi.org/10.1016/j.obhdp.2017.06.002

Yomiuri (2023). https://www.yomiuri.co.jp/sports/soccer/world-cup/20230219-OYT1T50076/

Photography permissions
in order of appearance

1. Ben Radford/Allsport UK/Getty Images

2. Franck Fife/AFP via Getty Images

3. Julian Finney/Getty Images

4. Bob Thomas Sports Photography via Getty Images

5. Quinn Rooney/Getty Images

6. Robin Jones/Getty Images

7. Mark Leech/Offside via Getty Images

8. Photo by James Gill - Danehouse/Getty Images

9. Sebastian Widmann/Bongarts/Getty Images

10. Michael Regan - FIFA/FIFA via Getty Images

11. Photo by Matthias Hangst/Getty Images

12. Juan Carlos Cardenas/EPA/Shutterstock

13. Elsa/Getty Images

14. Ryan Pierse - UEFA/UEFA via Getty Images

15. Laurence Griffiths/Getty Images

16. Alex Pantling/Getty Images

17. Alex Pantling/Getty Images)

18. Brian Murphy/Icon Sportswire via Getty Images

19. Mustafa Yalcin/Anadolu Agency via Getty Images

20. Harriet Lander - Chelsea FC/Chelsea FC via Getty Images

21. Matthew Ashton - AMA/Getty Images

22. Karim Sahib/AFP via Getty Images

23. Charlotte Wilson/Offside/Offside via Getty Images

24. SI Cover /Sports Illustrated/Getty Images

25. Mike Hewitt/Getty Images

26. Alex Pantling - FIFA/FIFA via Getty Images

27. David Geieregger/SEPA.Media /Getty Images

28. Alex Gottschalk/DeFodi Images via Getty Images

29. Atsushi Tomura/Getty Images

30. Norwegian Football Federation

31. Alex Grimm/Getty Images

32. Zhizhao Wu/Getty Images

Acknowledgements

This book, just like its main character, the penalty kick, may seem like a solo effort on the outside, but it is really a team effort, with pivotal contributions from many.

First, I am very grateful that Rebecca Nicolson and New River Books started the conversation. There have been others vying to create this book with me, but none as persuasive or convincing as Rebecca. It's been an honour and a pleasure collaborating with her.

I am also grateful to Aurea Carpenter and Giles Smith for their assistance at various stages with the editing of the text and to Susanna Lea, and her people, for bringing the book to a wider international audience.

Arsène Wenger is a leading global pioneer on psychology in football and has been an inspiration for decades. I am grateful for and proud of his contributions.

People involved in football at the highest level can be very closed-off and restrictive about what they think, feel, and do, particularly when this involves trade secrets that others can exploit. Thank you for sticking your necks out and sharing your insights Celso Borges, Yasuhito Endō, Erling Braut Haaland, Niklas Häusler, Alex Hodgins, Robert Lewandowski, Chris Markham, Maren Mjelde, Zećira Mušović, Ørjan Nyland, Fabi Otte, Hope Powell, and Martin Ødegaard.

Thank you for your assistance Frank Abrahamsen, Kaori Araki, Aksel Bergo, Christine Bolger, Lars Brotangen, Jan-Erik Buskerud, Thomas Cooper, Maud Craigie, Kuba Galanty, Peter Haberl, Thomas Elinam Jenssen, Pål Arne Johansen, Filip Kopeć, Bjørn Mannsverk, Alan McCall, Scott McLachlan, Anders Meland, Gareth Morgan, Barry Pauwels, Hans Erik Ramberg, Hege Riise, Jaeson Rosenfeld, Atle Røsseland, Christian Schönsberg, Sebastian Høyvik Skjold, Kenny Stamatopoulos, Viggo Strømme, Leif Gunnar Smerud, Bjørn Frode Strand, Rachel Vickery, Krzysztof Waloszczyk, Tania Wight, Takuma Yamanaka, and Egil Østenstad, as well as Lone Friis Thing, Kristin Andersen, and my great colleagues at the Department of Sport and Social Science, Norwegian School of Sport Sciences.

Acknowledgements

The book is also the culmination of years of academic research, where notable contributors are Marije Elferink-Gemser, Esther Hartman, Chris Visscher, Koen Lemmink, Gert-Jan Pepping, Tjerk Moll, Einar Sigmundstad, Philip Furley, Matt Dicks, and Foppe de Haan.

But the book would not exist at all if it wasn't for the brilliant Yanique Fletcher, whose big-picture views, forensic eye for detail and amazing support have been constant throughout.

277

Index

Diagrams are denoted by the use of *italic* page numbers.